Ideas, Policies and Economic Development in the Americas

Structuralism worked well in the Western Hemisphere and elsewhere for several decades but then was bypassed by events, particularly the debt crises to which it could not adequately respond. Its dominant successor, the Washington Consensus, is now moribund. A host of eminent international contributors address the urgent task of inventing a new structuralist economics to confront the challenges of the twenty-first century.

Ideas, Policies and Economic Development in the Americas examines the ideas of essential Latin American and Caribbean intellectuals such as Celso Furtado, Arthur Lewis, Raúl Prebisch, and some less well known like the José da Silva Lisboa and Alberto Pani and their influence on policy making. It also discusses the role of key structuralist ideas such as the Prebisch–Singer thesis, the notion of "development by invitation," inertial inflation, the differences between Latin American and Anglo-Saxon Structuralist tradition, and the debates with the liberal orthodoxies of their times, in particular the recent neoliberal tradition.

The essays in this book suggest that the recent shifts in broad political alignments in several important Latin American and Caribbean nations reflect the failure of the Washington Consensus agenda, and that a renewal of Structuralist ideas can play an important role in the future economic development of the region.

Esteban Pérez Caldentey is based at the Economic Commission for Latin America and the Caribbean in Port of Spain, Trinidad and Tobago. **Matías Vernengo** is in the economics department at the University of Utah, USA.

T0383589

Routledge studies in development economics

Ideas, Policies and Economic Development in the Americas

Edited by Esteban Pérez Caldentey
and Matías Vernengo

Routledge
Taylor & Francis Group

LONDON AND NEW YORK

First published 2007
by Routledge
2 Park Square, Milton Park, Abingdon, Oxfordshire OX14 4RN

Simultaneously published in the USA and Canada
by Routledge
711 Third Avenue, New York, NY 10017

First issued in paperback 2014

Routledge is an imprint of the Taylor & Francis Group, an informa business

Typeset in Times by Wearset Ltd, Boldon, Tyne and Wear

British Library Cataloguing in Publication Data
A catalogue record for this book is available from the British Library

Library of Congress Cataloging in Publication Data
A catalog record for this book has been requested

ISBN 978-0-415-77055-2 (hbk)
ISBN 978-1-138-80631-3 (pbk)
ISBN 978-0-203-96402-6 (ebk)

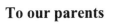

To our parents

The disparity between what we are and what we hoped to be has in no other period of our history been so large.

Celso Furtado, In *O Longo Amanhecer*

Contents

Figures

Tables

Contributors

Luiz Carlos Bresser-Pereira, Fundação Getúlio Vargas, São Paulo, Brazil.

James M. Cypher, Universidad Autónoma de Zacatecas, Mexico.

Kenneth P. Jameson, University of Utah, Salt Lake City, USA.

Julio López Gallardo, Universidad Autónoma de México, Mexico.

Carlos Mallorquín, Universidad Autónoma de Puebla, Mexico.

Ricardo Mansilla, Universidad Autónoma de México, Mexico.

Juan Carlos Moreno-Brid, Economic Commission for Latin America and the Caribbean, Mexico.

José Antonio Ocampo, United Nations Department of Social and Economic Affairs, New York, USA.

María Angela Parra, United Nations Department of Social and Economic Affairs, New York, USA.

Esteban Pérez Caldentey, Economic Commission for Latin America and the Caribbean, Port of Spain, Trinidad and Tobago.

Jaime Ros, Notre Dame University, South Bend, USA.

Diego Sanchez-Ancochea, University of London, UK.

Matías Vernengo, University of Utah, Salt Lake City, USA.

Foreword

There have been many structuralisms in economics. In the twentieth century, Keynes was a structuralist as were members of the first wave of development economists that emerged in the North after World War II – Rosenstein-Rodan, Myrdal, Hirschman, Chenery, and many others. Indian planners and economists – Mahalanobis, Rao, and Chakravarty – had strong structuralist inclinations.

Yet the label "structuralist" rightly emerged from the South, in the Western Hemisphere from interacting schools of thought that arose in the (then) *Economic Commission for Latin America* in Santiago and the Anglophone Caribbean in the decade following the War. The present volume edited by Esteban Pérez Caldentey and Matías Vernengo is a major contribution toward continuing this tradition.

Of course, structuralism does not exist in a vacuum. Structuralist lines of economic analysis have always been locked into an intricate dialectical dance with the orthodoxies of their times – notably monetarism and the Washington consensus in Latin America and the Caribbean – ever since they emerged a few hundred years ago. In their introduction, the editors rightly point out that living economic analysis can only emerge in the context of policy formulation and application, followed by an honest analysis of its successes and failures.

Structuralism worked well in the Western Hemisphere and elsewhere for several decades but then was bypassed by events including the debt crises to which it could not adequately respond. Its dominant successor, the Washington consensus, is now moribund. The authors in this book are addressing the urgent task of inventing a new structuralist economics to confront the challenges of the twenty-first century.

In my view they amply succeed.

Lance Taylor
New York, 2007

Acknowledgments

Slightly different versions of Chapter 2 and 7 were previously published by Comisión Económica para América Latina y el Caribe (CEPAL) as "Método y Pasión en Celso Furtado," and "México: las Reformas del Mercado desde una Perspectiva Histórica," *Revista de la CEPAL*, No 84 (LC/G.2258-P/E), Santiago de Chile, Diciembre de 2004.

1 Introduction

Ideas, policies and economic development in the Americas

Esteban Pérez Caldentey and Matías Vernengo[1]

The evolution of economies is a contingent historical process shaped to a great extent by the interplay of ideas and policies. Ideas are "more powerful than commonly understood" and can under certain circumstances have a definite and long lasting impact on policy.[2] In turn, policies both when they are deemed successful or unsuccessful provide a fertile ground for the development of new ideas or the re-casting of old ones. The economic history of Latin America and the Caribbean over the past 50 years exemplifies the symbiosis, by no means a linear one, between ideas and policies.

The economic history of Latin America and the Caribbean is characterized by a succession of policy phases associated with different conceptual frameworks embodying contrasting and at times contradictory visions of the workings of emerging market economies.

Following World War II, Latin America governments focused their efforts on policies to promote "industrialization" and growth. At this stage development was conceived as a process of factor accumulation and more specifically as a process of capital accumulation. Capital accumulation and industrialization was an essential requirement to break the cycle of poverty and "underdevelopment," especially for those countries that were most affected by declining terms of trade for primary commodities. The development strategy consisted of obtaining the supply of capital required for development, creating the inducement to investment and generating the savings capacity to finance that investment.

As the development focus shifted from physical capital to human capital,[3] greater interest was placed in social development objectives, including health, education and nutrition. The quest for growth and also that for social objectives depended on an efficient and flexible price mechanism in developing countries. This assumption was strongly questioned by the structuralist school. Structuralism argued that price, factor and market rigidities led to misallocation of resources and structural disequilibria.[4] Structural heterogeneity, duality and polarization were some of the key concepts coined and developed by structuralist thinkers.

The move away from policies associated with structuralism towards those of the Washington Consensus was spurred by Latin America's debt crisis in the 1980s, persistent macroeconomic disequilibria and high rates of inflation. The

Washington Consensus championed economic stabilization and structural reform policies which were seen as pre-conditions for the efficient functioning of Laissez-Faire.[5] The implementation of the Washington Consensus policies was accompanied by a reduction in inflation, but at the same time these managed to stifle growth and were not able to reduce inequality or improve economic and social welfare.

The Washington Consensus was questioned on that very basis leading to a revival and rediscovery of several insights of the old structuralist school.[6] Among these the most important include the change of the meaning of stabilization and to "reform" the structural reforms.[7]

More importantly the same international organizations such as the World Bank that advocated structural reform and orthodox macroeconomic policies have changed their views to champion the expansion of government expenditure on capital and human infrastructure as a key element in the development process much like the early development theorists. This represents a break with the very foundations of the Washington Consensus and signals its definitive demise.[8]

In Latin America and the Caribbean the interplay between ideas and policies seems to take the form of that of a circular flow. Either within the neoclassical economic literature or in the (neo)-structuralist tradition, much of the policy debate is about the re-casting of old ideas. The echoes and influence of the past seem to be forever present and much of what passes for new ideas are nothing but old ideas in new goat skins. As a result the current Latin American and Caribbean approaches are unprepared to confront new development challenges.[9] There is a growing divide between theory and reality; and no current development approach is able to bridge the gap. From the point of view of the editors of this book the lack of adequate attention paid to the relationship between ideas and policies explains part of this absence of progress.

Indeed, the history of economic ideas and their intricate relation to economic policies remains a relatively unexplored field in Latin American and Caribbean studies. This book contributes to this emerging literature.[10]

A unifying theme in all the contributions to the book is the understanding that there is a close relationship between the behavior of economies over time and the nature and evolution of ideas and that both are mediated by economic policy. Ideas shape policy and policy dictates to a large extent behavior. Also the interpretation of given historical episodes can alter the nature and scope of ideas. For this reason those interested in Latin American and Caribbean economic development should look back with a critical eye to the economic ideas of Latin American and Caribbean authors. Conventional wisdom, whatever the nature of its ideology – often based on ideas imported from abroad – misperceived the real obstacles to economic development in the past and the same may be happening at present.

Illustrative examples include the misconceived idea that free trade would have positive impact on growth, dominant in the aftermath of independence, or the lack of understanding of the importance of financial development were central in shaping institutions. Similarly ideas regarding proper exchange rate policy, the necessary degree of openness to foreign capital, and the appropriate policies to combat inflation had enduring effects on economic policies, and the resulting economic structures of the countries in the region.

A second important unifying theme in the book is that the limitations of the structuralist approach and the failure of the Washington Consensus to live up to its promise underscores the need to renew interest and develop critical perspectives on development economics. The contributors to this volume view economic history and history of ideas as a source fountain for the development of new and original ideas.

The point was hammered home by Celso Furtado. Furtado recounts Prebisch's farewell from ECLAC in a conference in Mar del Plata in 1963. Reflecting on the importance of intellectuals and of ideas in the process of economic development, Furtado ended his own speech at the conference suggesting that "for men that project themselves with creative thinking and that have the ability to influence reality with the power of their ideas there are no permanent departures, because they are always present" (Furtado, 1989, p. 167).

A third unifying theme is that reality can not be conformed to fit preconceived ideas, but that ideas should be modified and molded to fit a changing reality. An example is provided by ECLAC's changing conceptual framework. Over time the early preoccupation among ECLAC authors and the Latin American structuralists shifted from the technological gap with the center to the clear gap between Latin America and the more successful industrialization of East Asian economies – Fajnzylber (1983) being the most important mark of the intellectual change. The official report, *Transformación Productiva con Equidad* (ECLAC, 1990), was concerned with the successful integration of Latin America into the world economy. The changing structure of international markets, where the Fordist paradigm was transformed by flexible specialization techniques or Toyotism, is crucial in this view. Export orientation and a greater degree of openness were then seen as part of a strategy to reduce technological dependence.[11]

Last, but not least, the book takes seriously the role of ideas imported from abroad, and their effects on economic development. According to Roberto Schwarz (1992, p. 34) "it is true that the backwarderness and the attempts to keep up have internal causes, but it is also true that forms and techniques [. . .] that are adopted at times of modernization were created out of social conditions very different from ours and that their importation produces a maladjustment which is a constant trait of our civilization." It is in this context that the "indigenous" ideas of structuralists in Latin America and the Caribbean should be revaluated.

An outline of the book

First, Luiz Carlos Bresser-Pereira argues that the method that Celso Furtado utilizes is essentially historical and that his passion – a measured passion – was for Brazil. For Bresser, in the second half of the twentieth century no intellectual contributed more than Furtado for the understanding of Brazil. He was committed to its development, frustrated with its incapacity to achieve it, and always acute in analyzing the economic and political challenges that the country successively faced. In order to demonstrate these ideas, the chapter presents a broad review of Furtado's work.

In the following chapter James Cypher discusses whether neoliberal ideas and policies are *passé* in Latin America. Cypher argues that a paradigmatic shift in development policies requires a three-pronged attack on conventional wisdom. First, the old paradigm must be subjected to theoretical review and found to be demonstrably lacking in many of its formulations. Second, empirical evidence need be marshaled to demonstrate that the application of the theory has produced results inconsistent with the predictions of the theory. Last, but not least, an alternative theory must be put forward and there must be sufficient force behind this new set of ideas to displace or marginalize the earlier paradigm. According to the author the last movement is critical and determinant, and constitutes the crystallization of a defining political moment. Cypher suggests that recent shifts in broad political alignments in several important Latin American nations now suggest some likelihood of ringing down the neoliberal era.

The following chapter by Kenneth Jameson deals with the relevance of early twentieth-century Latin American economists in establishing exchange rate regimes and monetary institutions. The role of Latin Americans is contrasted to the better known participation of U.S. "money doctors," e.g. Edwin Kemmerer's role in the Andean region, in promoting certain foreign exchange and monetary regimes. Jameson enumerates some of the cases where Latin American analysts were active players and participants in analyzing exchange rate and monetary issues and in formulating domestic policy to address them. The role of Latin American economists in a variety of international monetary conferences and commissions from 1903–1922 is investigated. In addition, the chapter describes how Alberto Pani guided the formulation of Mexican economic policy after the Mexican Revolution and his ability to chart an independent course for Mexico. The conclusion is that there is evidence of "intense discussions of economic issues" based on Latin Americans' economic analysis. The role of foreign advisors was often to break the political impasse and to recommend the policy the inviting government wanted to implement.

In the following chapter Julio López Gallardo and Ricardo Mansilla provide a renewed view of structuralist theories of inflation. Starting with a structural model of inflation, as proposed by the Latin American structuralist school, the authors move on to an inertial model of inflation, where the price rise results from the pattern of wage bargain and price determination. They find that the initial price increase plays a crucial role as regards the rate of inflation. They suppose that an expansionary policy which provokes a current account deficit eventually brings about currency depreciation. In their model, the future rate of inflation is entirely determined by the extent of the initial currency depreciation. They conclude that this point helps to understand the different inflationary experiences of advanced vis-à-vis developing economies.

In the next chapter, Carlos Mallorquín discusses Raúl Prebisch's ideas after he left the Argentinean Central Bank in 1943 and before he entered the Economic Commission for Latin America (ECLA)[12] in 1949, and wrote his famous economic development "manifesto." Mallorquín analyzes the radicalization of Prebisch's ideas, in particular his macroeconomic thinking related to the nature of the business cycles, and how those ideas were to some extent frozen by the requirements of the more formal environment of the United Nations.

Juan Carlos Moreno-Brid and Jaime Ros take the Herculean task of discussing the recent pro-market reform in Mexico through the lens of the process of economic development since independence. They suggest that a recurrent problem in Mexican history has been the lack of understanding of the real constraints to economic development, and that this lack of vision might be a problem in the present too. In this context, they provide three main conclusions. First, the notion that the crisis was brought about by the exhaustion of past development strategies should not be taken for granted, even though they would be very far from defending every single aspect of past development strategies. Second, the solution to the new obstacles may require more and better, rather than less, state participation in the economy. As the authors have tried to show, the source of these new problems has to be found in part in the retreat of the state, in such areas as public infrastructure investment. But as a result of the shift in ideological climate, very little attention is being given to these problems and to what government policy can do about them while, at the same time, too much is expected from the efficiency gains of market reforms.

José Antonio Ocampo and María Angela Parra provide a critical review of the terms of trade debate that followed the development of the so-called Prebisch–Singer hypothesis. They suggest that Prebisch and Singer were correct on empirical grounds,[13] but that the validity of their hypothesis was not necessary to defend industrialization in developing countries. In their view, the excessive focus of ECLAC on the terms of trade problem sidetracked the discussion from what matters, namely that industrialization is necessary to take advantage of its dynamic economies of scale.

Esteban Pérez Caldentey, in his chapter, analyzes the policies inspired by the strategy of "industrialization by invitation" formulated by Arthur Lewis and their effects on the English-speaking Caribbean countries and Puerto Rico. The strategy consisted, in a nutshell, in attracting foreign capital through a series of incentives. Foreign capital was a means of overcoming limitations to industrial development imposed by the small volume of trade of Caribbean economies. It was also a means of acquiring entrepreneurial skills and capital resources which were lacking in small developing economies. The chapter argues that in both the English-speaking Caribbean and Puerto Rico the policies guided by the strategy of "industrialization by invitation" succeeded in attracting foreign direct investment. However, the expansion of foreign direct investment was accompanied by a stagnation of domestic investment. More important, the policies that followed actually increased the dependency of the economies in question on foreign capital flows.

Diego Sanchez-Ancochea analyzes the differences of Anglo-Saxon and Latin American structuralist ideas. The author claims that Anglo-Saxon structuralists deserve criticism for not paying enough attention to the relation between developed and developing countries, and because of their limitless faith in the capacity of the state to intervene efficiently in the economic system. Latin American structuralists, on the other hand, emphasized center–periphery interaction, and the ability to analyze the interaction between global processes and the domestic particularities of Latin American countries from a historical perspective makes this latter brand of structuralism particularly relevant in the current global era.

In the last chapter, Matías Vernengo criticizes the view according to which the relative backwardness of Brazil with respect to the United States in the nineteenth century was the result of the economic liberalism of its elites. The author argues that the defense of an open economy, integrated to the world economy, in which agricultural production would prevail over industrial interests, should be seen as a discourse for landowners and the mercantile class connected to the slave trade. It is also argued that, in contrast to Alexander Hamilton, José da Silva Lisboa, the Viscount of Cairú, and the Brazilian elites had a *naive* view of public finance that is central to understanding the backwardness of Brazilian financial markets. In that sense, political conservatism and financial underdevelopment are seen as at least as relevant as economic liberalism for explaining the relative backwardness of Brazil.

We would like to end by thanking everybody that made the conference and this volume possible, in particular to Mary Lesser and the Eastern Economic Association, who provided facilities for the conference sessions. We would also like to thank all the conference participants whose stimulating questions and comments added vibrancy to the sessions – including those that do not appear in this volume. Per Gunnar Berglund, Colin Danby, Pedro Páez and Frank Schroeder provided important insights for the organization of the conference, and Yongbok Jeon and the Routledge staff were instrumental in preparing the final version of the book.

Notes

1 Economic Commission for Latin America and the Caribbean, Port of Spain, Trinidad and Tobago, and the University of Utah, Salt Lake City, respectively. The opinions expressed are those of the authors and may not coincide with those of their respective institutions, ECLAC and the University of Utah. We thank Carlos Mallorquín for comments on a preliminary version.

2 John Maynard Keynes (1936, pp. 383–4) provided one of the most well known statements supporting the influence of ideas on policies: "ideas of economists and political philosophers ... are more powerful than commonly understood ... the world is ruled by little else. Practical men, who believe themselves to be quite exempt from any intellectual influences, are usually the slaves of some defunct economist ... It is ideas not vested interests, which are dangerous for good or evil." This point of view, of course, is not shared by all economists.

3 Anticipating as key the arguments of the endogenous growth theory, Hans W. Singer was one of the development economists who turned the focus of attention from phys-

ical to human capital. As he put it (1961): "the fundamental problem is no longer considered to be the creation of wealth, but rather the capacity to create wealth ... It consists of brain power."

4 The rigidity argument was emphasized by several structuralists (e.g. Chenery, Kalecki, Noyola and Sunkel). It can be argued that Prebisch's development manifesto, as well as his later paper in the *American Economic Review*, was ultimately based on a rigidity argument. For a recent presentation of structuralist ideas see Taylor (2004).

5 See Williamson (1990) and (2004).

6 For example Dani Rodrik's (1998) Eighth Raúl Prebisch Lecture at UNCTAD, in which he confesses to not having read Prebisch's work before being invited to give the lecture, he argues that "anyone who has read Prebisch more closely ... would object that the usual characterization of Prebisch as an advocate of protection ignores a lot of subtleties." In addition, for him "the development community has internalized the wrong lessons from the experience of countries that adopted the ISI strategy in Latin America and elsewhere." In particular, "ISI worked rather well for a period of about two decades, [bringing] unprecedented economic growth to scores of countries in Latin America, the Middle East, and North Africa, and even to some in Sub-Saharan Africa, [and] when the economies of these same countries began to fall apart in the second half of the 1970s, the reasons had very little to do with ISI policies per se or the extent of government interventions."

7 See Ocampo (2002) and Ffrench-Davis (2000).

8 In the past decade, the World Bank has changed its development orientation away from stabilization and structural reform, returning towards its original role of promoting project development. This, however, implies that governments will not be able to adhere to the type of orthodox fiscal policies recommended by the Washington Consensus.

9 Consider for example the idea that most economists share regarding the desirability of achieving fiscal surpluses in times of plenty to be used in times of scarcity. The argument applies at most to a barter economy, has little to do with a credit economy and has a strong religious connotation. The argument is actually more akin to religious beliefs than economic science.

10 For analyses of the relationship between ideas and policies in the United States and Europe see, for example, Peter Hall (1989), Bernstein (2001) and Barber (1996). With a few exceptions (such as Gabriel Valdés's 1995 study on the Chicago School of Economics in Chile) such studies are lacking in Latin America and the Caribbean.

11 For a review of the evolution of ideas at ECLAC see Bielschowsky (1998) and Love (2005). Vernengo (2006) describes a different path taken by Brazilian structuralists associated with Maria da Conceição Tavares that moved from an interpretation of capitalist development in the periphery that puts international money – and not technical progress – as the expression of financial capital domination over the periphery.

12 Later ECLA became ECLAC, when the Caribbean joined the Commission.

13 Interestingly enough conventional views on the terms of trade debate still get the facts wrong. For example, Coatsworth (2005, p. 134) argues that "Prebisch's hypothesis on the terms of trade was probably wrong."

References

Barber, William (1996) *Designs with Disorder*, Cambridge: Cambridge University Press.

Bernstein, Michael (2001) *A Perilous Progress. Economists and Public Purpose in Twentieth Century America*, Princeton: Princeton University Press.

Bielschowsky, Ricardo (1998) "Evolución de las Ideas de la CEPAL," *Revista de la CEPAL*, Numero Extraordinario, pp. 21–45.

Coatsworth, John (2005) "Structures, Endowments, and Institutions in the Economic History of Latin America," *Latin American Research Review* 40(3), October, pp. 126–44.

ECLAC (1990), *Transformación Productiva con Equidad*, CEPAL: Santiago de Chile.

Fajnzylber, Fernando (1983) *La Industrialización Trunca de América Latina*, México: Nueva Imagen.

Ffrench-Davis, Ricardo (2000) *Reforming the Reforms in Latin America*, New York: St. Martin Press.

Furtado, Celso (1989) *A Fantasia Desfeita*, Rio de Janeiro: Paz e Terra.

Hall, Peter (ed.) (1989) *The Political Power of Economic Ideas. Keynesianism Across Nations*, Princeton: Princeton University Press.

Keynes, John Maynard (1936) *The General Theory of Employment, Interest and Money*, Harcourt Brace, 1964.

Love, Joseph (2005) "The Rise and Decline of Economic Structuralism in Latin America: New Dimensions," *Latin American Research Review* 40(3), October, pp. 100–25.

Ocampo, José Antonio (2002), "Rethinking the Development Agenda," *Cambridge Journal of Economics*, No. 26, pp. 393–407.

Prebisch, Raúl (1959) "Commercial Policy in the Underdeveloped Countries," *American Economic Review* 49(2), May, pp. 251–73.

Rodrik, Dani (1998) "Globalization, Social Conflict, and Economic Growth," *The World Economy* 21(2), March, pp. 143–58.

Schwarz, Roberto (1992) *Misplaced Ideas*, London: Verso.

Singer, Hans W. (1961) "Education and Economic Development," in *International Development: Growth and Change*, New York: McGraw-Hill, 1964.

Taylor, Lance (2004) *Reconstructing Macroeconomics*, Cambridge: Harvard University Press.

Valdés, Juan Gabriel (1995) *Pinochet's Economists: The Chicago School in Chile*, Cambridge: Cambridge University Press.

Vernengo, Matías (2006) "Technology, Finance, and Dependency: Latin American Radical Political Economy in Retrospect," *Review of Radical Political Economics* 38(4), pp. 551–68.

Williamson, John (1990) "What Washington Means by Policy Reform," in J. Williamson (ed.) *Latin American Adjustment: How Much Has Happened*, Washington, D.C.: Institute for International Economics.

Williamson, John (2004) "The Strange History of the Washington Consensus," *Journal of Post Keynesian Economics* 27(2), pp. 195–206.

2 Method and passion in Celso Furtado

Luiz Carlos Bresser-Pereira

If there was an intellectual who, in the second half of the twentieth century, gave a most decisive contribution to the understanding of Brazil, I would not hesitate in stating that this intellectual was Celso Furtado. He did not just offer economic explanations for our development and underdevelopment. More than that, he situated Brazil in a world context, analyzed its society and its politics, and offered solutions for the major problems it faced. In order to achieve this task, as ambitious as frustrating – because, ultimately, Brazil fell short of his great expectations – Furtado used method as well as passion. He was rigorous in his method, but this did not prevent him from viewing with passion the subject matter of his study, which has always been a republican project of life as well: the development of Brazil.

One of the books by Carlos Drumond de Andrade is called *A Paixão Medida* [The Measured Passion]. This oxymoron, so deftly used by the great poet, helps us to understand Celso Furtado. The passion is strong, making his work and life full of energy and desire of economic and political transformation, but it is a measured passion, which weights costs and trade-offs – as economists usually do – and does not overlook political restrictions.

Celso Furtado was an economist devoted to development theory and to the analysis of Brazilian economy. In those two areas he always thought independently, using mainly the historical method rather than the logical-deductive one. He has a powerful ability to infer and deduct, but he always starts from the observation of reality, avoids starting from general assumptions on human behavior – and tries to infer the theory from this reality and its historical movement.

In this chapter I will not make a general evaluation of Celso Furtado's work. I will only focus on three issues of that work. One issue is well known – his independence of thought; the second one has not been much studied – the method; and the last one is somehow present in all the analyses of his work – the passion, but it always appears in a measured way, through expressions such as love for Brazil, personal and intellectual integrity. Furtado is all this, but is more than this. His struggle for the development of Brazil and for overcoming backwardness in his homeland – the Northeast of Brazil – was conducted with such an intensity and determination that only passion could explain.

Theoretical independence

Celso Furtado was a development economist. He was part of the group of "pioneers" of the modern development theory, along with Rosenstein-Rodan, Prebisch, Singer, Lewis, Nurkse, Myrdal and Hirschman.[1] His theoretical contributions focused on the understanding of the process of economic development and underdevelopment. And to achieve it, he used in the first place, as we will see, the most suitable method to the study of development: the historical-inductive one. But, before examining the method he uses, it is important to point out the theoretical independence that characterizes his intellectual path.

He used the economic theory he learned with the classics, among which Ricardo and Marx play an outstanding role, together with Keynes. He owed little to the neoclassicals. Furtado, however, was not to be taken for a Marxist, or a Keynesian. He learned with the classics and with Keynes, but he had independent thought, and had always absolutely prized this independence. He was identified with Latin American structuralism, to the extent that he was one of its founders.[2] But we must bear in mind that structuralism is not, nor has it intended to be, an all-encompassing economic theory. It was an influential economic doctrine in Latin America in the 1950s and 1960s because it offered an interpretation for the underdevelopment of countries that, in the mid-twentieth century, experienced the transition from pre-capitalist or mercantile forms to industrial capitalism, and presented to their government leaders a consistent development strategy.

The theoretical independence of Furtado's thought enabled him to use the theories he considered relevant to solve the problems presented by the interpretation of the economic facts that he faced. Marxism was important for him to the extent that it offered a powerful view of history and capitalism, but Marx's contribution to economic theory was less significant. When describing his Marxist studies, in France, in the late 1940s, he stated:

> The remarkable view provided by Marx on the genesis of modern history cannot leave indifferent a curious mind. Yet his contribution in the field of economics seemed less important for someone familiar with Ricardo's thought and acquainted with modern economics.
>
> (Furtado, 1985, p. 31)

On the other hand, he did not believe in pure economic theory, whether neoclassical or Marxist. Furtado had never been interested in this aspect of economic theory. For him, economic theories existed to solve actual problems. From his point of view, economics was "an instrument to penetrate social and political realms and further the understanding of history, particularly when it was still displayed before our eyes" (Furtado, 1985, pp. 15 and 51).

But how did Furtado intend to understand the world around him? Not by applying without criticism any system of economic thought. Nothing is more opposed to Furtado than the stereotyped thought of orthodox intellectuals, whatever orthodoxy they adopted. He wanted to see the world with his own eyes. To use the instruments of economic analysis without losing his own freedom of thought and creation, which was his greater asset. As observed by Francisco Iglésias (1971, p. 176),

> it is absurd to point him as neoclassical, Marxist, Keynesian, labels that are frequently assigned to him. From every author or trend he takes what is, from his point of view, correct or adaptable to Brazilian or Latin-American reality. He adopts the models that seem correct to him, without trying to apply them mechanically to different cases, without orthodoxy.[3]

Furtado did not intend by that to reconcile those theories, nor was he being undefined, as suggested by those who wish a single and integrated view of economic theory: he was only saying that, according to the problem we face, one school of thought or the other may be more useful. As for Keynes, Furtado was, as observed by Bielschowsky (1980, p. 60), an "atypical Keynesian" because he classically characterized underdevelopment as a problem of savings shortage. The shortage of demand would apply primarily to developed countries. Notwithstanding, when describing the development process, Furtado, instead of adopting the attitude which was typical among the pioneers of development of imagining that the concentration of income was a condition for the beginning of development, assigned to wage growth a fundamental role in ensuring the increase of aggregate demand and capitalists' profits. At this point he was already being fully Keynesian.

His concern with the independence of his thought appears clearly when he decided to leave Rio de Janeiro and work in Santiago, at the *Comisión Económica Para América Latina* (CEPAL), which had just been created. CEPAL was then still an empty project. Furtado did not know Prebisch, who had not yet formulated his view of the development of Latin America. Even so, he decides to leave, in order to "escape the siege, gain an open horizon, even if he had to wander in search of a lost Atlantis" (Furtado, 1985, p. 50). He made this statement in *A Fantasia Organizada* [The Organized Fantasy] (1985), and afterwards manifested his conformity to Sartre and his philosophy of responsibility, according to which if we based our real choices only in reason, there would be no choices, and everything would be predetermined.

By deciding to go to Santiago, Furtado was telling himself that his own life was not predetermined. And he was, thus, consistent with his broader view of society and the economy. Since he never believed that a single economic theory was able to explain everything, he always rejected all kinds of determinism as well: whether Marxist determinism, based on the "laws of history," or the neoclassical one, based on the principle of rationality, which, by postulating the maximization of interests, leaves no room for decisions, for choices.[4] On the contrary, if in the debate between determinism and voluntarism Furtado committed a sin, it was the sin of voluntarism, expressed in the belief in the ability of human reason of imposing its will on the economy and society through planning. More broadly, he always attributed the key role to decisions when it comes to the macroeconomic system. The market had a fundamental role, but the decisions taken were no less important.

This view is very clear in *Criatividade e Dependência na Civilização Industrial* [Creativity and Dependency in Industrial Civilization] (1978, p. 18):

> The profile of an economic system is defined from the identification of the centers from which are issued those decisions, destined to harmonize the initiatives of the multiple agents, who exert power in different degrees.

This refusal of determinism, including market determinism, was related to the individualism and idealism of the great intellectual who decides to intervene in reality. He started from the conviction that he was part of the intellectual elite, of the *Intelligentsia*, that would be able to reform the world. In this field, his master was Karl Mannheim. As he said:

> By following Mannheim, I had a certain idea of Intelligentsia's social role, particularly in periods of crisis. I felt to be above the determinants created by my social insertion and was persuaded that the challenge consisted in inserting a social purpose in the use of such a freedom.
>
> (Furtado, 1985)

Gerard Lebrun, in his analysis of *A Fantasia Organizada*, points out Furtado's idealistic voluntarism, expressed by his unshakeable belief in planning – a planning that would totally eliminate the unpredictability of decisions. Well, observes the philosopher, "his idea of power (in a democracy, of course) seems so abstract, so well adjusted, *a priori*, to his ideal of a neutral planning, that he apparently hardly conceives that the planner might become a technocrat" (Lebrun, 1985).

As a matter of fact, this outstanding economist was a scientist, but was also a bureaucrat in the best sense of the word, a man of State, a public policymaker who only ceased to be inserted in the State apparatus when the military dictatorship suspended his political rights. Celso Furtado started his professional life at the *Departamento Administrativo do Serviço Público* (DASP), as a public administration technician. He overcame that phase, became an economist and a university teacher, but never gave up believing in the rationalizing power of bureaucracy, including medium bureaucracy. He often said that the sole social group that was able to act as an interlocutor with international powers was the State bureaucracy. And for him it was essential to strengthen bureaucracy in democratic regimes in order to maintain public policies and the very effectiveness and legitimacy of the State power. As he said in *A Fantasia Desfeita* [The Faded Fantasy]:

The process of bureaucratization does not just mean the growth of the State apparatus, it also means significant changes in the political processes. By increasing the effectiveness of power, bureaucratization consolidates it at lower levels of legitimacy.

(Furtado, 1989, p. 185)

With this thought, Furtado is faithful to what he learned from such different thinkers as Mannheim, Sartre and his teacher Cornu (Furtado, 1985, p. 31). In capitalist democracies intellectuals may free themselves from ideologies and use their freedom to intervene in the world in a Republican way. He knew that this was always a relative freedom with which we may build our own lives, but we cannot have any illusion regarding social and political determinants to which we are subject. For great intellectuals such as Furtado, the dialectics between freedom and socially conditioned behavior could be more conscious and, if accompanied by the virtue of courage, as in his case, it would be more favorable to freedom, but just more favorable: nobody escapes his own circumstances.

Intellectual courage was expressed primarily in moments when it was necessary to differ from one's environment and group. In 1962, right in the middle of the country's political radicalization, Celso Furtado published *A Pré-Revolução Brasileira* [Brazilian Pre-Revolution]. After praising the humanistic nature of Marx's work, Furtado does not hesitate in declaring:

Since Marxism-Leninism is based on the replacement of a class dictatorship with another, it would be a regression, from a political point of view, to apply it to societies having reached more complex forms of social coexistence, that is, to modern open societies.

(Furtado, 1972, p. 27)

Likewise, in the *Triennial Plan* of 1963 he did not hesitate in proposing a fiscal adjustment and a strict monetary policy, although he knew that he would be called "monetarist" by the groups that supported the Goulart administration.

The use of freedom gained full meaning in Furtado because it was marked by the gift of creativity. Furtado's contribution to economic theory and to the analysis of Brazilian and Latin-American economies may be explained in terms of method, but it is, in the first place, the result of an enormous personal ability to think and create. Furtado knows it, and it is certainly not by chance that the epigraph of one of his books is a quotation of Popper in which he acknowledges that "scientific discovery is impossible without faith in ideas which are of a purely speculative kind, and sometimes even quite hazy."[5]

Creativity would be one of the bases of his intellectual independence from orthodoxy. Lebrun, writing on *A Fantasia Organizada*, remarks: "it is the odor of heterodoxy that makes this book even more fascinating and makes Celso Furtado a great writer, as well as a thinker." As observed by Bourdieu (1976, p. 145), if in economic theory there is a *doxy*, "a set of assumptions that antagonists regard as evident," there is also an orthodoxy and a heterodoxy. The heterodox intellectual does not deny his science's most general assumptions, but refuses to subordinate his thought to the dominant one. The right and the conventional economists insist on giving heterodoxy a negative meaning, identifying it with economic populism, but, in fact, to innovate in economic theory and analyses almost always involves some heterodoxy.

To be heterodox is to develop new theories, often from the identification of new historical facts that modify a certain economic and social setting and make pre-existent theories inadequate. When Celso Furtado opted to use mainly the historical-inductive method, and when he became one of the two founders of Latin American structuralism, he was opting for heterodoxy and for independence of thought. In the next section, I will briefly present my view of the two methods in economic theory, and subsequently I will continue the analysis of the method in Celso Furtado.

Two methods in economics

Orthodoxy, or neoclassical mainstream, is primarily logical-deductive. It intends to deduce the balanced operation of market economies from the sole assumption that economic agents maximize their interests. If we classify sciences as adjectival or methodological, there is no substantive science more logical-deductive than neoclassical economic science, in spite of the statements that it is a positive science. Paradoxical as it may seem, not even physics is as logical-deductive. The supremacy of the logical-deductive method is such that I always recall the observation of a former student, who returned from a scholarship in a foreign university. When I told him that, for me, in certain fundamental areas, such as macroeconomics and economic development, the economist should use predominantly the historical-inductive method instead of the logical-deductive one, he immediately replied: "but in economics, the logical-deductive method is always dominant; we do not study history, we study economic theory." For him, as for the whole neoclassical thought, economic theory is by definition logical-deductive.

Economic theory is abstract by definition, and cannot be confused with history. In economics we try to find models, theories, which should explain the stability and variation of economic aggregates, the short-term economic cycle and development, inflation or deflation and the balance of payments, the variation of relative prices, of interest rate and of exchange rate. The subject matter of economic theory, therefore, is clear, as it is clear that the aim is to generalize with respect to the behavior of relevant variables, and, through this generalization, to be able to predict the behavior of economic variables. Therefore, it is important to acknowledge that, according to the subject discussed, the most applicable method will sometimes be the logical-deductive one, sometimes the historical-inductive one.

In another paper, I advocated the idea that macroeconomics is irreducible to microeconomics because the former uses predominantly the historical-deductive method whereas the latter uses the logical-deductive method. The statement that the advance of knowledge depends on the connected use of the two methods is part of philosophy's introductory classes. In the process of knowing, individuals make permanent use of induction and deduction, one following the other and vice versa. Induction and deduction are not, therefore, methods of knowledge, or, more precisely, opposite mental operations. They are complementary. This doesn't mean, however, that sciences use one method or the other with the same intensity. Mathematics, for instance, is only logical-deductive, and sociology, mainly historical-inductive. In mathematics everything is deduced from a few identities; in sociology and in the other social sciences, with the exception of the neoclassical variant of economics (recently extended to political science), the observation of the social fact and its evolution in time is the fundamental method of research, although the researcher is permanently forced also to use the deductive method to perform his analysis.

Therefore, I am not corroborating the dominant belief in the nineteenth century that the use of the inductive method would distinguish true science. This latter would begin with the observation of facts and with experiments to reach ultimately general laws. As Hume's "problem of induction" made clear, we may infer general laws from induction, but the inferences thus performed do not become logically demonstrated.[6] The historical-inductive method does not exclude the logical-deductive one. In macroeconomics and in the theory of economic development, however, it takes precedence over the logical-deductive method, whereas the opposite is valid for microeconomics.

I consider the neoclassical theory of general equilibrium a remarkable contribution to the understanding of how market economies operate. But this does not mean that the whole economic theory may be subordinated to it. A second branch of the economic theory – macroeconomics – cannot be reduced to microeconomics because one deals with the behavior of economic agents, and the other, with economic aggregates – this is only a definition. Microeconomics, or, more precisely, the general equilibrium model that provides its basis, approaches economy from a logical-deductive perspective, deducing the way by which resources are allocated and income distributed in a market economy from a single assumption, the agents' rational behavior. Macroeconomics, on the other hand, was born and continues to bear its bigger fruits when it observes the behavior of economic aggregates, verifies how this behavior tends to repeat itself, and generalizes therefrom, building models or theories. Subsequently, macroeconomists try to find a logical reason, a microeconomic fundamental for the behavior of macroeconomic aggregates, but at most they will find ad hoc explanations. The neoclassical hope of reducing macroeconomics to microeconomics cannot be achieved, because the methods prevailing in each of those branches of economic science are different.[7] As it is impossible to reduce the third major branch of the economic theory – the theory of economic development – to microeconomics or to macroeconomics.

The core of the thought is still classical in this case, as is neoclassical the core of microeconomic thought, and Keynesian, the core of macroeconomic thought. The economic theory tries to explain and predict the behavior of economic variables. It is necessary, however, to determine the variable in which we are interested. If we want to understand and predict the behavior of prices and the allocation of resources in the economy, the microeconomic theory, with its logical-deductive basis, will be more effective; if we want to understand the distribution of income in the long run in the capitalist system, the reversion of the classical theory, by placing the profit rate as given and the wage rate as a residue, will have a higher predictive power; on the other hand, if we want to understand the behavior of economic cycles, the Keynesian-based macroeconomics will be the instrument par excellence; finally, in order to understand the dynamics of development, the classical historic-based development theory will be the one with the highest power of explanation and prediction.

According to this reasoning, it is impossible to have an absolutely integrated view of economic science. Economic science has three major branches: microeconomics, macroeconomics and the development theory. Each one of them provides us with a view of the operation of the economic system from a certain perspective, and using one prevailing method. Of these three branches, only in microeconomics the logical-deductive method is and must be dominant. It was this method that made it possible to build the microeconomic models of partial and general equilibrium, which constitute one of the major scientific achievements of the universal thought. Through it we can understand how a market economy allocates resources. Yet the theory of economic development, which explains the growth process of capitalist economies in the long run, and macroeconomics, which shows how economies behave in the economic cycle, although they use the logical-deductive method, were built from the observation of historical phenomena. Smith and Marx, who found the former, observed the transition from pre-capitalist forms to capitalism, and theorized on the basis of this observation. The classical theory of income distribution also has a historical nature, although, with the change in the behavior of the wage rate, from the mid-nineteenth century on, it only continued to make sense when it was inverted: the long-term profit rate proved to be stable enough to be considered constant, and therefore it is possible to predict that the wage rate will increase with productivity as long as the technical progress will be neutral. Keynes and Kalecki, who were responsible for the appearance of macroeconomics, began with the observation of the economic cycle after World War I, and theorized from there on: they also primarily used the historical-inductive method. Ricardo's great contribution to the theory of economic development – the law of comparative advantages in international trade – was a great logical-deductive effort, but even in this case it was based on the observation of what happened in England and took into account its business interests, rather than the rational behavior of economic agents.

Friedman's criticism of the Keynesian macroeconomic policy – the discovery that through adaptive expectations the economic agents would partly neutralize that policy – started rather from the observation of reality, although it has an obvious microeconomic foundation. This criticism didn't invalidate macroeconomic policy but limited its scope. When, however, macroeconomic theory detached itself from reality and radicalized the logical-deductive approach, as happened with the rational expectations hypothesis, we have an absurd and empty theoretical construct, despite its apparent consistency, which transforms economic theory in a mere ideology. According to this distortion suffered by the economic theory, macroeconomic policies would be completely ineffective, since they would be neutralized by the agents' rational expectations. Well, this assertion contradicts daily experience, in which we see the economic authorities of all nations actively involved in economic policy. The radical use of the logical-deductive method led theory to ignore historical reality. The economic policymakers, in the ministries of finance and in the central banks, for some time in the 1980s, accepted the radical version of monetarism proposed by rational expectations, but since the beginning of the 1990s they abandoned monetarism and started to adopt the pragmatic strategy of inflation targeting.

Another common distortion that arises from the pretension of using the logical-deductive method to explain all economic phenomena is the one resulting from the insistence on employing a certain model when reality does not conform to it. At that moment, economic theory becomes an obstacle rather than an instrument for the analysis of what is happening. When he manages to overcome this obstacle and actually think, analyzing the new facts that demand new analyses, he is forced to abandon the pre-existent models. In this case, as observed by Tony Lawson, "the only thing that remains intact is an adherence to formalist and, therefore, deductivist closed systems of modeling."[8]

Therefore, I see with skepticism the attempts to unify microeconomics, macroeconomics and the development theory. Those approaches are not mutually reducible because they start from different methods. Trying to unify them is mere intellectual arrogance that results in the impoverishment of economic theory. There is no need to find a model that unifies everything. We may perfectly well use one theory or the other, according to the point that we are trying to explain. A strictly neoclassical macroeconomics is a contradiction: it is macroeconomics without the very object of the discipline: the economic cycles. A purely neoclassical theory of economic development makes still less sense, since the general equilibrium model is essentially static. When the neoclassical economists finally reached a compatible model of development – the Solow model – this model advanced substantively little compared with what Smith, Marx, Schumpeter and the "pioneers of the development theory" of the 1940s and the 1950s had taught us on development. The same may be said of the Keynesian model of development of Harrod and Domar. Both models had, as a great merit, the fact of being consistent with their corresponding theories, rather than the fact of explaining the development process. The Solow model eventually proved to be more profitable, not due to that logical-deductive consistency, but rather because, since it was based on a Cobb–Douglas function, it was possible to conduct a great deal of empirical research, not precisely historical, but predominantly inductive.

The method

One way through which Furtado evidenced his independence of thought was keeping faithful to the historical-inductive method, despite the fact that orthodoxy, in these eighty years, became more and more logical-deductive. Of course, he used abundantly his logical-deductive ability, but he always did it from the historical facts and their tendency to repetition, not from the presumption of a rational behavior. As an economic historian, it was natural for him to use predominantly the historical-inductive method, but this is also true when he takes on the role of a development and underdevelopment theorist. Therefore, I am not suggesting that Furtado belongs to Gide's German historicist school, or to Veblen's American institutionalism. Those schools were characterized by the refusal of economic theory, and by the search for the analysis of economic facts on a case-by-case basis, whereas Furtado uses the available economic theory and tries to make it advance in the understanding of economic development.

Even as an economic historian, Furtado was, above all, an economist rather than a historian. He does not recount the history of the Brazilian economy, he analyzes it. No one made use of economic theory more brilliantly to understand the evolution of Brazilian economy than Furtado in *Formação Econômica do Brasil* [Economic Growth of Brazil] (1959). As remarked Francisco Iglésias (1971, pp. 200–1), a historian, although this is a book on economic history, it is a book from an

> economist's point of view ... in this analysis of economic processes one arrives at a great simplicity, at an ideal model, at forms that sometimes look as abstract. This is what happens in many excerpts of Celso Furtado's book; the rigor of construction of this book is such that ... it makes the reading difficult for those who lack a vast historical information and a certain knowledge of economic theory.

Along the same lines, Lebrun points out: "history, as it is practiced by Celso Furtado, is only worthwhile for its extreme *accuracy* [author's emphasis] ... This is his method: no assertion that isn't based on facts or on statistical data." But, I would add, data that are used with great intelligence and inference ability. One of the features that make *Formação Econômica do Brasil* (1959) a masterpiece of history and economic analysis is Furtado's ability to deduce, from the scarce available data, the other variables of the economy and their dynamic behavior. But, by doing that, Furtado is not abandoning the primacy of the historical-inductive method. He is only being able to combine his creativity with his logical rigor in order to present, from the available data, a general picture of the historical evolution of Brazilian economy hitherto unsurpassed. *Formação Econômica do Brasil* is for me the most important book published in the twentieth century on Brazil because in it Furtado was able to use economic theory and the other social sciences not to describe, but to analyze the economic history of Brazil.

I will give an example of his independence and method in that book. From chapter 16 on Furtado writes about the nineteenth century. First of all, although he had just participated in the foundation of Latin American structuralism in Santiago de Chile, he was not led by imperialist explanations of our underdevelopment, and declares, with respect to the 1810 and 1827 privileged agreements with England: "the common criticism made to these agreements, that they precluded Brazilian industrialization at that stage, seems to be unfounded" (Furtado, 1959, p. 122). From the country's exports data and exchange relations, he observes that the century's first half was a period of stagnation: in fact, the per capita income must have fallen from US$50 to US$43 (at the exchange rate of the 1950s). The next 50 years, however, show a great expansion, thanks to the exports increase and to the substantial improvement in the terms of trade. Once again the analysis starts from some historically verified facts, in order to infer the economy's general behavior, and, of course, to connect it with the social aspects.

The landowners are not undifferentiated, as it is usually seen. The new ruling class of coffee growers is very different from the old patriarchal class of the sugar plantations. It has commercial experience, and therefore the interests of production and trade are intertwined. On the other hand, he dedicates four chapters to the problem of labor, stressing the importance of immigration and wage labor. This fact may seem obvious, but it deserves the emphasis from someone who does not transform the economy into mere abstractions, and thinks it as a historically situated political economy.

The second example, I will pick it from his leading theoretical book: *Desenvolvimento e Subdesenvolvimento* [Development and Underdevelopment] (1961). In chapter 1, he summarizes his broader methodological view, and remarks that economic theory must be at the same time abstract and historical:

> The effort towards higher levels of abstraction must be followed by another effort, which tries to define, based on historical realities, the validity limits of the inferred relationships. The fundamental duality of economic science – its abstract and historical nature – appears, therefore, in its entirety in the theory of economic development.

The fact that economics was, and still is, taking on a more and more abstract nature, according to Furtado, was due to the fact that, from Ricardo on, its aim has been virtually limited to the study of product division, leaving in the background the issue of development. However, he points out, "economic development is a phenomenon with a sharp historical dimension" (Furtado, 1961, p. 22). He would repeat this statement numerous times throughout his vast work, because it was a key issue to his thought. After introducing the "mechanism of development," in which a few abstractions required for the understanding of development were presented, we have in chapter 3 one of the most remarkable texts I know on "The historical process of development."

In this chapter, which was no longer reissued – in my opinion, due to mistaken judgment – and which was lost during the transformation of *Desenvolvimento e Subdesenvolvimento* into another one, more systematic and didactical, *Teoria e Política do Desenvolvimento Econômico* [Theory and Politics of Economic Development] (1967), Furtado shows how the way of using the economic surplus will determine the emergence of the development process. In precapitalist formations, the surplus was primarily used for war and for religious temples. With the advent of capitalism, the surplus obtained by merchants will be transformed into capital accumulation, which will now be intrinsic to the economic system. With the industrial revolution, however, capitalism extends itself to the sphere of production. In a world in which technical progress starts to speed up and the competition is widespread, the reinvestment of profits no longer satisfies the businessman's wish for increased profits, but becomes a condition for the survival of enterprises.

Development acquires a self-sustainable nature. In his words:

> When the production surplus of the social organization becomes a source of income, the accumulation process will tend to become automated ... The strategic points of this process are the possibility of increasing productivity and the appropriation of the fruits of this increase by minority groups.
>
> (Furtado, 1961, pp. 120–1)

The idea is simple and powerful. But we should not imagine that Furtado would present only its bare bones. He was presenting a historical process through which we watch development emerging along with capitalism, and with all the complex changes of social, institutional and cultural nature that are inherent to it. The economic phenomenon of productivity increase was a key issue, but it is intrinsically connected to the emergence of new social classes and new institutions.

The importance of institutions, which became a key issue in the 1990s for the study of development, was already clear for Furtado in *Desenvolvimento e Subdesenvolvimento*. He explained, for instance, the economic decline that follows the collapse of a pre-capitalist empire such as the Roman Empire in terms of the collapse of the Roman State apparatus, of its military power and of its long matured institutions. Surplus was appropriated by Roman citizens, and particularly by its patricians, through the collection of tributes on the colonies, and gives birth to a large trade warranted by Roman law. When this whole system collapses, economic decline is inevitable.

> The destruction of the enormous administrative and military machinery that constituted this Empire had profound consequences for the economy of the vast area it occupied ... Once the administrative and military system was dismantled, the security conditions that made trade possible disappeared; on the other hand, tributes having disappeared, the main source of income of urban populations, who lived on subsidies or rendering services, was over.

Institutions are, therefore, a fundamental thing, but they did not develop alone. First of all, they are part of the State, which, in the Roman case, took on the form of an Empire. Second, it is not just a question of ensuring economic activity – trade – but of making feasible a way of appropriating the surplus. Since we still do not have capitalism and surplus value or capitalist profit, the surplus is appropriated by force, by means of tributes.

Development in the historical sense of the word only occurs when the expansion of Islamism forces Byzantium to turn to Italy. Powerful trade economies are then formed in the Italian city-states, and alongside aristocracy, or in its place, a new bourgeois class appears. And this trade promotes political integration, which would eventually lead to the emergence of nation-states. Institutions in this case emerge rather as a consequence than as a cause of development. Furtado was explicit about it, and remarks that whereas in the Roman Empire political integration led to trade and development, in Europe it was long distance trade, adventurous and insecure, that would cause political integration. The latter, however, will soon become a decisive factor of development itself.

Institutions and their stability are a fundamental issue for development – especially the greatest of them all, the nation-state, from which the others depend. In this case Furtado was not being original, since there was a broad consensus about it. He added, however, that the capitalist system would produce not only the nation-state, but will tend to adopt democratic institutions. This view appeared clearly in Furtado's following book, *A Dialética do Desenvolvimento* [The Dialectics of Development] (1964), in which he criticizes the Marxist idea that in bourgeois society the limitations to freedom derive from the need to defend the privileges of the class that has the ownership of capital goods. On the contrary, he argued, democracy arises from capitalism and from the increasing institutional stability it provides. Such stability not only leads the bourgeoisie to adopt democracy as the political regime, but would also ensure the system's economic dynamism. According to Furtado:

> The reason for the progress of liberties in democratic capitalist societies was their increasing institutional stability. The revolutions that were directly caused by class struggles in Western Europe completed their cycle in the third quarter of the last century [the nineteenth] ... Now, this institutional stability is due to the existence of a powerful class – the owner of the capital goods – with broad created interests to protect ... The progress of civic liberties in bourgeois societies resulted less from the effective participation of the working class in political decisions, than from the confidence that the capitalist class acquired in a setting of flexible political institutions.
>
> (Furtado, 1964, p. 45)[9]

Furtado's political economy, always based on the historical method, was remarkable. Not only development, but also democracy derived from capitalism. The workers' struggle plays in it a fundamental role, not only in furthering democracy but also in ensuring, through the fight for better wages, the growth of aggregate demand, as profits grow. In the process of developing bourgeois democracy, which is initially just liberal, the essential role lies with the bourgeoisie itself and with the institutional stability it achieves. Perhaps the institutional stability is less due to the broad created interests to be protected, and more to the fact that the bourgeoisie is the first social class that was able to appropriate the surplus without direct use of the force of levying tributes and enslaving colonized populations – which led it to become an agent of the liberal rule of law and to become open to the advance of democratic institutions. But in any case it was remarkable to observe the connected analysis of the role of the capitalist class in achieving institutional stability, a stability that promotes development, which, in turn, strengthens the democratic trends existing in society, thus establishing a virtuous circle of self-sustainable development.

For Furtado, the historical method was a key issue for his analysis of development, to the extent that it enabled him to combine the great view of the historical process with the specificities of each moment and each country. The ability of predicting facts, which was required from every social theory, was present here through the analysis of the historical process of development. The abstract definition of development, as the increase of productivity from the capital accumulation and from the incorporation of technical progress, acquires historical substance, that is, was complemented by political, institutional and social elements. Development was not just capital accumulation, but it was also the incorporation of technical progress, which depended on the class structure, the political organization and the institutional system. Therefore, there was no development outside history; there was no economic development without political and social development.

By adopting the historical method, Furtado approaches Hegel's dialectics and Marx's historical materialism, although remaining independent from them, primarily because he attributes a greater role to human will. He argued that "the importance of dialectics for the understanding of historical processes derives from the fact that history ... cannot be reconstructed from the multiple phenomena that are part of it." However, through it man "intuits in the historical process this all-encompassing view that is able to give multiplicity a unity." Marx had boldly adopted this dialectical principle when he divided society into infrastructure and superstructure, and into two social classes. This strategy "had an extraordinary importance as a starting point for the study of social dynamics ... However, it is necessary to admit that, at this level of generality, an analytic model is hardly worth it as an instrument of practical orientation. And the purpose of science – he concludes, evidencing the pragmatism that has always guided him – is to produce guides for practical action" (Furtado, 1964, pp. 14–15 and 22).

I extracted those passages from *Dialética do Desenvolvimento* (1964), a book that Furtado writes amidst the crisis of the Goulart Administration, after resigning from the Ministry of Planning, and when he was again only in charge of *Superintendência de Desenvolvimento do Nordeste* (SUDENE) [Northeast Development Agency]. Among his autobiographical books this is perhaps the book that deserved his greater attention: a full summary (Furtado, 1989, pp. 182–90). In *A Fantasia Organizada*, Furtado clearly states that one of his purposes was to delimit the utilization of Marxism and dialectics in the analysis of development. By doing it, he restates his commitment to the rigor of scientific method:

> The second goal [of *Dialética do Desenvolvimento*] would be to determine the scope of dialectics, which had come into fashion again with Sartre's *Criticism*, but manifesting that its use would not exempt us from applying the scientific method with rigor in the approach of social problems.
>
> (Furtado, 1989, p. 182)

To adopt the scientific method with rigor, however, does not mean to adopt analytic models based on the assumption of the stable equilibrium, as it is so common in economics. To analyze development we need dynamic models, such as the "cumulative principle" proposed by Myrdal. More generally, Furtado concluded:

> Even if we had made progresses in modeling, we must admit that, to build models, we always start from a few intuitive hypotheses on the behavior of the historical process as a whole. The most general of those hypotheses is the one provided by dialectics, by which history is something that necessarily is part of the course of development. The idea of development appears as an hypothesis that organizes the historical process – as a "synthesis of several determinations, unity in multiplicity," in Marx's expression – from which it is possible to achieve an efficient effort of identification of relationships between factors and of selection of those factors in order to reconstruct this process through an analytic model.
>
> (Furtado, 1964, p. 22)[10]

With this exemplary text – which shows Furtado's elegance and ability of synthesis to express his thought – he makes clear his conception of the historical and dialectical nature of the scientific method he adopts. I could have begun the analysis of his method by this quotation, but I preferred to use it at the end. I conclude therefore my analysis with his words.

Passion

In the way Celso Furtado worked with economic science there was not only a rigorous method, there was also passion. There were great expectations, and the corresponding frustration. Usually reason and emotion are seen in opposition. However, this is a misguided way of understanding the process of thought. Great scientists were very often people passionate about their work, their research. The really great economists hardly failed to be passionate not only about their science, but also about its results. Some of them fell in love with the achievement of economic stability, others, with a fairer distribution of income, and most of them, with the development of their country.

Furtado's passion was the development of Brazil, a passion that was fed by the belief that this development was within the reach of his country in the historical moment when he graduated as an economist, in the late 1940s. World War II had just come to an end. New theories of economic development appeared. A great hope was beginning to take shape before the eyes of the young man from Paraíba who had just achieved his PhD in economics in France (1948). Brazil, already experiencing accelerated industrialization, would overcome the structural imbalances of its economy, and with the help of economic theory and economic planning, would reach the stage of a developed country.

Only this passion – the passion for the idea of the development of Brazil – explains the strength of his thought, particularly in his first books, from his first fundamental paper on Brazilian economy – "Características Gerais da Economia Brasileira" [General Characteristics of Brazilian economy] (1950) – and his first book – *A Economia Brasileira* [Brazilian Economy] (1954) – up to *Dialética do Desenvolvimento*, written in a moment when hopes began to be shattered by the imminence of the crisis. All these works have a theoretical strength and a power of analysis that do not derive just from creativity, from a great culture, from the independence of thought, and from the preferential use of the historical-inductive method: they are clearly related to a life project identified with the project of development. In *Ares do Mundo* [Airs of the World] (1991, p. 63) he makes clear that his life project was directly related to the conviction that he developed in the late 1940s that "a favorable international scenario – a consequence of the Great Depression of the 1930s and of the world conflict of the 1940s – had opened a crack through which perhaps we could sneak in to achieve a qualitative change in our history."

This qualitative change was the industrialization and the development of Brazil. But, Furtado argued, recalling 1964, when he arrived in Chile as an exile, that already in that year he was persuaded that, although "the intellectual has, as a characteristic, the boundless ability of devising reasons to live," his life project, which was based on the existence of that crack, was, ultimately, "an illusion . . . that was now vanishing" (Furtado, 1991, pp. 45 and 63). The fantasy was gone. There had been a great hope, but the disenchantment and the frustration were even greater. Frustration and disenchantment that were going to be expressed in his next book, *Subdesenvolvimento e Estagnação na América Latina* [Underdevelopment and Stagnation in Latin America] (1966) – a dense and pessimistic book, that later proved to be mistaken, as Latin-American economies enter a new development cycle.

The mistake, however, would eventually prove to be a relative success. The development cycle, that was then beginning, was artificially financed by foreign debt – a debt that made Latin-American economies prisoners of international financial capital, and that eventually led them to the great crisis of the 1980s, and to the near-stagnation that continues to date. I say a "relative success" because the book's key assumption, which is influenced by Marx and Keynes, still seems to me to be ill-placed. The stagnation or the development at very low rates would be due on one hand to the increase in the capital–labor ratio, and on the other hand to the decrease in the product–capital ratio, as a result of the capital-intensive nature of investments and their allocation to consumer durables. Capital productivity would then be falling (Furtado, 1966, p. 80). This theory underestimates, in my opinion, the increased technical progress, which saves not only labor, but also capital, that is, it is a technical progress that increases the efficiency of capital.

In *Subdesenvolvimento e Estagnação na América Latina* the idea that the concentration of income was preventing the operation of capitalism's virtuous circle, caused by the rise in wages as productivity increases, already appears. In two other books, Furtado answers indirectly to his critics. In *Análise do Modelo Brasileiro* [Analysis of the Brazilian Model] (1972) he incorporated into his thought, with great elegance and accuracy, the new dependency theory that had come out from the critique of his works. This does not prevent him from clearly restating, in *O Mito do Desenvolvimento* [The Myth of Development] (1974), his theory on the consumption shortage in the long run. The concentration of income in the middle and upper classes did not solve the problem of demand in the process of development. In his words:

> My basic assumption is that the system has not been able to spontaneously produce the profile of demand that could assure a steady growth rate, and that long-term growth depends on government exogenous actions … Although those two groups [the big companies and the modernized minorities] have convergent interests, the system is not structurally prepared to generate the kind of expansion of demand that is required to ensure its expansion.

Now, this theory, as Keynes showed when he criticized Say's law, is valid in the short run, to explain the economic cycle. And it is only valid for me in the long run to the extent that the development rate attained in that time lapse depends on keeping the demand at a constant tension with the supply in the short run. The new model of techno-bureaucratic capitalist development that was then being established in Brazil, producing an industrialized underdevelopment, eventually failed, but not due to a problem of lack of demand, but rather to an irresponsible excess of foreign indebtedness.

Hope would still be present for Celso Furtado when, in 1968, before the Institutional Act No. 5, which definitely established dictatorship in Brazil, he was invited by the Brazilian House of Representatives to present his view of what could be done. He could not resist, and wrote *Um Projeto para o Brasil* [A Project for Brazil] (1968), in which he proposed the resumption of development from a substantial increase in tax burden and public savings. However, if again there was hope – the refusal to accept dependency and underdevelopment – pessimism was still the same. The pessimistic analysis of the Brazilian situation was consistent with the one in *Subdesenvolvimento e Estagnação da América*

Latina – so much so that the first criticisms of this perspective, showing that the resumption of Brazilian development was taking place thanks to the concentration of income in the middle and upper classes, which created a demand for luxury consumer goods, were made from the analysis of those two books.

The optimistic passion that fed the action became now the great frustration of someone who recognized not only that he no longer directly influenced the country's destiny, but that the country itself had lost the ability of endogenous development. The economic theory he now used became debatable as it involved a twofold pessimism: regarding the ability of underdeveloped economic systems to have capital-intensive technical progress, but a capital saving progress or at least a neutral one (not involving, therefore, a decrease in capital productivity), and regarding the ability of supply to create demand in the long run.

His pessimism appears in the quotation below, extracted from *Ares do Mundo*, in which he recalls his first months in Santiago after the exile:

> I could not escape the idea that history is an open process, and that it is *naïve* to imagine that the future is absolutely contained in the past and in the present. But, when every relevant change is a result from the intervention of external factors, we are confined to the setting of a strict dependency ... The trends that appeared in Brazil led to the thought that the significant changes would no longer be the result of the action of endogenous factors.
>
> (Furtado, 1991, p. 63)

Um Projeto para o Brasil was Furtado's last clear manifestation of hope.[11] His work, from then on, according to Francisco de Oliveira (1983, p. 23), "may be called 'philosophical'." I would say that it becomes serene, to the extent that the exile, first in Chile, then in the United States, in England, and finally, for a long time, in France, imposes an emotional detachment. On Latin America, Furtado would still publish in 1969 a fundamental work, *Formação Econômica da América Latina* [Economic Formation of Latin America], but afterwards he became once again interested in the analysis of the historical process of development, and in the changes that international economy underwent.

He returned to the development process in *O Mito do Desenvolvimento* (1974), *Pequena Introdução ao Desenvolvimento: Enfoque Interdisciplinar* [Small Introduction to Development: Interdisciplinary Approach] (1980), "Underdevelopment: to Conform or Reform" 1987a) and in many other works. Yet the changes in world economy were analyzed in a 1968 paper, "A Preeminência Mundial da Economia dos Estados Unidos Pós-Guerra" [The Global Preeminence of the United States Economy in the Post-war Period].[12] In 1981, in the first issue of the *Revista de Economia Política*, of which he became one of the patrons (along with Caio Prado Jr. and Ignácio Rangel), appeared "Estado e Empresas Transnacionais na Industrialização Periférica" [State and Transnational Companies in Peripheral Industrialization]. All his other works on the subject will be later gathered in *Transformação e Crise na Economia Mundial*

[Transformation and Crisis in Global Economy] (1987b) and *O Capitalismo Global* [Global Capitalism] (1998).

In the 1970s Furtado once again took part actively in international meetings in which the developing countries demanded "a new international division of labor." This movement was successful for a while, but, with the foreign debt crisis, and the neoliberal wave that took over Washington and the world from the beginning of the 1980s, also that project did not bear the expected fruits. It was the beginning of the great crisis of the 1980s for Latin America. With the crisis Celso Furtado's passion strongly returns, as indignation. His books *Não à Recessão e ao Desemprego* [No to Recession and Unemployment] (1983) and *Brasil: A Construção Interrompida* [Brazil: The Interrupted Construction] (1992), are the evidence of such an indignation.[13]

The return from exile and the participation in the Sarney administration, as Culture Minister, did not allow him to modify his feelings of frustration and indignation.[14] But in 1999, when stabilization was reestablished, and when there were signs of some resumption of development, hope returned, although he remains a strong critic of the economic policy of the Cardoso administration. In his last book *O Longo Amanhecer* [The Long Sunrise] (1999), he pointed out strongly his disenchantment: "in no other moment in our history was so big the distance between what we are and what we intended to be." He restates his criticism of globalization, that, through an irresponsible foreign indebtedness, led the country to the great crisis, but he observes that globalization itself and its lack of control are not responsible for our inability to resume development, but rather the way our elites have reacted to it, by deciding to "acritically adopt an economic policy that privileges transnational companies, whose rationality can only be assessed in a setting of a system of forces that goes beyond the specific interests of the countries that are part of it." An example of this alienation is the proposal made by CEPAL itself, in February 1999, for the dollarization of Latin American economies, a process that, according to that international organization, was already advanced (Furtado, 1999, pp. 18, 23 and 26)

In his short speech in a seminar conducted in São Paulo in his honor, "Reflections On Brazilian Crisis" (2000), his criticism was not only directed against governments, but more broadly against Brazilian elites. He particularly rejected the "explanations [for the nearly stagnation] that pretend to ignore the moral responsibilities of the elites." In face of words favorable to dollarization that were then current in the press (today probably forgotten in view of the Argentinean crisis), he remarked that "if we surrender to dollarization, we will revert to the semi-colonial status." But, as in his last book, in this chapter we see that hope was back at last. In the book, in which there is a section whose title is "What To Do?" he stressed the need to revert the process of concentration of income, to invest in human capital, and, above all, to cope with the problem of globalization by strengthening the national State, which is "the privileged instrument to deal with structural problems." In his brief speech he restates one of his key ideas: the importance of political creativity. "Only political creativity impelled by collective character shall engender the breaking of the impasse" (Furtado 1999, pp. 32–44; Furtado, 2000, p. 4).[15]

The great master continues to think along that line. I don't always agree with him, as I have made apparent in a few places in this chapter, but I always admire him. Celso Furtado was one of my masters, when – still very young – I became interested in economics. I still learn from him. His contribution to the understanding of Brazil is unparalleled; his analysis of development and underdevelopment, a landmark in contemporary thought. In this text, which is not a general overview of his work, I only tried to define a few points regarding the author, the political economist: Furtado has never made compromises with respect to his independence of thought; his method has always been rigorous and mainly historical-inductive; he never ceased to see and think with passion of Brazil and his Northeast.

Notes

1 The identification of the "pioneers of development" was made by Gerald Meyer and Dudley Seers in two books (1984, 1987).

2 Joseph Love (2001) incisively postulates Furtado's role as co-founder of Latin-American structuralism, although Furtado has always insisted on paying his tribute to Raúl Prebisch.

3 It may seem amazing to consider Furtado also as a neoclassical, but this is what we see, for instance, in Mantega (1984, p. 90): "in the first place, there is a certain imprecision and even a good dose of indecisiveness in this thinker, who wavers between classical and neoclassical fundamentals, for me irreconcilable."

4 The deterministic nature of neoclassical thought was shaken only when microeconomics textbooks included game theory – that is, decision theory. Game theoretical authors are then healthily taking a relativist view of the maximizing postulate of neoclassical theory.

5 Epigraph to the *Prefácio a Nova Economia Política* [Preface to New Political Economy] (1976a).

6 See Blaug (1980, pp. 11–12). He uses Hume's problem of induction to reduce its role in economic theory. As most economists, he presumes that there is only "one" economic theory, and therefore the predominant use of one method or the other depending on the approach – microeconomic, macroeconomic or of economic development – makes no sense for him.

7 See Bresser-Pereira and Tadeu Lima (1996).

8 See Lawson (1999, pp. 6–7). Lawson adds: "mainstream's insistence in the universal application of formalist methods presumes, for its legitimacy, that the social world is closed everywhere, that event regularities are ubiquitous."

9 In 1976, in the *Prefácio à Nova Economia Política*, Furtado once again attributed to the classical concept of economic surplus a fundamental role in his analysis of the process of capitalist accumulation.

10 Marx's quotation is from the *Contribution to the Criticism of Political Science.*

11 In *O Brasil Pós-Milagre* [Brazil After the Miracle] (1981a: 56–90) there was still hope, when, after mentioning the bad governments of the 1970s, he wrote two sections in which he looked to the future: "Os Desafios dos Anos 80" [The Challenges of the 1980s] and "Esboço de uma Estratégia" [Outline of a Strategy].

12 In Furtado (1968).

13 Between those two books he wrote his already mentioned three remarkable autobiographical books: *A Fantasia Organizada* (1985), *A Fantasia Desfeita* (1987) and *Ares do Mundo* (1989).

14 In 1984 Furtado published a collection of essays under the title *Cultura e Desenvolvimento em Época de Crise* [Culture and Development in an Era of Crisis], whose key subject was still the crisis of the Brazilian economy, but that should have inspired President José Sarney to invite him for the Ministry of Culture. I was then his fellow minister, between April and December 1987, when I occupied the Ministry of Finance. He was enormously concerned about the failure of the democratic government to cope with the crisis, and to deepen it, instead. As concerned as he felt impotent in view of the facts – since he was located in a ministry that made it possible for him to support me decisively when I needed, but which did not allow him to modify the directions of Brazilian economy. Eventually, I served little time in the administration, and I was also unable to stabilize the Brazilian economy.
15 In this chapter I was not concerned about eliminating prejudices regarding Celso Furtado. This last quotation, however, leads me to point out that one should not infer from it that Furtado is a partisan of state control – the usual accusation the right uses to make of someone who defends the importance of a reconstructed State, able to promote the country's economic and political development. There still are a few partisans of state control, but this is definitely not the case here. In a debate promoted by the newspaper *O Estado de São Paulo*, for instance, Furtado said: "the point is, therefore, to abandon the old idea that the State should solve all problems. We know perfectly well that when the State controls everything, few control the State" (1976b: 39).

References

Bielschowsky, Ricardo (1980) *Pensamento Econômico Brasiliero*. Rio de Janeiro: IPEA/INPES.
Blaug, Mark (1980) *The Methodology of Economics*. Cambridge: Cambridge University Press.
Bourdieu, Pierre (1976) "O Campo Científico," in Renato Ortiz (org.) *Pierre Bourdieu – Sociologia*. São Paulo: Editora Ática, 1983.
Bresser-Pereira, Luiz Carlos e Gilberto Tadeu Lima (1996) "The Irreducibility of Macro to Microeconomics: a Methodological Approach." *Revista de Economia Política* 16(2), April.
Furtado, Celso (1950) "Características Gerais da Economia Brasileira." *Revista de Economia Brasileira* 4(1) March.
Furtado, Celso (1954) *A Economia Brasileira*. Rio de Janeiro: Editora A Noite.
Furtado, Celso (1959) *Formação Econômica do Brasil*. Rio de Janeiro: Fundo de Cultura.
Furtado, Celso (1961) *Desenvolvimento e Subdesenvolvimento*. Rio de Janeiro: Editora Fundo de Cultura.
Furtado, Celso (1962) *A Pré-Revolução Brasileira*. Rio de Janeiro: Editora Fundo de Cultura.
Furtado, Celso (1964) *Dialética do Desenvolvimento*. Rio de Janeiro: Editora Fundo de Cultura.
Furtado, Celso (1966) *Subdesenvolvimento e Estagnação na América Latina*. Rio de Janeiro: Editora Civilização Brasileira.
Furtado, Celso (1967) *Teoria e Política do Desenvolvimento Econômico*. São Paulo: Companhia Editora Nacional.
Furtado, Celso (1968) *Um Projeto para o Brasil*. Rio de Janeiro: Saga.
Furtado, Celso (1969) *Formação Econômica da América Latina*. Rio de Janeiro: Lia Editor.

Furtado, Celso (1972) *Análise do 'Modelo' Brasileiro*. Rio de Janeiro: Editora Civilização Brasileira.

Furtado, Celso (1974) *O Mito do Desenvolvimento*. Rio de Janeiro: Editora Paz e Terra.

Furtado, Celso (1976a) *Prefácio a Nova Economia Política*. Rio de Janeiro: Editora Paz e Terra.

Furtado, Celso (1976b) "Uma Transição Metódica e Progressiva". Debate promoted by *O Estado de S. Paulo*, 8 August, 1976.

Furtado, Celso (1978) *Criatividade e Dependência na Civilização Industrial*. São Paulo: Editora Paz e Terra.

Furtado, Celso (1980) *Pequena Introdução ao Desenvolvimento*. São Paulo: Nacional.

Furtado, Celso (1981a) *O Brasil 'Pós-Milagre'*. Rio de Janeiro: Editora Paz e Terra.

Furtado, Celso (1983) *Auto-retrato Intelectual*. São Paulo: Ática.

Furtado, Celso (1984) *Cultura e Desenvolvimento em Época de Crise*. São Paulo: Editora Paz e Terra.

Furtado, Celso (1985) *A Fantasia Organizada*. Rio de Janeiro: Editora Paz e Terra.

Furtado, Celso (1987a) "Underdevelopment: to Conform or Reform," in Gerald Meyer (ed.) *Pioneers in Development, second series*. New York: Oxford University Press for the World Bank.

Furtado, Celso (1987b) *Transformação e Crise na Economia Mundial*. São Paulo: Editora Paz e Terra.

Furtado, Celso (1989) *A Fantasia Desfeita*. Rio de Janeiro: Editora Paz e Terra.

Furtado, Celso (1991) *Ares do Mundo*. Rio de Janeiro: Editora Paz e Terra.

Furtado, Celso (1992) *Brasil: a Construção Interrompida*. São Paulo: Editora Paz e Terra.

Furtado, Celso (1998) *O Capitalismo Global*. São Paulo: Editora Paz e Terra.

Furtado, Celso (1999) *O Longo Amanhecer*. Rio de Janeiro: Editora Paz e Terra.

Furtado, Celso (2000) "Reflexões sobre a Crise Brasileira." *Revista de Economia Política*, 20(4), October, pp. 3–7.

Iglésias, Francisco (1971) *História e Ideologia*. São Paulo: Editora Perspectiva.

Lawson, Tony (1999) "Connections and Distinctions: Post Keynesianism and Critical Realism." *Journal of Post Keynesian Economics* 22(1), Fall, pp. 3–14.

Lebrun, Gérard (1985) "Os Anos de Aprendizado." São Paulo: *Jornal da Tarde*, September 7.

Love, Joseph (2001) "Furtado e o Estruturalismo," in Luiz Carlos Bresser-Pereira and José Márcio Rego (eds) *A Grande Esperança em Celso Furtado*. Sao Paulo: Editora 34, pp. 221–52.

Mantega, Guido (1984) *A Economia Política Brasileira*. São Paulo e Petrópolis: Livraria e Editora Polis e Editora Vozes.

Marx, Karl (1859) *Contribución a la Critica de la Economia Política*. Buenos Aires: Ediciones Estudio, 1970.

Meyer, Gerald (org.) (1987) *Pioneers in Development, Second Series*. New York: Oxford University Press for the World Bank.

Meyer, Gerald and Dudley Seers (orgs) (1984) *Pioneers in Development*. New York and Oxford: Oxford University Press.

Oliveira, Francisco de (1983) "A Navegação Aventurosa," in Francisco de Oliveira (org.) *Celso Furtado*, São Paulo: Editora Ática.

3 Shifting developmental paradigms in Latin America

Is neoliberalism history?

James M. Cypher[1]

> One of the strangest silences of development thinking is the silence about internal integration. We should distinguish between "external integration" and "internal integration" (or articulation), and recognize that the development of a national economy is more about internal integration than about external integration."
>
> Robert Wade, 2005 p. 94

Preface

First in Chile in 1973 and soon after in Uruguay and Argentina, military coups imposed a new set of economic policies – particularly as they pertained to the role of labor, industry and the state – that subsequently became known as "neoliberalism" (Cypher, 2005; Valdés, 1995; Winn, 2004). Liberalism, the strong faith that many in Latin American – particularly the Chilean elite – registered in support of unconstrained international trade and investment policies throughout much of the Nineteenth Century, was cemented as a policy during an era of improving terms of trade for exported primary products (Bulmer-Thomas, 1994; Pinto, 1962). *Neoliberalism*, consisted of a vague and theoretically empty condemnation of import substitution industrialization and an equally vague championing of export-oriented macroeconomic policies without regard to the massive literature demonstrating the validity of the declining terms of trade argument and related critiques of neoliberalism as originally presented by Raúl Prebisch and Hans Singer (Ocampo, 2004).

Gradually, through the late 1970s and early 1980s, neoliberalism spread, becoming the paradigmatic perspective in virtually all of Latin America and, not incidentally, at the World Bank and International Monetary Fund – where the renascent perspective was commonly known by the (then) less pejorative term, the Washington Consensus. At its height of influence in the 1990s Ha Joon Chang depicted the sweeping hegemony of neoliberalism in the following fashion:

> Neoliberalism has established a near-total worldwide intellectual dominance during the last 25 years. In political debate critics of neoliberalism are routinely dismissed as "economically illiterate" . . .. Even in academia there

has been a remarkable degree of intolerance of dissenting views ... The academic rollback has been particularly vicious in development economics ...

(Chang, 2003a, p. 3)

John Williamson, who had earlier synthesized the basic tenants of neoliberalism in a systematic fashion, served to corroborate Chang's statement on several occasions:

The Washington Consensus represents the common core of wisdom embraced by all serious economists. The superior economic performance of countries that establish and maintain outward-oriented market economies subject to macroeconomic discipline is essentially a positive question. The proof may not be quite as conclusive as that the Earth is not flat, but it is sufficiently well established as to give sensible people better things to do with their time than to challenge its veracity.

(Williamson, 1993, pp. 1334, and 1330)

The Washington Consensus should become ... a part of the basic core ideas that we hold in common and do not need to debate endlessly.

(Williamson, 1998, pp. 11)

As criticisms of some core propositions of neoliberalism were eventually mounted by outstanding practitioners of orthodox development economics – such as Joseph Stiglitz and Dani Rodrik – even they were accused of superficiality and myopia:

Although Stiglitz and Rodrik, and a plethora of others, are correct to criticize the results of the liberal reforms in Latin America, their use of "Washington Consensus" reflects its journalistic meaning (cutting the size of the state and becoming more market friendly) rather than the academic definition, which spelled out a consensus that still exists among mainstream economists proposed by Williamson more than a decade ago ...

(Spanakos and McQuerry, 2004, p. 260)

Introduction

As the above citations record, the neoliberal/Washington Consensus – at least in its *academic version* remains *among mainstream economists* the dominant, unquestionable paradigm governing development theory and (correct) policy for Latin America. Those who dissent from this paradigm are "flat-earthers," "insensible," "non-serious" and unable to distinguish between "journalistic" meanings and "correct" meanings. All this should serve to confirm strikingly Ha-Joon Chang's portrayal of the current environment in development economics as "vicious" and "intolerant."

The Chicago School has provided (directly and indirectly) the core personnel and ideas behind neoliberalism in many Latin American nations and has commonly used a rhetorical device whenever their pet ideas have met challenges – empirical or theoretical: "Our ideas/theories were not applied correctly." Apparently, then, even such eminent economists as Joseph Stiglitz and Dani Rodrik simply cannot find and evaluate the true "essence" of neoliberalism: By offering modest dissent, they have *ipso facto* fallen into an intellectual/theoretical morass, myopically mired in a "journalistic" labyrinth.

While such rhetorical flourishes – long used in economic "science" to propel polemics – have their demonstrable purposes, the increasing shrillness of the neoliberal defenders is clearly a sign of the slippage of the great neoliberal Washington Consensus.

John Williamson notwithstanding, Latin America has experienced paradigmatic shifts through its long history, suggesting that the neoliberal Washington Consensus will eventually be replaced by something else. It is argued in this chapter that the transition from one paradigm to another demands a threefold movement. First, the old paradigm must be subjected to theoretical review and found to be demonstrably lacking in many of its formulations – or at least so presented. Second, empirical evidence need be marshaled to demonstrate that the application of the theory has produced results inconsistent with the predictions of the theory. Third, another conceptualization must be put forward and there must be sufficient force behind this new matrix of ideas to displace or marginalize the earlier paradigm. The third movement is critical and determinant and constitutes the crystallization of a defining political moment. It is the third movement that precipitates the legitimation of the theoretical critique and the justification for the selective interpretation of the empirical evidence which now serves to under-grid the new paradigm. Thus, beginning in the 1980s it became "understood" that import substitution industrialization (ISI) was "exhausted" in Latin America and that it was a "failure" – in spite of evidence to the contrary in many nations (Bruton, 1998; Moreno-Brid and Ros in this volume).[2]

Given the threefold division posited above, this chapter is divided into three parts: The first entails a theoretical confrontation wherein even the most cherished shrine of orthodoxy, Static Comparative Advantage theory, is challenged, and the premises behind export-oriented industrialization (EOI), as postulated by the New Growth Theory (NGT), are examined. The second surveys some of the more striking empirical "anomalies" of the neoliberal paradigm. By definition, a degree of selectivity is employed in an attempt to portray what would hopefully constitute a "representative" array of data, relationships, trends and interpretations. In the final section it is maintained that a revision and reformulation of Industrial Policy holds the greatest promise for sustainable, forward movement in economic development. Whether there can be sufficient political will to move the agenda in this "neostructuralist" direction, however, remains an open question. Recent shifts in broad political alignments in several important Latin American nations now suggest some likelihood of ringing down the neoliberal era.[3] But such a policy shift – propelled by the need to confront the "Polanyi

Problem" – cannot be a "return" to past forms, processes and structures of the ISI era (Cypher, 2004a).

The international financial institutions (IFIs), however, will not be passive observers of such tendencies. Furthermore, the theory of Path Dependence informs us of the conditioning legacy of the past. In this instance it is important to recall that the neoliberal era has served some deeply entrenched national interests – many large Latin American conglomerates (or grupos) have adapted and prospered as the primary focus of accumulation has shifted from the growth of the national market to the possibilities of international markets in finance, the service sector and raw-materials based manufacturing exports.

Theoretical formulations

It is no simple task to attempt to pin down the essential meaning of neoliberalism (Saad-Filho and Johnston, 2005). It is commonplace for researchers to make reference to the work of Friedrich von Hayek and Milton Friedman, yet their works only seem to set some broad underlying parameters. For Latin America, Friedman's colleague Arnold Harberger clearly played a major role in transmitting the fundamental ideas of the "Chicago School" to Chile many years prior to the arrival of the Pinochet dictatorship in 1973 (Huneeus, 2001; Valdés, 1989, 1995). The Chilean case is instructive and indicative: the zeal of the earliest students of Chicago to influence the inner circles of power during the onset of the Chilean dictatorship was tempered by both the restraining power of an entrenched professional military cadre of officers (who were nationalists often positively inclined toward the ideas of state-promoted industrialization) and the tremendous crisis that the Chicago School economists brought upon Chile in 1982–1983. We can term what followed from the mid-1980s to the present (2006) in Chile as "pragmatic neoliberalism" to be distinguished from the "dogmatic neoliberalism" of the 1973–1984 period.[4] Most noted at the onset of the "pragmatic" period, for example, was Chile's willingness to impose capital controls.

More generally, we can see this Chilean progression in various forms throughout Latin America: the dogmatic Chicago/Washington Consensus ideas of the 1980s have given way to "second generation" policies that focus on a range of issues that often entail "institutional" or "structural" change, while folding-in some matters that cannot be dealt with in a purely market framework – such as prioritizing poverty reduction. The World Bank has shifted from structural adjustment and policy-based lending to "second stage structural adjustment" with a prime focus on a vague and questionably oriented emphasis on "institutions" (Cypher, 2003a). Under the guise of its "market friendly approach" the World Bank is no longer focused on the rollback of the State or on the absolute delegitimization of all forms of regulation, but rather it insists that government policies be constrained to those that lead to the enhancement and strengthening of market forces.

At the same time, a second tendency – only mildly distinguished from the market friendly, second-stage structural adjustment approach – is that of Stiglitz's "Post-Washington Consensus," a largely rhetorical construct which highlights many themes long associated with Stiglitz's research on market failures, particularly due to asymmetries, most of which call for more activist state interventions (Stiglitz, 2002).

Yet, at the bedrock level, stripped of all nuance, there is strong convergence between the pragmatic neoliberalism of Chile after 1984, the "market-friendly" "institutional change" approach of the World Bank and the "market-enhancing" tendency advocated by Stiglitz – all seek to clear the way toward the achievement of a dominant role of "market forces" in an "open economy." But, for what purpose? Presumably, development. And, by what means – "spontaneous" market-led development? No, this was the strict Chicago School "dogmatic neoliberal" approach. The present underlying premise is not in the least contemporary – development is to be achieved in an export-led model. This export-led model, or export-oriented industrialization (EOI) is, in turn, premised on both the fundamental hypotheses of David Ricardo's nearly universally celebrated theory of comparative advantage, and a number of theoretical flourishes that are associated with the New Growth Theory. *In short, the term "neoliberalism" has metamorphosed and continues to evolve, while the practitioners of neoliberalism seek to distance themselves from the term itself.*

Although it is no longer fashionable to do so, the analysis in this chapter will continue to make use of the original term – neoliberalism – in lieu of a variety of other terms such as the Washington Consensus, export-oriented industrialization or the post-Washington Consensus. This usage implies acceptance of the continued *evolution and plasticity* of the concept, as well as acknowledgment of the intellectual gymnastics of major proponents of neoliberalism such as John Williamson who recently disclaimed any connection to "quintessentially neoliberal ideas" such as capital account liberalization, monetarism, supply-side economics and the minimal state to his widely cited "Washington Consensus" concept (Williamson, 2002).

Comparative advantage or absolute advantage?

Neoliberal analysis claims that development will be driven by the successful establishment of preferred specializations which arise via market forces in the context of open international trade. Positing the win/win assumption of Ricardian comparative advantage plus the assumed externalities arising from open trade according to the New Growth economics (learning-by-doing, transmission of best practices via the competitive effects of cheap imports and the competitive demands of quality and delivery placed on exporters along with technology transfers via direct foreign investment, etc.), Neoliberal analysis pivots on key implicit assumptions behind the Ricardian "law." First is the assumption of trade balance. In the event this does not occur, it is assumed that price adjustments and quantity adjustments are sufficient – via market forces – to suppress imports and accelerate exports (the assumption of "balanced trade"). Further, as countries move toward specialization based upon trade, businesses that are suppressed by competition are somehow matched by businesses that are stimulated by export opportunities such that export producers, suppliers and employees are all shifted, while none are left unemployed. (That is, full-employment is assumed both before and after nations open to international trade and investment.) Assuming all this to be true, the quantitative impact of opening to free trade is viewed as being relatively modest. CGE models in some instances suggest a short-term boost to real GDP growth rates of one percent or so for a few years.

Hence the emphasis on the New Growth Theory – with these formulations EOI policies are assumed to have much stronger consequences, lasting much longer. Instead of a modest "one-off" boost, the trade opening constitutes what Irma Adelman terms the "X-factor" – the *determinant constraint* that when overcome will yield economic development. According to the New Growth Theory this occurs via increasing returns in the trade sector, arising in part from "learning-by-doing" and "synergistic" effects, technological spillovers, R&D externalities, economies of scale in the export sector, etc. (Adelman, 2001).

In his critique of orthodox trade theory Anwar Shaikh argues that the assumed basis for trade specialization rests on comparative costs of production, but:

> Once nations engage in international trade, relative prices of commodities are *no longer* regulated by their relative costs of production. At the opening of trade, competition in each nation would have produced relative prices regulated by relative costs. Hence the terms of trade, which are merely international relative prices, would initially also be regulated by the relative cost of exports and imports. But comparative cost theory requires that the terms of trade subsequently move in such a way as to balance trade. It follows that they can no longer be regulated by relative costs. They cannot serve two masters.
>
> The theory of real competition comes to the very opposite conclusion. Competition forces prices, and hence the terms of trade, to be regulated by relative real costs at all times. In a country that enjoys an initial trade surplus, the resulting inflow of funds would enhance the availability of credit, which would lower interest rates. Conversely, in the country with the initial trade deficit, the fund outflow would tighten the credit market and raise the interest rate. With interest rates lower in the surplus country and higher in the deficit country, profit-seeking capital would flow from the former to the latter. Thus the surplus country would become a net lender on the world market, and the deficit country a net borrower. Instead of eliminating trade imbalances, this would end up offsetting them with capital flows. Trade imbalances would be *persistent* . . .
>
> (Shaikh, 2005, p. 47).

Under what Shaikh terms "the theory of real competition" the ability to compete in internal trade is determined by the cost of production which arises from real factors: real wages, the level of technological capability, institutions such as business organizations and governmental structures and managerial practices, and resources. According to the New Growth Theory, the dynamic benefits of trade – far exceeding the static benefits – would have to flow disproportionately to the highly industrialized countries since they have a cost advantage in technological development and in institutional structures. It is precisely in this area that we find the greatest degree of applicability for the various virtuous circles and positive cumulative causation processes imagined in this theory. Thus Latin American nations would be forced under the theory of real competition to either seek trade specializations based upon cheap labor or resources – thereby ensuring limited export possibilities in most cases. This sets up the probability, sooner or later, of the Latin American nations suffering from chronic trade deficits, to be covered (temporarily) by capital account flows. Development cannot occur either because it is necessary to continue to suppress wages in order to stay internationally competitive (the race to the bottom scenario), or because resource-based exports suffer from long-term adverse shifts in the terms of trade. Furthermore, shifting to trade-based specializations would not ensure that jobs created in the trade sector(s) would equal jobs lost. National producers would likely increase importations of inputs, in the form of capital goods and especially intermediate products, thereby constraining national employment (and the trade balance). Large firms, national or foreign, would have the capacity to meet the complexities of foreign marketing (increased quality control and delivery capabilities, increased demand for working capital, etc.). These firms would generally operate with more advanced capital-intensive production systems, normally substituting capital for labor and thereby reducing the demand for labor even in labor-intensive production activities.[5]

Meanwhile, in the surplus (advanced industrial) countries, the lowering of the interest rate and the inflow of funds from abroad will also (according to neoclassical theory) lead to a higher investment rate, which should lead to expanding the technological base, which should further distance the surplus country's national system of production from that of the deficit country by lowering its costs of production. This latter point was made long ago by Joan Robinson. It is once again confirmed in Latin America where in 1985 average per capita income (p.c.i.) was 22.9 percent of the US level, falling to 17.7 percent in 1999 (Hausmann and Rodrik, 2003, p. 604).

As Alfredo Saad-Filho states:

> Neoliberalism implies that the main reason why poor countries remain poor is not because they lack machines, infrastructure or money but, rather, because of misconceived state intervention, corruption, inefficiency and misguided economic incentives. Neoliberals also claim that international trade and finance – rather than domestic consumption – should become the engines of development.
>
> (Saad-Filho, 2005a, p. 114)

Yet, Shaikh's critique of neoliberal/neoclassical trade theory, and related comments above, force analysis to move in another direction: even in the absence of "rent seeking" at the state level, and poor national policies, opening to trade is neither a necessary nor sufficient condition for economic development.[6] Whatever gains can be conjured from a policy of openness – such as the idea that "best practices" will be adopted by exporters and subsequently spread through the production system of the poor nation – have to be judged in a larger context:

> Whereas neoliberals often calculate the costs of state intervention in order to press the case for market reforms, they systematically fail to consider the cost of the neoliberal policies. These include the loss of dynamic benefits resulting from permanently lower growth rates, the social and economic costs of high unemployment, foreign currency waste in imports of luxury goods and capital flight, and the negative impact of the contraction of the industrial base which invariably follows the neoliberal reforms.
>
> (Saad-Filho, 2005a, p. 116)

But, to return to the critique of Ricardian trade theory, the failure to demonstrate the validity of the two key assumptions – (1) full employment before and after a trade opening; (2) balanced trade, with adjustments to surpluses/deficits occurring automatically through relative price increases in surplus nations (thereby destroying the surplus) and price declines occurring in the deficit nation (thereby destroying the deficit) – opens the door to an older theory of international trade. Absolute advantage is the appropriate theoretical formulation for trade relations in the neoliberal era according to both Shaikh and William Milberg (Shaikh, 1996, 2005; Milberg, 1994, 2004). Milberg argues that even among the advanced industrial nations the empirical evidence does not show that trade is based upon Ricardian principles of relatively factor endowments, based in "labor coefficients" (Milberg, 1994, p. 222). On these, and other, grounds Milberg finds the theory of comparative advantage wanting. In its stead, he argues for the replacement of the theory with one of absolute advantage based in technological capabilities. In this trade environment technological capabilities determine success or failure in trade, and these capabilities are determined by the institutional matrix of the nation, including the existence or non-existence of a national system of innovation and the capacity to incorporate and adapt technologies via "upscaling," according to Alice Amsden's research on Asia (Amsden and Chu, 2003; Amsden, 2004). Critical in the final analysis is the State: "the state is in the crucial position of providing organizational, skill-development and innovation incentives to promote growth and competitiveness" (Milberg, 1994, p. 233).

In a world of absolute advantage, countries that are ahead technologically tend to stay ahead in matters of trade. That its, the low cost producer of the product is expected to be the nation most able and likely to plow back part of the surplus from trade into R&D, innovation adaptation, upscaling and diversification. Other nations, in this case Latin America, are crowded-out of the high value-added activities given that the largest firms (the conglomerates) have an antipathy toward reinvesting their profits in R&D and the Latin America States (particularly in the neoliberal era) lack the vocation to fill the void left by the private sector in the area of technological innovation (Mouguillansky, 2002). In a world where trade is based in absolute advantage:

> Modernization is the only remaining alternative, both in theory and in practice. It is only by raising both the level and the growth rate of productivity that a country can, in the long run, prosper in international trade. This may be done through internal means, through (directed) foreign investment, or with the help of other nations. But it will not happen by itself, through the magic of the market. On the contrary, precisely because free trade reflects the uneven development of nations, by itself it tends to reproduce and even deepen the very inequalities on which it was founded. It follows that success in the free market requires extensive and intensive social, political and infrastructural support. While this may seem like heresy to the free marketers of the world, it is nothing new to those familiar with the actual history and practices of successful capitalist nations.
>
> (Shaikh, 1996 p. 76)

Nations that do not follow the path recommended by Amsden, Milberg and Shaikh – a path that would clearly eschew a strong, unidirectional focus on the external sector in favor of the internal market/regional market as a first order priority – are condemned in the world of absolute advantage to fleeting booms in commodities and intensive attempts to accommodate foreign capital's interest in cheap labor production processes that relegate host nations to the low end of the global production chain. Latin American nations can only seek greater participation in foreign trade through strategies that further lower the cost of their laborers and/or their resources.

The pratfalls of commodity-dependent strategies are well known and well documented both at the theoretical and empirical level, with Aníbal Pinto's dissection of the failures of the Chilean elite to harness commodities booms being perhaps the classical statement of the failure of the State to seize the many incredible opportunities at hand (Pinto, 1962). What would appear to be new is the surge in "manufactured" exports, including "high and intermediate technology exports" from Latin America – particularly from Mexico – in the past 25 years. Behind the appearance of a drastically revised export sector, no longer dependent on low value-added commodity exports subject to the devastating effects of the long-run deterioration in the terms of trade, is the fact that the global production/value chain has been "sliced" in such a way that transnational corporations (TNCs) can now operate a globally integrated production system without transferring significant production skills to Latin American nations. In autos, electronics and a host of other production processes now involving Latin America in portions of the value-added process, it is profitable to import semi-finished inputs, add cheap labor and re-export finished products (or products that have reached a higher stage of completion) without greatly disseminating advanced forms of "learning" or technological spin-offs. William Milberg's recent analysis of this process highlights the growing role of subcontracting (or outsourcing) within the context of the globally integrated production system (Milberg, 2004). The recent growing emphasis on subcontracting further undercuts the likelihood of synergistic effects arising from direct foreign investment as assumed by the New Growth Theory (NGT) for the simple reason that increasingly TNCs are able to subcontract with supplier firms (often other TNCs) within a structure wherein the prime producers/buyers (the lead firms) in the global production chain operate under conditions of oligopoly/oligopsony while the subcontractors function under essentially competitive conditions:

> In sum, there are two, seemingly incongruous, tendencies that can be discerned in the evolving structure of global industry. On the one hand, and despite the popular association of globalization with greater competition, there is a strong tendency towards greater concentration of industry globally. On the other hand there is evidence that more and more developing countries are entering manufacturing industries at the low end of the value chain. This constitutes the asymmetry of market structures in global commodity chains.
>
> (Milberg, 2004, p. 13)

For many suppliers/subcontractors the means to stay competitive is not to innovate through the introduction of advanced production processes, but rather to squeeze the workforce. Instead of creating the capacity to innovate and "upscale" the production process, most Latin American nations engaging in globally integrated production processes are trapped in a global pyramid structure of dominant and subordinate firms – with the Latin American producers specializing in processes that receive few if any positive externalities as imagined by the NGT, while bearing the brunt of the negative externalities associated with such practices: that is, productivity increases are essentially "exported" as they move up the production/value chain, captured through the pricing structure that forces suppliers to forfeit control/receipt of productivity increases. This exportation of increased productivity means that profit margins are too thin to support R&D outlays, while wage levels are too low to sustain a broad mass market in commodities that would engender economies of scale and/or other conceivable externalities. When profit margins are not thin firms rarely plow their surpluses into technological innovation because the major Latin American firms are not structurally organized around an R&D ethos, they do not have the support needed from the State for such activities and they do not have a cadre of personnel capable of sustained technological innovation. Under conditions of absolute advantage there are only two essential ways to remain competitive: (1) lowering costs through technological innovation, or (2) lowering costs through the intensification of the labor process. With the path to technological innovation blocked, the emphasis on the cheap labor strategy remains the foremost option. Engineering a "strategy switch" from low value-added activities – abandoning a given export market through a strategy of upscaling – can only be achieved if a nation has the capability of altering institutions and organizational structures to a sufficient degree to ensure quick adaptation to global demand (Amsden and Chu 2003, p. 263). To engage sequentially in this process it is necessary to have the capability of creating new mechanisms of discipline and control which are binding both for the private sector and for the agents of the public sector. State assistance to facilitate upscaling (or a "strategy switch") away from cheap labor/resource intensive activities demands State/private institutional procedures and organizational structures that demonstrate integrity.[7]

In this larger context it is important to determine if the many cases of privatization of infrastructure or national industrial firms has resulted in the fragmentation of either the infrastructure base or the national production system, thereby raising relative costs and making the nation even more uncompetitive in trade areas or sectors. This has been exactly the case in Argentina as documented by Daniel Azpiazu: Azpiazu shows that both national and international capital was drawn to the rentier possibilities of acquiring State properties (usually natural monopolies) at subsidized prices, and then succeeding through cost-cutting strategies, asset sell-offs and price increases in attaining the highest rate of profit within the economy (Azpiazu, 2005, pp. 45–79). Thus, with ever more fragmented and dysfunctional systems of infrastructure, Latin American nations seeking to achieve or sustain an absolute advantage in "sliced" global production/value chains in manufacturing are ever-more dependent on the cheap labor strategy because an innovation-intensive, R&D-intensive alternative (as imagined by the NGT) implicitly assumes a high and increasingly functional infrastructural system – most particularly in the area of education.

Neoliberalism, in particular, has no theory of production, and as a *sphere of circulation* based theory, it fails to account for the long-run costs of the fragmentation of the production base built-up painstakingly during the ISI era. Rather than attempting to build upon this base, the theory of openness required the abolition of all forms of restraint on imports, and this led to the shattering of a web of complex production commodity chains – webs that often interwove para-state firms with the private sector. The theory of comparative advantage suggests that this underlying matrix of the production base will be simply *shifted* from one set of specializations to another. The dynamic process of *shifting* from a production system based on meeting the demands of the home market to one geared to the demands of the external market is assumed to be benign and symmetrical. Nothing, however, could be further from the case. After having reviewed much of the recent discussion and econometric "evidence" relating to the neoliberal period – including the effects of "second generation" Washington Consensus proposals, Dani Rodrik concluded that:

> The purpose of inserting an economy into the global economic system should be envisioned as a means to accelerate growth and development, not as an end in itself. Maximization of foreign trade and the flow of international capital is not, nor can it be, the policy objective of development.
>
> (Rodrik, 2004b, p. 116)

In fact, Rodrik finds only one reason to tighten linkages with the international economy – at least for nations of any size: there is a conceivable functional relationship between more trade and development when this leads to the importation of capital goods that are produced substantially cheaper abroad. But this link requires an "export-investment nexus" a relationship well-established in East Asia (and largely absent in Latin America) not due to market forces but rather to industrial policies – discussed below (Cypher, 2003b). That is, only if there exists a functional structure within the economy – in terms of the role of the State, the expansion of the necessary infrastructure, a national system of innovation and a nationally oriented *industrial* elite – will expanded exports result in expanded importation of capital goods that will be utilized to expand the national production base.

Although Rodrik does not explicitly focus on the limits of absolute advantage in the structural context of Latin America (as discussed above) his research shows that the suppositions of openness based on comparative advantage theory as a strategy for development (as fostered by neoliberalism) cannot be empirically demonstrated. After completing an exhaustive study of the research concerning the central hypotheses of neoliberalism, Rodrik finds that:

> The nature of the relationship between trade policy and growth continues for the most part to be an open question. … In fact, there are reasons to doubt the existence of a general, unequivocal, relationship between openness to foreign trade and economic growth waiting to be discovered. What is most probable is that this relationship is contingent and dependent upon a series of external and internal characteristics.
>
> (Rodrik, 2004b, p. 117)

Empirical issues of neoliberal policy

One outstanding result of the effects of opening throughout Latin America is the fact that as their economies have *shifted* toward trade the "resources freed up" through greater import competition and through the "shrinkage" of the State sector have *not* been absorbed. In particular there has been an explosion of the "informal" sector along with the destruction of the institutional matrix of the ISI era, resulting in a new empirical relationship in the neoliberal era: countries with large informal sectors grow more slowly than those with strong institutional structures and small informal sectors (Larraín, 2004, p. 189). To move in the opposite direction – to construct an export-investment nexus – national policies of technological advance, not the assumed automatic forces of the market, must be put into place, or maintained and expanded. But that is not enough – investment cannot merely be of a "capital-deepening" nature as they were under ISI, according to Carlota Pérez:

> There are no magic formulas to attain developed status without technological capabilities – as understood in a basic sense as the incorporation at

the level of the human actors of the requisite social, technical and economic *"know how."* This reality, clearly recognized in the past, was lost from view within the context of the unique conditions of the policies of import substitution industrialization. These policies enabled, for a limited time period, many countries to achieve extraordinary results in terms of economic growth, making investments in plants, equipment and mature technologies, without having to make great efforts to advance the level of learning or training.

(Pérez, 2004, 228)

Having used-up these quick-returns options, presently the *shifting* of the national production system would require massive State intervention in the area of R&D and science policy far beyond that achieved in Latin America in the ISI period. Due to the pervasive differences between the private rate of return and the social rate of return from R&D – the classic market failure case – neoliberal policy bent on trade opening and hosting foreign direct investment (FDI) condemns Latin American economies to cheap labor and/or resource-intensive activities. That empirical evidence shows this for Latin America in the resource area (when Mexico's exports are excluded) was highly predictable. Throughout Latin America the emphasis on openness has been accompanied by greater volatility and this has acted further to undermine progress in closing the technological/science gap:

> Today, the context of a volatile and uncertain macroeconomic environment has generated a defensive microeconomic environment, with a low propensity both for investment and technical change, resulting in a reduced number of new manufacturing plants, and scarce examples of productivity improvement, which fails to constitute the consolidation of an adequate capability to reach levels of international competitiveness.
>
> (Cimoli and Katz, 2004, p. 242)

Ironically, Rodrik's best case for opening – financing the importation of capital goods – leads to perverse effects according to the broad, detailed research of Mario Cimoli and Jorge Katz: as the importation of cheaper capital goods proceeds so too does the decline of the internal technological capacity of the nation (Cimoli and Katz, 2004, p. 253). As they note, in a fivefold division of the industrial sectors (1. metal working industries, excluding autos; 2. the auto sector; 3 and 4. food processing, tobacco and natural resource processing; and 5. labor-intensive industries) for Argentina, Brazil, Chile, Colombia and Mexico essentially *all* sectors have shrunk except 3 and 4 between 1970 and 2000 (excluding Mexico) (Cimoli and Katz, 2004, Cuadro 9.1, p. 249). Latin America is steadily shifting toward activities that demand a relatively low density of knowledge, relegating Latin America to an "overwhelmingly subsidiary role" as the neoliberal policies are incorporated.

José Antonio Ocampo, observing these same trends, puts great emphasis on the "heterogeneous" (but not dualistic) nature of the economy. This "disarticulated" economy has created a complex double movement within the national production base: there are now in Latin America more firms that are 'world class', many if not most of which are subsidiaries of TNCs. But, at the same time there are more firms engaged in low-productivity activities – activities that now absorb six of every ten urban workers. What this means is that the degree of heterogeneity is *rising* with consequences that are the exact opposite of those anticipated by the neoliberals: rather than "market signals" that provide the basis for the notion of "automaticity" in an economy, as heterogeneity rises so does the likelihood that possible spillover effects are less frequently found. *Only in a homogeneous structure of national production can it be anticipated that spillover effects and externalities will be captured and utilized by other firms.* New Growth Theory assumes a homogeneous national production system, but in Latin America in the instances where "world class" firms have emerged this has not led to general spread effects (Ocampo, 2004).

In his important essay "Industrial Policy for the Twenty-First Century" (to be examined further in the next section) Dani Rodrik finds that the benefits of the neoliberal opening were restricted to some exporters, the financial sector and skilled workers. The price for these limited sectoral benefits was steep; labor and total factor productivity growth rates fell below levels achieved under the ISI strategies. Further, seemingly in accordance with Ocampo's evidence of growing heterogeneity and the lack of transmission signals and effects within the national production base, Rodrik finds that innovation spread effects are not all (or primarily) on the supply-side: entrepreneurs in the real economy cannot anticipate the benefits of innovation and therefore do not provide a "demand" for it. Investment in science and technology has atrophied because it is failing to realize its role owing to a lack of demand. There is also a weak demand for schooling (and a consequential "oversupply" of educated workers/professionals) (Rodrik, 2004a, pp. 3–5).

As might be expected, Latin American nations have deviated from the neoliberal program in many instances. EOI has involved a broad range of subsidies, benefits and incentives targeted at exporters and FDI. But, the spillover effect anticipated by way of the New Growth Theory has for the most part not been realized. Hanson's research shows this to be particularly the case regarding FDI – while Milberg shows that TNCs now have a lower tendency to engage in FDI as outsourcing/subcontracting structures have become more profitable (Hanson, 2001; Milberg, 2004). While neoliberal policy has upheld openness and export-led growth and FDI as the engines of growth:

> Economic research provides little support for this presumption. In has been known for a while that exporting firms tend to be more productive and technologically more dynamic than firms that sell mainly to the home market. We now know that the reason has to do . . . not with any benefits that accrue from the activity of exporting *per se*, but simply with selection effects. It is the better firms that are able or choose to export. Consequently, subsidizing

exports can do very little to enhance overall productive or technological capacity. Similarly, careful studies have been able to find very little systematic evidence of technological or other externalities from foreign direct investment, some even finding negative spillovers.

(Rodrik, 2004a, p. 30)

Robert Gwynne's research of firm-level dynamics in the neoliberal era adds another dimension to Rodrik's analysis: Gwynne finds that in the course of the 1980s in Brazil an array of intermediate level national firms producing auto-parts, known for their propensity to plow back their profits into further investments, were absorbed by a small number of TNCs. This shift – noted also in Chile – left more and more of the process of technological advancement within the framework of the TNCs who, with their tendency to "internalize" and control, were less likely to be sources of technological spillovers, diffusion of learning or other external effects. At the same time at the national level, Neoliberal policies forced a reduction in programs of technological advancement, and national firms only rarely served to close the gap left by receding outlays on the part of the State (Gwynne, 2004, pp. 245–6). The spin-offs, externalities, forms of learning and other aspects of "increasing returns" championed by the NGT did not emerge – but disarticulation did:

[Neoliberalism] did not solve, and quite probably increase two problems associated with the nature of firms in Latin America. First, investment continued to be concentrated among large entrepreneurs that have not shown the capacity to develop backward and forward linkage with smaller firms. This has made the development of localized clusters of technologically dynamic firms much more difficult to achieve. Secondly, local supplier chains were destroyed by the quest for competitiveness through increasing imported inputs.

(Gwynne, 2004, p. 246)

This led to a more restricted flow of information exchanges and limited cooperation between firms at the local level, along with slowing job formation, since the smaller supplier firms had a greater propensity to create employment. Further, firms *without* extensive local networks – such as backward linkages – tended to be more flexible in meeting the requirements of buyer-driven commodity chains. "The more embedded a firm is in local supply networks, the less likely that firm is to compete on the global economic stage" (Gwynne, 2004, p. 248). Under such conditions, the likelihood of technology sharing, learning and other virtuous circle effects assumed by the NGT are not going to appear.

EOI policies designed to drawn in FDI have been at cross-purposes with neoliberal polices of shrinking the State due to the fact that FDI correlates positively and significantly with social outlays on education – particularly secondary education according to the findings of Tuman and Emmert (2004, p. 22). Tuman and Emmert's research also reveals a darker side of neoliberalism – in the race to attract FDI nations in Latin America that do more to suppress human rights, particularly Argentina, Brazil, Chile and Mexico, are able to receive more FDI. Suppression of human rights (including labor's right to organize) was found to be an important variable determining levels of FDI in the 1979–1996 period (Tuman and Emmert, 2004, p. 21).

Interestingly, during the neoliberal era, as Latin America nations have been led to increase their specialization level in trade it has become established that there is an *inverse* relationship between trade, specialization and per capita income (Imbs and Wacziarg, 2003). Successful nations tend to move from high levels of specialization at low levels of income to much greater degrees of diversification – only at very high levels of p.c.i. does this diversification trend modestly reverse.[8] Once again, supporting Shaikh's analysis, the Ricardian premises of the neoliberal model are undercut. Most interesting is the fact that it is in precisely those areas where EOI has been successful – in Mexico in autos, computers and electronics; in Brazil in shoes, steel and aircraft; and in Chile in wine, salmon, forestry and copper – that we find industries built, strengthened and adapted through ISI policies (Cypher, 2005; Moreno-Brid and Ros, in this volume). These industries exhibit an historical trajectory the opposite of what would be predicted by the neoliberal model.

Why are the spread effects so weak in Latin America? Hausmann and Rodrik contend that there is no way for business owners to capture the benefits of adoption, modification or adaptation of technologies: whenever a business firm exhibits a successful innovation it will not be able to claim proprietary rights. The innovation will quickly be copied and the potential excess profit from this activity will be eradicated. Knowing this, business firms do not generally bother to search out strategies of adaptation, modification and application/adoption. This is the case too under ISI unless a counterstrategy is deployed, but matters are worse under neoliberalism to the degree that under this regime it is relatively easier for firms to jump from sector to sector or move within a sector, making it even more difficult to realize the benefits of adoption/adaptation of technological investments. Breaking this vicious circle would demand State policies. However, "[u]nder ISI, Latin America was marked by plenty of promotion, but too little discipline. In the 1990s, Latin America had considerable discipline (provided through competitive markets and open trade) but too little promotion" (Hausmann and Rodrik, 2003, p. 628).

On the empirical level the emphasis on openness and FDI led to a brutal process of deindustrialization, often partly arising due to a policy of overvaluation of the exchange rate:

> Cheap imports badly harmed local industry. In Argentina, Brazil and Mexico, the proportion of manufacturing value added to GDP reached, respectively, 31 percent (1989), 35 percent (1982) and 26 percent (1987). By 2001, this ratio had declined to 17, 21, and 19 percent (1987). Industrial sector employment also fell, especially in Argentina, where it declined from 33 to 25 percent of the labor force between 1991 and 1996. In Brazil, more

than one million industrial jobs were lost between 1989 and 1997. During the neoliberal era, open unemployment across Latin America increased, *on average*, from 5.8 percent to nearly 10 percent of the workforce – but this excludes underemployment and informal employment which may reach half of the labor force. Finally, average wages fell by 16 percent in Argentina, 8 percent in Brazil and 4 percent in Mexico between 1994 and 2001.

(Saad-Filho, 2005, p. 226)

Equally undesirable, but perhaps more directly in non-conformance with Neoliberalism, both savings and investment fell in Latin America's largest and most economically important nations. From the mid-1980s to the late 1990s the investment/GDP ratio fell by one-third in Argentina, it dropped by 25 percent in Brazil from 1989 to 2001 and fell by more than 25 percent in Mexico between 1981 and 2001. Meanwhile, in the same time periods the ratio of savings/GDP fell even more (Saad-Filho, 2005, p. 226).

Exhibiting the "Polanyi problem" – undercutting of social expenditures and opening to market forces leads to the rise of social opposition and the subsequent rise of a social safety net – social expenditures went up across most of Latin America, a trend most apparent in many respects in the very origin of the neoliberal model – Chile (Cypher, 2004a). Overall, in the 1990s social expenditures went up from 10.4 percent of GDP to 13.1 percent, which put the level of social expenditure *above* that of the ISI era in 1981 (Hueber and Solt, 2004, p. 161). With more recent adjustments to the Washington Consensus model proponents might claim that this is all consistent with the new focus on poverty eradication, but the impetus for these shifts arises from social forces mobilized in opposition to the neoliberal model. Hueber and Solt make use of the "Morley Index" of neoliberal policies (the degree to which government interventions in trade, finance, taxation and state ownership have declined) to analyze the relationship between imposition of the neoliberal agenda and general macroperformance. The latest update of the results shows that for the 16 Latin American nations in the index on average the degree of conformance to the model rose by 71 percent while p.c.i. declined by 23 percent from 1985 to 1999 (Hausmann and Rodrik, 2003, p. 604). Meanwhile, Hueber and Solt show that:

> Higher levels of liberalization and more radical processes of liberalization are associated with higher levels of inequality and poverty. The changes in inequality are impressive: The countries with the more liberalized economies as of 1995 started out around 1982 with lower levels of inequality than the countries with the less liberalized economies as of 1995, but the two sets of countries switched position with the more liberalized economies ending up with higher levels of inequality around 1995 than the less liberalized economies. ... The more radical reformers increased their Gini index twice as much as the more moderate reformers."

(Hueber and Solt, 2004, p. 156)

In what appeared to be a debate format, Michael Walton of the World Bank critically analyzed the Hueber and Solt critique, claiming that "The reforms were good for growth," he presented some surprising concessions:

> Advocates of a shift to greater market orientation in Latin America [anticipated that] ... growth would be spurred ... income distribution would improve through the reductions in the opportunities for rents and corruption ... and [that there would be] rising rewards to unskilled labor from greater trade. ... The shifts to a greater dependence on markets were ... probably disappointing relative to the expectations of advocates, and certainly incomplete as a development strategy. ... A broad neoliberal view, in the sense of the radical retreat to the minimalist state, is generally bad for development.
>
> (Walton, 2004, pp. 168 and 165)

Yet, consistent with Williamson's 2002 revision of the Washington Consensus, Neoliberalism might be abandoned in name but not in essence. Thus Walton offers more focus on the positive role of state intervention claiming, as has the World Bank against all possible evidence, that the East Asian successes are actually good examples of "market friendly" neoliberalism (Amsden, 2001, 2004; Cypher, 2003a, 2003b).

Neoliberalism committed errors in its understanding of the role of the State, it is "hopelessly incomplete as a development strategy" but Walton concedes very little, particularly he does not concede that the neoliberal model was erroneous, and based on unsupported theoretical assumptions and premises – most particularly in its embrace of Ricardian/orthodox trade theory.

No nation in Latin America has received as much support from the World Bank, the IMF, the IADB (all International Financial Institutions) and the U.S. government to adopt the neoliberal model as Mexico. Mexico's macrofundamentals have largely improved, with the notable and not accidental exception of the structural trade balance which has been in constant deficit aside from crisis years (when imports have collapsed and exports have surged due to devaluations). Viewing the weak growth of per capita income, which has consistently registered a level of less than 50 percent of that achieved in the 1940–1980 ISI period in the years 1990–2005, and a broad range of similar trends – including a 20 percent drop in the real manufacturing wage, 1980–2001 – a recent paper by Enrique Dussel presents several major conclusions regarding the neoliberal experiment:

> [The] net penetration of imports reflects one of the main characteristics of manufacturing since [the onset of the] liberalization strategy: its increasing dependency on imports, and, as a result, an increasing rupture of backward and forward linkages and value-added chains. ... In terms of industrial organization, the learning effects, as well as positive impact on employment, productivity, value-added and technological development, are very limited for the rest of the economy. However the effects of import liberal-

ization, the overvaluation of the exchange rate and the fall in financing to the productive sector have been very negative for the rest of the economy, and particularly for firms, branches sectors, and regions not linked to exports ... this process affects a process of low employment generation [and] ... low quality of the generated employment ... Thus liberalization strategy has generated a process of increasing socioeconomic polarization and is, in the medium and long run, unsustainable. NAFTA, from this perspective is not the cause, but one of the most significant elements for deepening this process during the 1990s.

(Dussel, 2004, pp. 19 and 26)

Finally, the theme of the firm needs to be incorporated into the analysis of the impact of neoliberal policies in Latin America. As Eva Paus and Helen Shapiro have noted, neither the New Growth Theory (NGT) nor the Washington Consensus have an explicit analysis of the role of the firm (Paus, 2003; Shapiro 2003). NGT pivots on the incorporation of technical changes, yet is silent on how this might occur in the context of Latin America. As Paus emphasizes, the empirical record is sufficiently complete on this point: Incorporation/adaptation of technical change does not occur in the vacuum of perfectly competitive markets (which in any case do not describe Latin American production conditions). Rather, as Paus demonstrates, mere openness to FDI and trade yield nothing in terms of technological dynamism and, hence, productivity growth. Key underlying institutional conditions – absent in the neoliberal model – must be present. Uppermost is an adequate infrastructure, which is largely a function of public sector policy and expenditures. Public education is the bedrock foundation for (1) "domestic ability to adopt new technology to domestic circumstances" (know-how) and, (2) "domestic ability to develop new technology" (know-why) (Paus, 2003, p. 430). The re-primarization of exports and the reliance on cheap-labor assembly mitigates whatever passive effect that might be anticipated via a policy of openness to FDI and trade because these activities are least likely to require or nurture technological advances.

Shapiro's focus on the firm emphasizes the "conceptual schizophrenia" that exists between firm level policies and practices as advocated by business schools and business consultants and those who uphold the tenets of the Washington Consensus. Following the ideas advanced by Michael Porter (author of the widely cited *Competitive Advantage of Nations*) the business school approach is to assume that firms exist within an environment of oligopoly power where, rather than passivity under market-induced conditions of comparative advantage, firms must strive for competitive advantage – emphasize technological mastery and dynamism, brand-name identification, product quality, delivery and service. Firms are, in the Porter model, not price-takers, but price-makers. In Porter's view, an absolute advantage based in natural resources, low wages or devaluations is simply not sustainable (Shapiro, 2003, pp. 247–8). Shapiro argues that the international financial institutions (IFIs) have grudgingly shifted some of their focus from comparative advantage to competitive advantage analysis, but (like Porter) the modest shift in emphasis remains constrained in crucial areas: the IFIs, consistent with their neoliberal orientation are hostile to the State and particularly industrial policy (discussed below) and they are silent on the effects of the TNCs. Porter's model assumes that a competitive advantage can be created in an open economy, but three of the underlying conditions for the creation of competitive advantage are a strong set of supplier industries surrounding the major export (oligopoly) firms and the existence of both large amounts of skilled labor and a "deep" infrastructure. Yet, up-to-date, versatile, well-financed supplier firms are virtually absent in Latin America. This has been the major reason why in many nations when exports have grown rapidly, imports – particularly of intermediate goods – have grown even faster. The missing link in Porter's analysis is the necessary role that the public sector must play in creating an environment for innovations – namely, building the national supplier base, the infrastructure and developing the requisite labor skills. Amsden's research has demonstrated in detail that the ingredients for the construction of a successful policy of competitive advantage can be found, but only through the allowance for a determinate role for State policy – a position of anathema for the IFIs and the business school/Porter approach (Amsden, 2001, 2004; Amsden and Chu, 2003). The IFI/Porter approach denies the vital positive role played by import substitution industrialization, which provided the legacy for currently successful export industries throughout much of Latin America. Instead of a historical approach to the issue of competitive advantage, the IFI/Porter approach assumes that all the necessary elements of a successful strategy of competitiveness will arrive in a nation via market structures. Yet, openness to FDI has clearly resulted in deindustrialization and the destruction of the national supplier base, while failing to foster a national innovation system. Instead, intra-firm transactions have increased, and most recently a new emphasis on outsourcing has created new structures wherein the economic surplus accumulated by supplier firms is increasingly appropriated via monopsony/oliogopsony structures by dominant TNCs operating globally integrated systems of production (Milberg, 2004).

Geske Dijkstra's dense empirical and theoretical analysis, preceding the work of Paus and Shapiro, reaches many of the same conclusions as their research (Dijkstra, 2000). Regarding the re-primarization effect throughout Latin America, Dijkstra emphasizes that one of the major dynamic effects of openness – economies of scale for exporters – is much less in agriculture and cheap-labor manufacturing, and more limited in primary processing activities than in manufacturing (Dijkstra, 2000, p. 1570). Meanwhile, great competition from imports leads to the substitution of imports and consequently a decline in outlays at the national firm level on science, research and development – at the same time that neoliberal policies force a reduction in State outlays for R&D (Dijkstra, 2000, p. 1570).

> Theory suggests that dynamic efficiency effects will occur mainly in countries that already have a firm industrial base or that are far ahead in the

industrialization process. Otherwise, the reallocation of resources in keeping with static comparative advantage that results from trade liberalization will lower long-term growth prospects. This is the result of a lower income elasticity of demand for these goods, and a lower potential for internal and external economies of scale, learning effects, and R&D investment. Countries that do not have this industrial base are expected to miss out on these long-run effects.

(Dijkstra, 2000, p. 1580)

Towards a new paradigm?

The previous section was not presented with the intended purpose of encapsulating a systematic critique of neoliberalism in its pragmatic form. Rather, in consonance with the understanding of the nature of a paradigmatic shift, the purpose has been to present as concisely as possible, a body of research that conveys the many "anomalies" found to exist regarding the predicted effects of the neoliberal Washington Consensus. It is not relevant, but it is to be anticipated, that no array of anomalies will be sufficient to convince neoliberals to pronounce their conceptions "unsustainable." But, these anomalies do function on two important levels. First, the defenders of the paradigm face a dwindling audience, and their less-committed compatriots tend to distance themselves from association with the paradigm even as the defenders attempt to introduce ever more *plastic* nuances into their position in the hope of forestalling the impending demise of the paradigm. Second, the more marginally committed and the opponents of the paradigm now initiate a search for a new paradigm and commence a struggle to achieve hegemony. This section deals with the search for the new paradigm, commenting on some of the most theoretically compelling ideas that have been advanced.

Neostructuralism

The neostructuralist critique of neoliberalism was advanced in the early 1980s, long before a mass of empirical evidence accumulated on the disarticulating and retarding effects of neoliberalism in Latin America. By 1987 ECLAC had produced a special issue of the *CEPAL Review* (No. 34) devoted both to Prebisch and to expositions by Norberto González, Osvaldo Rosales, Ricardo Ffrench-Davis and Sergio Bitar, while Osvaldo Sunkel had repeatedly advocated a "development from within" strategy.[9]

Sunkel argued that the ISI period was driven by the structure of demand and the growth of demand which meant that Latin America attempted to build sectors and industries that would be viable given the highly unequal distribution of effective demand in Latin America. In contrast, he urged a new strategy designed to create a "basic endogenous nucleus" of industries designed to meet both broader-based domestic and external demands, with a focus on the "creation and dissemination of technical progress" (Sunkel, 1990, p. 156). But, the timing and place of this critique limited or defeated its impact: the Cepalistas were physically located in Santiago where Pinochet's economists were determined to marginalize all critical perspectives – purging the universities and research centers as well as the means of communication of nearly all heterodox economic ideas. At the same time, while the neostructuralist critique gained some traction with the devastating Chilean crisis of 1982–1984, the following economic expansion that turned into a ten-year boom tended to silence some critics and de-legitimize others. While the boom ended in late 1997, it was not until several years later when the evasions of the neoliberals had lost credibility that the echo of the neostructuralist critique was once again to be heard.

In recent years José Antonio Ocampo has become a major proponent of a renewed neostructural approach. Ocampo has placed emphasis on the need to build an investment-export nexus and on finding and supporting industries or sectors that propagate technological progress – finding the "dynamic nucleus" of firms and sectors that engender productivity growth and diffusion through a given period of time (Ocampo, 2004, p. xxv). His vision of such a transformation, however, would seem to pivot on a successful process of negotiation with external agencies such as the WTO, the World Bank and the IMF in order to permit the imposition of temporary forms of assistance in key areas.

> A [neostructuralist] policy requires recognition on the part of the international community that [these] strategies are an essential component for dynamic growth; this implies "special and differential treatment" in three areas: (1) programs of protection for intellectual property that helps in the creation of technology transfers; (2) temporary development of industries that will serve to substitute for imported products, and (3) particularly given current conditions, temporary support for new exports (from potential industries) through the use of incentives designed to diversify exports, as well as mechanisms that will allow for the increase in the level of national content of goods exported . . .
>
> (Ocampo, 2004, pp. xxvii–xxviii)

Both Ocampo here, and Sanjaya Lall elsewhere, have made similar calls for a new "international policy regime" – a request that would seem to rest on the not inconsiderable intellectual legitimacy of the case for the negation of the neoliberal paradigm (Lall, 2005, p. 63). Yet, operationalizing key elements of the Neostructuralist paradigm through the good will or volition of the IFIs – institutions that have been in the lead in imposing pragmatic neoliberalism – would seemingly hold little promise.

Industrial policy – following the East Asian lead

More promising it would seem is the modification and adoption (at the national level) of a broad host of strategies demonstrated to have been highly effective in East Asia. Obviously, Latin America is not and cannot become a mere follower of strategies adopted in East Asia. In part, the East Asian moment has passed – the current historical conditions, not the least the neoliberal era, impose deep structural constraints. Yet, the East Asian strategies reveal key proven aspects of policy innovation that Latin America could adopt/adapt. As Chang has demonstrated, the East Asian successes have not been based on "Asian values" – values that Latin America will not attain. Rather, following Chang, the "secret" of Asian success has to do with their degree of success at importing/ adapting/assimilating institutions and technologies (Chang, 2003d, pp. 119–21). Concretely, this process demands the building of industrial policies in Latin America (Chang, 2003b, 2003c; Lall, 2005; Rodrik, 2004a).

In this regard, while the work of Ha-Joon Chang (cited above) is fundamental in many respects, limitations of space require primary focus here on an import-ant work of Rodrik, "Industrial Policy for the Twenty-First Century": Rodrik raises a central issue that has been treated extremely circumspectly in Latin America – the relationship between private initiative and public policy. This relationship, at best has been distant and testy – at worst it has been poisonous, with Chile serving as an excellent example. In this area the Chicago Boys have resorted to their "Public Choice" theories to posit the implicit self-seeking (rent seeking) nature of all aspects of public policy. By their definition all attempts to shape policy, even neoliberal attempts, are reducible to no more than self-seeking gambits. Beyond this cul-de-sac of nonsense, however, lies a great body of empirical knowledge that policy *does matter, can be effective, has been effective and continues to be* (even in Chile). Rodrik advocates:

> Strategic collaboration between the private sector and the government with the aim of uncovering where the most significant obstacles to restructuring lie and what type of interventions are most likely to remove them.
>
> (Rodrik, 2004a, p. 3)

The issue is not getting policy outcomes or prices right, "but getting the policy process right." This means *embeddedness*: state policy must be *both* embedded by way of constant close cooperation with the private sector, and *sufficiently autonomous* to avoid capture by the private sector. In this process the State will often have to take a leadership role due to the general weak level of the private sector. But the shift toward viable industrial policies is not very remote – a step beyond reorientation would seem to be within reach:

> Unlike what is commonly believed, the last two decades have not seen the twilight of industrial policy. Instead, incentives and subsidies have been refocused on exports and direct foreign investment, in the belief (largely unfounded as it turns out) that these activities are the source of significant positive spillovers. Therefore, the challenge in most developing countries is not to rediscover industrial policy, but to redeploy it in a more effective manner.
>
> (Rodrik, 2004a, p. 5)

For Latin America this means venturing into some non-traditional activities and into a diversification of these economies. In this conjuncture the State has to serve as the means for overcoming (1) negative informational externalities and (2) coordination externalities. Negative informational externalities exist when businesses cannot patent or monopolize "discoveries" that certain goods that are broadly produced in the global market can in fact be produced cheaper domestically – given some modest levels of investment to support adaptation and innovation. Thus, *first movers* will find that their investments/innovations are quickly copied/appropriated. To overcome this expectation on the part of domestic producers that they cannot reap the short-term economic rents from their investments, the State will need to find the means to subsidize these potential non-traditional forms of production. The issue is not finding the optimal policy outcome, but rather to implement the policy process. The State will finance some losers, but most fundamental to the policy process is that *reciprocity* be the key to any and all forms of assistance. Assistance can only be extended under the condition that the private sector meets certain predetermined targets (for export volume, or employment or output, etc.). The State must be *sufficiently autonomous* to castigate firms that fail to meet performance targets. But it must be sufficiently embedded within the private sector to have these actions of *enforcement* accepted as legitimate. Latin America has generally failed at imposing *reciprocity*, East Asia has generally excelled.

Overcoming coordination externalities is not a new idea in development economics. At times a sectoral "big push" is required. Investments in one area cannot be made unless upstream or downstream or infrastructural investments are made at the same time. The State has to play the role of *coordinator* and *first mover*. But this has to be conditioned on *reciprocity* on the part of the private sector. Deep networks of communication, "social learning," practices that engender mutual trust, including the professionalization of public sector policy makers, are necessary to achieve the coordination function. The State and the private sector have to achieve "strategic collaboration" based on a flexible "horizontal" structure, not on a principal (the State)/agent (the firms) structure. Rodrik emphasizes that priority should be placed on projects where there is high likelihood of achieving technologies with scale potential and/or agglomeration effects.

A new institutional architecture must be built to "institutionalize" industrial policy. This would include a cabinet-level advocate of industrial policy who is accountable, and a broad array of public/private coordination councils where communication and therefore trust would be established and where the likelihood of targeting meaningful investment priorities would be high. Rodrik offers "Ten Design Principles for Industrial Policy" – premised on the negation of the Neoliberal assumption that the most important externalities normally reside in either exports or FDI:

- Incentives should be provided only to "new" activities (to diversify);
- There should be clear benchmarks for success and failure;

- There must be built-in sunset clauses;
- Activities, not sectors, must be targeted;
- Subsidized activities must have clear potential spillover effects;
- Competence/merit are preconditions for industrial policy agencies;
- IP agencies must be monitored by an accountable cabinet-level leader;
- Two way "horizontal" communication between IP agencies and private sector;
- Anticipate and accept "failures"/minimize losses;
- IP agencies incubate "self-sustaining" processes.

Side-stepping or stepping over the WTO?

It is a commonly held view that "globalization" and particularly the recent and increasing institutional powers of the WTO have made it impossible for Latin American nations to seek "special and differential treatment," a necessary ingredient in the construction of a viable industrial policy. Yet, a recent body of research, while conceding some ground to this argument, has made a solid analytical case for well-managed forms of State intervention. Of note in this regard is the position of Alice Amsden who maintains that the WTO's strictures do not prevent certain major initiatives that could prove crucial to Latin America assuming the existence of adequate leadership and political will. Amsden notes three major areas where nations can develop policies in regard to the influx of imports: (1) when aggregate imports destabilize the balance of payments, (2) when nations face a surge of imports in individual industries and (3) when nations face dumping or other "unfair" trade practices (Amsden, 2005, p. 217). Further, nations can impose domestic origin requirements, even within the context of the WTO's TRIM (Trade Relate Investment Measures) Agreements (Amsden, 2005, p. 220). Developing countries can:

> Retain trade balancing stipulations and the 100 percent export requirement of export processing zones, both of which are forms of exports promotion. ... Safeguards can also be used to protect an infant industry, with eight years of protection virtually guaranteed.
>
> (Amsden, 2005, p. 220)

Extending the analysis, Amsden also finds wide latitude for allowed subsidies under the WTO when they (1) facilitate R&D outlays, (2) foster regional development and (3) advancing environmental sustainability (Amsden, 2005, p. 221). "Any high-tech industry, therefore, can receive unbounded subsidies for the purpose of strengthening [science and technology] (Amsden, 2005, p. 221).

Developing nations can employ performance standards linked to subsidized credit from development banks in order to professionalize their managerial cadre. Subsidies can be used to set policy standards in areas of national strategic priority such as raising the level of local content. It is also possible to employ "performance standards, as they operate in the area of science and technology, as designed to increase national skill formation and the generation of firm-specific knowledge-based assets" (Amsden, 2005, p. 227). In short, Amsden believes that the WTO is not the major barrier it is thought to be – rather, the real barrier is "the lack of a culture or vision to 'get the job done,'" a condition that certainly describes the neoliberal regimes of Latin America, including some that came under the sway of "socialist" or "labor" governments in the course of the 1990 or early 2000s.

Robert Wade is much more critical of the new structures imposed both by the WTO and the tendency of the powerful nations, particularly the US to construct bilateral accords:

> The rules being written into multilateral and bilateral agreements actively prevent developing countries from pursuing the kinds of industrial and technology policies adopted by the newly developed countries of East Asia and by the older developed countries when they were developing policies aimed at accelerating the "internal" articulation of the economy. ... Today reverse-engineering, imitation, and many strategies of innovation to develop technology are either outlawed or made significantly more difficult by the high level of patent and copyright protection mandated by TRIPS [Trade Related Aspects of Intellectual Property Rights].
>
> (Wade, 2005, pp. 81 and 85)

Certainly Wade is on solid ground regarding the trends and intentions of the recent wave of multilateral and bilateral agreements governing trade, investment and other areas. Amsden, however, takes up the issue from a perspective that is rarely presented – special provisions do exist within the general framework of the WTO that will permit certain aspects of industrial policy to be pursued. For the rest, the question in Latin America is not if but when some of the more restrictive forms of bilateral agreement will yield to renegotiation. The long-term impacts of NAFTA in Mexico, for example, could provide the opportunity for a path-breaking reconsideration of bilateral agreements spearheaded by the large industrial/commercial "grupos" (conglomerates) in Latin America and their counterpart elements – the US-based TNCs – in the US.

Further, the status of the WTO currently appears to be one of disarray – introducing the possibility that the powers of the WTO can be reduced, modified or side-stepped. Sanjaya Lall presented a detailed argument for selective industrial policy with broad and detailed reference to successful cases in Asia (Lall, 2005). At the same time, Lall recognizes that the WTO and other policies adopted by the IFIs have made conditions extremely difficult for nations that would seek to replicate or follow the path taken in Asia. What this leads to, although the concept is not developed by Lall, is a clear case for "a desirable international policy regime" that would permit adequate "policy space" for the development of the capability to inaugurate a viable industrial policy (Lall, 2005, pp. 62–4). With the WTO operating under increasing degrees of critical scrutiny and opposition, with the US agenda for a Free Trade Area for the Americas now sidelined after the critical North-South encounter in Mar de Plata in late 2005, and with political regimes throughout Latin America successively shifting away from the most ardent neoliberal policies, the compelling necessity and likelihood for a major shift toward selective industrial policies in many Latin American nations is high.

Conclusions

If the transcendence of a paradigm is premised on the three ingredients hypothe-sized in the introduction – (1) a theoretical critique of the existing paradigm, (2) a sustained and proliferating process of uncovering "anomalies" in the existing paradigm through an accretion of empirical information and (3) the creation of a plausible new paradigm – it would seem that the conditions now exist to wave neoliberalism into history. There are, of course, other attempts underway to present a post-neoliberal paradigm, and Stigliz's formulation has been men-tioned (Fine, 2002; Gore, 2000). Potentially, neostructuralism could incorporate the industrial policy strategies first developed in East Asia and make them pivotal. Yet, there is a tangible paucity of focus in Latin America on the role of the private sector, the sphere of production and technology. Overcoming these institutionalized biases will not be easy and is far from foreordained.

Beyond these concerns is something far more fundamental. Past paradigm shifts in Latin America have mandated the mobilization of a broad social base – at least in some instances. The advancement of the neoliberal agenda demanded the marginalization of broad social interests. And this, once again, brings in the "Polanyi problem," this time into the sphere of production rather than the realm of distribution. The missing fourth ingredient in the formulation posited in the Introduction is the mass social consensus/ social accord/social contract that must underlie a socially sustainable paradigm. Given modern interdependencies and the fragilities of the Latin American nations, a critical mass of society must be sufficiently mobilized finally to inter the neoliberal/Washington Consensus. The question then becomes whether with recent progressive governmental changes in Argentina, Bolivia, Brazil, Ecuador and Uruguay along with potential allies in Chile and (for better or for worse) Venezuela, these nations can generate a *crit-ical mass* of social and intellectual ferment sufficient to overcome the ever weakening hegemonic grip of neoliberalism. The stunning electoral victory of anti-neoliberal forces in Bolivia's presidential election in late 2005 certainly illustrates the fact that there exists a broad social support for fundamental change in economic policies. Perhaps a catalytic event would tip the balance at this point in history. Certainly an outspoken foe of neoliberalism, elected as President of Ecuador in 2006, currently adds to the momentum serving to derail and bury the Washington Consensus. Meanwhile 2006 brought to power a deter-mined cadre of arch neoliberals in Mexico. Nevertheless, the Neoliberal model, in its guise as EOI has imposed terrible social costs on Mexico, thereby giving rise to a fractured, fragile and fluid situation that could facilitate the further unwinding of Neoliberalism in Latin America. Obviously the situation is mercurial, but what is most remote to conjecture now is the continuation or renewal of the neoliberal paradigm in Latin America.

Notes

1 Profesor-Investigador, Programa Doctorado en Estudios del Desarrollo, Universidad Autónoma de Zacatecas. Several individuals – none of whom have either read the following or are in any way responsible for the analysis – kindly responded to my request for suggestions at the onset of the research stage of this chapter: I thank Arthur MacEwan, Ha-Joon Chang, Sara Babb, Enrique Dussel Peters and Osvaldo Sunkel. I am also grateful to Oscar Muñoz, María Angela Parra, Esteban Pérez Caldentey and Matías Vernengo, for comments on an earlier draft.

2 This is not the place to reassess the nature of the ISI era. An interesting perspective is offered by Juan Carlos Moreno-Brid and Jaime Ros in "Mexico's market reform in historical perspective" (Moreno-Brid and Ros, in this volume). As the authors show, there is a very strong link between the limited success Mexico has shown in the export of manufactured products in the last 25 years and the sectoral-specific industrial policies designed to generate new industrial activities that arose from the extension of ISI policies in Mexico in the 1970s and early 1980s. Their findings are consistent with research on Chile and Argentina regarding the origins of "successful" industrial sectors (Cypher, 2005; Schorr, 2004).

3 By December 2005, with the stunning presidential victory of Evo Morales in Bolivia, press accounts claimed that 300 of South America's 365 million inhabitants were now guided by "leftist" political agendas. The lack of homogeneity of these governments, however, was as striking as their determination to explore (sometimes limited) economic and/or social policies that diverged from the neoliberal project. In 2006 the trend to move away from the Washington Consensus was reinforced by the re-election – with broad support – of Lula in Brazil and Chavez in Venezuela, while Ecuador elected a staunch opponent of neoliberal policies and Mexico's left party came within a hair's breadth of victory. For a more skeptical perspective see (Vernengo, 2005).

4 Enrique Dussel Peters makes a similar distinction. He maintains that the Austrian/Chicago focus on incentives and unconstrained market forces gave way in short order to a more "pragmatic" emphasis on export-oriented industrialization which had greater conformance to perspectives adopted by more moderate neoliberals such as Anne Krueger (Dussel Peters, 2004, and personal correspondence October 2004)

5 Outsourcing can involve extremely primitive labor-intensive activities, but this eventuality is far afield of the conventional application of the Ricardian assumption of full employment. It is assumed that open international trade is "welfare enhancing," not a process that leads to even greater levels of degradation of workers through the adoption of thought-to-be bygone forms of production.

6 Yet, as noted by Oscar Muñoz, small nations face special problems to the degree that a balanced, or broad, range of manufacturing industries would seem to be beyond their capacities (Personal interview, Santiago, Chile, 27 May 2005). While this matter is beyond the scope of this chapter, the question of outward-oriented vs. inward-oriented policies cannot be a matter of absolutes, particularly for small nations. Various alternatives need to be explored, among them strong economic unions, or common markets that are not asymmetrically structured – such as NAFTA.

7 In "late-coming nations": "The government becomes the leading actor in promoting the import substitution of high-tech components and parts. It leads in the development of advanced technologies to the point where their commercialization is possible once they mature. In Taiwan the government targeted key sectors and directly intervened

in them. The model in electronics was to create spin-offs from a government-owned research institute. . . . As for discipline, when the government wielded power over the purse, discipline operated through the imposition of performance standards on subsidy recipients *and subsidy providers* – bureaucrats in state-owned banks, for example, were held personally responsible in terms of their salaries and promotion, for the health of their loans" (Amsden and Chu 2003, p. 276).

8 In the ISI era Latin America had too great a level of diversity – which in no way negates the misspecifications of the neoliberal model regarding specialization.

9 Sanjaya Lall encapsulates some of the major differences between the neoliberal and the neostructuralist position, although he adopts the term "structuralist": "the *structuralist* view puts less faith in free markets as the driver of competitiveness and more in the ability of governments to mount interventions effectively. It questions that free markets account for the industrial success of the East Asian Tigers. Accepting the mistakes of past strategies, it argues that greater reliance on markets need a more proactive role for the government . . . . Structuralists accept that some industrialization policies have not worked well in the past. For the neoliberals this is a reason for denying any role for proactive policy: if there are market failures, the costs are always less than those of government failures. Structuralists . . . see a vital role for policy; past policy failure is not a reason for passive reliance on deficient markets but for improving policymaking capabilities" (Lall, 2005, p. 34).

References

Adelman, Irma (2001) "Fallacies in Development Theory and Their Implications for Policy." In *Frontiers of Development Economics*, edited by Gerald Meier and Joseph Stiglitz, Washington: The World Bank and Oxford University Press, pp. 103–83.

Amsden, Alice (2001) *The Rise of "the Rest."* Oxford: Oxford University Press.

Amsden, Alice (2004) "La substitución de importaciones en las industrias de alta tecnología: Raúl Prebisch Renace en Asia." In *El Desarrollo Económico el Los Albores del Siglo XXI*, edited by José Antonio Ocampo, Bogotá: Alfa-omega, pp. 259–82.

Amsden, Alice (2005) "Promoting Industry under WTO Law." In *Putting Development First*, edited by Kevin Gallagher, London: Zed Books, pp. 216–32.

Amsden, Alice and Wan-Wen Chu (2003) "'Getting the Structure Right' Upscaling in a Prime Latecomer." In *Development Economics and Structural Macroeconomics*, edited by Amitava K. Dutt and Jaime Ros, Cheltenham, UK: Edward Elgar, pp. 263–81.

Azpiazu, Daniel (2005) *Las privatizaciones I.* Buenos Aires: Capital Intelectual.

Bruton, Henry (1998) "A Reconsideration of Import Substitution." *Journal of Economic Literature* 36 (June), pp. 903–36.

Bulmer-Thomas, Victor (1994) *The Economic History of Latin American Since Independence*, Cambridge: Cambridge University Press.

Chang, Ha-Joon (2003a) "Introduction." In *Rethinking Development Economics*, edited by Ha-Joon Chang, London: Anthem Press, pp. 1–18.

Chang, Ha-Joon (2003b) "Trade and Industrial Policy Issues." In *Rethinking Development Economics*, edited by Ha-Joon Chang, London: Anthem Press, pp. 257–76.

Chang, Ha-Joon (2003c) "The Market, the State and Institutions." In *Rethinking Development Economics*, edited by Ha-Joon Chang, London: Anthem Press, pp. 41–60.

Chang, Ha-Joon (2003d) "The East Asian Development Experience." In *Rethinking Development Economics*, edited by Ha-Joon Chang, London: Anthem Press, pp. 107–24.

Cimoli, Mario and Jorge Katz (2004) "Reformas Estructurales y Brechas Tecnológicas." In *El Desarrollo Económico en Los Albores del Siglo XXI*, edited by José Antonio Ocampo, Bogotá: Alfa-omega, pp. 242–58.

Cypher, James (2003a) "Recent Tendencies in Development Economics: Bringing Institutions Back In?" In *Institutional Analysis and Economic Policy*, edited by Marc Tool and Paul Bush, Boston: Kluwer Academic Publishers, pp. 549–76.

Cypher, James (2003b) "The State in the Context of an Internationalizing Production System." *International Journal of Development Issues* 2(1), pp. 1–16.

Cypher, James (2004a) "Pinochet meets Polanyi?" *Journal of Economic Issues* 38(2), pp. 527–36.

Cypher, James (2005) "The Political Economy of the Chilean State in the Neoliberal Era." *Canadian Journal of Development Studies* 31(4), pp. 763–79.

Dijkstra, Geske (2000) "Trade Liberalization and Industrial Development in Latin America." *World Development*, 28(9), pp. 1567–82.

Dussel Peters, Enrique (2004) "The Mexican Economy Since NAFTA: Socioeconomic Integration or Disintegration?" Available at www.dusselpeters.com.

Fine, Ben (2002) "Economics Imperialism and the New Development Economics as Kuhnian Shift?" *World Development* 30(12), pp. 2057–70.

Gore, Charles (2000) "The Rise and Fall of the Washington Consensus as a Paradigm for Developing Countries." *World Development* 28(5), pp. 789–804.

Gwynne, Robert (2004) "Clusters and Commodity Chains: Firm Responses to Neoliberalism in Latin America." *Latin American Research Review*, 39(3), pp. 243–55.

Hanson, Gordon (2001) *Should Countries Promote Foreign Direct Investment?* G-24 Discussion Paper, Geneva: UNCTAD, pp. 1–31.

Hausmann, Ricardo and Dani Rodrik (2003) "Economic Development as Self-Discovery." *Journal of Development Studies* 72(2), pp. 603–33.

Hueber, Evelyn and Fred Solt (2004) "Successes and Failures of Neoliberalism." *Latin American Research Review* 39(3), pp. 258–74.

Huneeus, Carlos (2001) *El Régimen de Pinochet*, Santiago: Editorial Sudamericana.

Imbs, Jean and Romain Wacziarg (2003), "Stages of Diversification." *American Economic Review* 93(1), pp. 63–86.

Lall, Sanjaya (2005) "Rethinking Industrial Strategy: The Role of the State in the Face of Globalization." In *Putting Development First*, edited by Kevin Gallagher, London: Zed Books, pp. 33–68.

Larraín, Felipe (2004) "Estructura, Políticas e Instituciones: Una Visión del Desarrollo Latinoamericano." In *El Desarrollo Económico en Los Albores del Ssiglo XXI*, edited by José Antonio Ocampo, Bogotá: Alfa-omega, pp. 173–204.

Milberg, William (1994) "Is Absolute Advantage *Passé?*" In *Competition, Technology and Money*, edited by Mark Glick, Aldershot, UK: Edward Elgar, pp. 219–35.

Milberg, William (2004) "The Changing Structure of Trade Linked to Global Production Systems." *International Labour Review* (Spring–Summer), Vol. 143, pp. 1–34.

Moguillansky, G. (2002) "Inversion y Volatilidad Financiera en América Latina," *Revista de la CEPAL* (agosto) No. 77, pp. 47–65.

Ocampo, José Antonio (2004) "Introducción." In *El Desarrollo Económico en Los Albores del Siglo XXI*, edited by José Antonio Ocampo, Bogotá: Alfa-omega, pp. xiii–xli.

Paus, Eva (2003) "Productivity Growth in Latin America: The Limits of Neoliberal Reform," *World Development* 32(3), pp. 427–55.

Pérez, Carlota (2004) "Cambio Tecnológico y Oportunidades de Desarrollo Como Blanco Mobil. In *El Desarrollo Económico en Los Albores del Siglo XXI*, edited by José Antonio Ocampo, Bogotá: Alfa-omega, pp. 205–40.

Pinto, Aníbal (1962) *Chile: un Caso de Desarrollo Frustrado.* Santiago: Editorial Universitária.

Rodrik, Dani (2004a) "Industrial Policy for the Twenty-First Century." Kennedy School of Government, Harvard University. Available at www.ksg.harvard.edu/rodrik/.

Rodrik, Dani (2004b) "Estrategias de Desarrollo para el Nuevo Siglo". In *El Desarrollo Económico en Los Albores del Siglo XXI*, edited by José Antonio Ocampo, Bogotá: Alfa-omega, pp. 89–124.

Saad-Filho, Alfredo (2005) "The Political Economy of Neoliberalism in Latin America". In *Neoliberalism: A Critical Reader*, edited by Alfredo Saad-Filho and Debora Johnson, London: Pluto Press, pp. 222–9.

Saad-Filho, Alfredo and Debora Johnston (eds) (2005) *Neoliberalism: A Critical Reader*, London: Pluto Press.

Schorr, Martín (2004) *Industria y Nación*, Buenos Aires: Edhasa.

Shaikh, Anwar (1996) "Free Trade, Unemployment and Economic Policy." In *Global Unemployment and Economic Policy*, edited by John Eatwell, Armonk, New York: M.E. Sharpe, pp. 59–78.

Shaikh, Anwar (2005) "The Economic Mythology of Neoliberalism." In *Neoliberalism: A Critical Reader*, edited by Alfredo Saad-Filho and Debora Johnson, London: Pluto Press, pp. 41–9.

Shapiro, Nina (2003) "Bringing the Firm Back In?" In *Development Economics and Structural Macroeconomics*, Amitava K. Dutt and Jaime Ros, Cheltenham, UK: Edward Elgar, pp. 247–62.

Spanakos, Anthony and Elizabeth McQuerry (2004) "Political Economy in a Time of Capital Outflows." *Latin American Research Review* 39(2), pp. 258–74.

Stiglitz, Joseph (2002) "Whither Reform? Towards a New Agenda for Latin America," *The Prebisch Lecture*, Santiago: ECLAC (August), pp. 1–67.

Sunkel, Osvaldo (1990) "Reflections on Latin American Development." In *Progress Toward Development in Latin America*, edited by James Dietz and James Dilmus, Boulder, Co.: Lynne Reinner, pp. 133–58.

Tuman, John and Craig Emmert (2004) "The Political Economy of U.S. Foreign Direct Investment in Latin America: A Reappraisal." *Latin American Research Review* 39(3), pp. 9–28.

Valdés, Juan Gabriel (1989) *La Escuela de Chicago: Operación Chile.* Buenos Aires: Grupo Editorial Zeta.

Valdés, Juan Gabriel (1995) *Pinochet's Economists: The Chicago School in Chile*, Cambridge University Press.

Vernengo, Matías (2005) "Latin America's Left off Track." *Dollars and Sense*, (May/June) No. 259, pp. 21–5.

Wade, Robert (2005) "What Strategies are Viable for Developing Countries Today?" In *Putting Development First*, edited by Kevin Gallagher, London: Zed Books, pp. 80–101.

Walton, Michael (2004) "Neoliberalism in Latin America: Good, Bad or Incomplete?" *Latin American Research Review* 39(3), pp. 165–84.

Williamson, John (1998) "Latin American Reform: A View from Washington." In *Economic Reform in Latin America*, edited by Harry Costin and Hector Vanolli, Orlando: Dryden, pp. 106–11.

Williamson, John (1993) "Democracy and the 'Washington Consensus'." *World Development* 21(8), pp. 1329–36.

Williamson, John (2002) "Did the Washington Consensus Fail." Available at www.iie.com/publications/papers/williamson1102.htm

Winn, Peter (2004) *Victims of the Chilean Miracle*, Durham, N.C.: Duke University Press.

4 Exchange rate regimes from a Latin American analytical perspective

Kenneth P. Jameson

Introduction

In the introduction to her economic history of twentieth century Latin America, Thorp (1998, pp. 10–11) notes the various actors, such as government, business, the military and external entities. She finishes by asking where "ordinary people" appear. We might ask "where are the Latin American economists in such a history?" While Thorp (1998, p. 10) mentions CEPAL, the "homegrown international organization," Latin American economists seem to have had little role in charting the direction of the economic history of the century.

The choice of exchange rate regime has been a recurrent problem for Latin America, and is one area where economists have generally played a central analytical role. Politicians faced with external challenges have relied on economists to suggest an exchange rate regime that allows them to attain the domestic goals they seek. Most notably, in recent years Latin American economists have played an important role in understanding the implications of different regimes and in effecting their implementation. Thus Domingo Cavallo was central to Menem's convertibility, Fernando Henrique Cardoso (an honorary economist) gained the presidency of Brazil by developing the Real Plan. Even so, much of the debate was dominated by "northern economists": John Williamson's "Washington Consensus" that encouraged greater flexibility (1990), or Stanley Fischer's (2001) suggestion that the bi-polar policy, flexible or hard fixed rates, should be adopted.

The twentieth anniversary of the publication of McCloskey's *Rhetoric of Economics* (1985) should make us sensitive to the role that ideas and argument have in policy formulation and decision, and should lead us to wonder whether there was a similar interaction around issues of exchange rate regime in earlier periods. This is an interesting question particularly in the period from 1900 through the 1920s, since the story of foreign influence on exchange rate regime is so well-known, thanks to the work of Drake (1989) and Seidel (1972). The broader story of "dollar diplomacy," and economic policy influence, has been told extensively by Rosenberg (1999).

This chapter sets out to show that there was debate and that Latin American economists were writing on the issues around exchange rate regime choice in the first decades of the twentieth century. Their role in the debate and the apparent dominance that US and other foreign economists ultimately established is a complex story that probably says more about economic and political power than about the power of economic ideas. But that is part of a broader set of questions. The chapter documents the activity and contributions that Latin American economists made to understanding and developing policy in this important area.

The chapter begins with a brief survey of exchange rate regimes in Latin America in the first decades of the last century, highlighting their diversity and their links with domestic monetary systems. The following section focuses on the work of Mexican economists and the debate on exchange rates that swirled around the Mexican silver peso prior to the Revolution and in its immediate aftermath. The Mexican Revolution represented a chaotic break with any previous economic policies, and the role of one particular economist, Alberto Pani, provides an example of the creativity and of the contribution that Latin American economists made to dealing with such revolutionary challenges. He is the subject of the next section. While Mexico faced some unique challenges, the period after 1915 saw a movement toward a more uniform set of policies, incorporating the gold exchange standard and Central Banks that were to be the guarantors of the exchange regime. While Kemmerer and others had an influence in this process, there is evidence that such proposals antedated the international money doctors. The final section asks what the roots of these earlier proposals were. It attempts to find them in the Latin American participation in a series of international conferences on financial issues. The end result, as shown in the conclusions, is to shed light on the rhetoric of economics in this area and to show the actual and active role of Latin American economic thinkers in the early years of this ongoing debate.

Exchange rate regimes and analysis at the turn of the century

McKinnon (1993) provides a useful starting point for understanding the question of exchange rate regime at the turn of the twentieth century. Though he concentrates on the industrialized countries, his division of the century into "monetary systems" is certainly relevant to Latin America, its choice of exchange rate regime, and the institutional structures around exchange rates. Let us start with McKinnon's earliest period that he characterizes as "The International Gold Standard, 1879–1913." He writes: "By 1879 ... the gold standard had become *inclusively international* – covering all the major industrial economies, and most smaller agrarian ones" (McKinnon 1993, p. 3). The reality in Latin America was actually more complex and at variance with what McKinnon claims.

Evidence does suggest that this was the period of greatest "globalization," as measured by the share of trade in total output (Hoogvelt, 1997). Williamson (2002, p. 5) found that capital market integration today has not reached the level it attained in this period. However, as a result of defaulting on earlier loans, primarily from Britain, Latin America was viewed with skepticism and caution.

Financial crises of the 1870s and 1890s had led to *de jure* ownership of the countries' most important assets by British bondholders (Glade, 1969, Ch. 7). Turmoil in Central America and the Caribbean had raised European fears that their loans would never be repaid and prompted the 1904 "Roosevelt Corollary" to the Monroe Doctrine. It asserted that "when states of the Western Hemisphere conducted their economic affairs irresponsibly enough to raise the possibility of European intervention (to control customs or banking systems), the United States would assume the role of an 'international police power'" (Rosenberg and Rosenberg 1987, p. 62). In Haiti, Nicaragua and the Dominican Republic, the US pressured governments to install US representatives to control their banking, taxation and trade as well as to ensure "responsible" economic policy. The carrot accompanying the pressure was loan agreements that provided external resources. The agreements also allowed the intervener to command the resources necessary to service the loan and to allocate national resources to satisfy international demands.

So in Latin America the "monetary system" or exchange rate regimes were quite diverse from country to country. Trade had expanded rapidly as globalization proceeded after 1850, and control of export proceeds and tariffs on imported goods were the major foreign exchange issues. On the other hand, instability resulted in a variety of domestic monetary systems. Some had currency or banknotes convertible to gold, others to silver, and some with foreign gold and silver coins circulating freely (Crosby, 1915). In Panama the dollar circulated alongside the silver/nickel balboa, at a 1:1 rate, because of the US role in Panama's creation. The same was true in Cuba. Kemmerer (1917) claimed that all of the 21 countries except Honduras were legally on a gold standard in 1915, and thus a unified monetary system based on the dollar was possible and desirable. He was immediately challenged by Latin American economists whose position was that such an outcome was impossible – and undesirable (Gonzalez, 1917).

Peru provides a good example of the order's effect on a South American country. As the gold standard period began, Peru backed its currency with silver, an important domestic product. Between 1883 and 1898 this led to a 40 percent depreciation against its main trading partner, Britain, because silver depreciated when the US quit supporting silver after 1892 (Thorp and Bertram, 1978, pp. 29–30). In 1898, Peru moved to the gold standard par, and British gold circulated freely in Peru as legal tender.[1] Most other South American countries had similar systems, usually accompanied by a domestic paper currency theoretically convertible into gold or silver (Crosby, 1915).

The most interesting case was Mexico, whose silver peso was used throughout the world until the gold standard became preferred, and until the conscious US policy to supplant the peso was successful around the turn of the century (Andrew, 1904). This was not an accident and there were many Mexican economists writing on the issue, as will be noted below.

The outbreak of World War I in 1914 completely disrupted this already inchoate monetary system. The Latin American paper currencies had become inconvertible by 1915 as the reversal of globalization had begun. Countries turned inward in an effort to maintain economic activity. To resist the contractionary effects of decreased exports, governments began to issue more paper currency, leading to domestic economic instability (Crosby, 1915). As an extreme example, during the Mexican Revolution, economic disruption spawned 21 types of paper money, none with widespread acceptance (Ortiz, 1982, p. 441). The end result was domestic inflation and loss of value of the domestic currency. By 1921 Chile's currency was 60 percent of its prewar value vis-à-vis the dollar, Colombia's 80 percent, Bolivia's 60 percent and Peru's 75 percent (Seidel, 1972, p. 523).

This earlier period of globalization captures a pattern that recurs in the contemporary globalization process: continued efforts by Latin American countries to establish domestic financial and international exchange rate policies and systems that provide stability and facilitate participation in the international monetary order. This was generally guided by national "economists" who were able to analyze their domestic reality, as we will see below. However, external changes in the international monetary order undermined the countries' efforts, led to domestic economic instability, and forced the adoption of increasingly ad hoc exchange rate regimes.

So what were Latin American economists writing and thinking about this situation? What were their analyses of the exchange rate regime that would be appropriate in these circumstances? Obviously, this varied from country to country and played out as part of the competition between the US and Britain for dominance in Latin America. In Central America and the Caribbean, much of the writing was polemic in nature, reacting to and resisting the imposition of US "pro-consuls" and pointing out how little of the loans that were offered were actually delivered to the countries involved. So in many ways, the key issue was a familiar one: the cost of the increased debt and its effect on the exchange rate regime and its stability.

Further south, there was more ability to analyze the economics involved in the situation and to suggest policies. Thus there were analyses of bi-metallic regimes carried out in Peru and other countries and analyses of currency substitution and the use of foreign currencies in the domestic economy were realized. All have a contemporary ring and suggest that the Latin American economists were in the forefront of dealing with issues that recurred in modern periods.

To document the activity of Latin American economists in this period, let me focus on Mexico and economists who analyzed the issues of the exchange rate in the first decades of the twentieth century.

Mexican economists' analyses of exchange rate regimes at century's turn

Mexico, like Peru, was severely affected by the US decision to abandon bi-metallism and to adopt the gold standard. Its economic policy also became an object of concern and action on the part of the United States.

From 1900 to 1905, the United States laid the groundwork for a financial policy that sought to create a bloc of gold-standard countries ... whose coinage was denominated on the U.S. gold dollar; whose gold reserves were deposited in the United States; and whose exchange transactions took place through New York banks.

(Rosenberg, 1985, p. 170)

Mexico was particularly important to this effort because of the continued importance of the silver Mexican peso. The effort was coordinated by the members of the US Commission on International Exchange, which was formed in 1903 primarily to move Mexico and China to a gold standard. However, Mexican economists had already been studying these issues, in response to the devaluation of their silver-based money owing to the decline in silver's price. As Rosenberg (1985, 188) writes: "Unlike other countries [US advisor Charles Conant] advised, Mexico had its own accomplished currency experts, and the Commission on International Exchange played only a minor consultative role, even though the Mexican initiative had brought it into being." Why did Mexico present a pattern so different from Panama, Cuba, the Philippines, Puerto Rico, the Dominican Republic or China? One answer is the analysis of the exchange rate system and its effects on the domestic economy that had been carried out by Mexican economists at the turn of the century.

This story starts with the Porfiriato and the role of the "científicos." Today we would call them the "técnicos" such as the recent PRI presidents of Mexico. Under the leadership of José Yves Limantour, born of a French immigrant in Mexico City in 1854, they adopted the positivist view that scientific analysis could provide the basis for governance. Limantour became Secretary of the Treasury in 1893 and was the key adviser to Porfírio Díaz until his fall in 1911. While he did not write analytically about the issues of exchange rate, his role was to establish the mechanisms that would facilitate understanding the problems Mexico faced and their potential resolution. There were numerous Mexican economists who were writing about the exchange rate problem. For example Kemmerer (1916) and Cerda (n.d.) refer to the following:

- Casas, S. J., *La Reforma Monetaria en Mexico* (1905)
- Casas, S. J., *Las Reformas a la Ley de Institucions de Credito* (1908)
- Gurza, J., *Apuntes Sobre la Cuestion de la Plata en Mexico* (1902)
- Gurza, J., *Nuestros Banco de Emision* (1905)
- Macedo, P., *Tres Monografías* (1905)
- Casasús, J. D., *El Peso Mexicano y sus Rivales en los Mercados del Extremo* Oriente (1904)
- Casasús, Joaquín D., *La Reforma Monetaria en Mexico* (1905)
- Sobral, Enrique Martinez., *La Reforma Monetaria* (1910)

So, as can be seen, there was an active discussion of the exchange rate problem and how Mexico might deal with it. Limantour's approach to policy development was to create a Comisión Monetaria in 1903 with 44 members. It followed on the Comisión de Cambios Internacionales de la República Mexicana, which had been established on the prodding of the US government. The later commission compiled extensive data on banks and the whole range of monetary and foreign exchange issues. Kemmerer (1916) provides an extensive treatment of the analysis carried out by the Comisión, a fact which shows again the high level of analytical ability available in Mexico. It became the key factor in the Mexican move away from a flexible exchange rate to a gold exchange standard in 1905, with the value set at one peso equal to 0.75 centigrams of gold. This was accompanied by the creation of the Comisión de Cambios y Moneda designed to regulate the relation of domestic money and foreign exchange by controlling foreign exchange (Ortiz, 1982, p. 441).

The policy was not successful, since silver's price increased, starting in 1904 and accelerating in 1905. This upset the parity that had been set as the value of silver in bullion increased over its coin value and led to the export of large amounts of silver. This forced the government to allow the circulation of gold coins and to the effective movement to a gold standard. In addition, negative external shocks in 1907 contributed to a stagflation that played an important role in the Mexican revolution of 1910 (Cerda, n.d., p. 5).

Nonetheless, Kemmerer (1916, p. 539) noted the caliber of the analysis that had been undertaken by the Comisión Monetaria:

> While this phenomenal advance in the price of silver came as a surprise to the Mexican authorities, it cannot be said they were unprepared to meet it. The thoroughness with which the Monetary Commission had gone into the entire subject of monetary reform had not stopped short of formulating ... tentative plans by which to meet such an emergency.

So the ability of Mexican economists to analyze and adapt to the new world that was coming into being was notable. They stood out among the countries that had been on silver standards and that had been targeted by US policy makers for imposition of the gold standard. The fact that Mexico finally ended up adopting the system that the United States was attempting to force on countries was attributable not to better analysis by foreign economists, but was more the result of the successful use of US political power to impose its gold standard throughout the world. Mexico's effort to chart its own course was notable, though not unique in Latin America. As Rosenberg notes (1985, p. 202): "Mexico requested American advice but, like many other Latin American nations that went onto a gold basis around the turn of the century, Mexico undertook reform because of internal decisions and politics, not in direct response to American pressures."

It is ironic that the presentation at the Second Pan American Scientific Congress (1917, p. 32) by Joaquín Casasús, Mexican economist and former Mexican Ambassador to the US, turned Kemmerer's proposal for a system based on the dollar into a revalidation of that role as previously played by the Mexican peso. As he wrote: "That Mexican Peso ... that for nearly a century gave prestige to the government that created it . . . will always have to be considered by the civilized world as a lasting historical monument and as an exceptional money of commerce.

This same evidence of extensive and capable analysis of issues of exchange rate by Mexican – and Latin American – economists will appear again in later years of the first decades of the twentieth century. In this case, the backdrop will be the chaotic years after World War I and the Mexican revolution. Kemmerer (1916, p. 547) lamented "The story of the subsequent breakdown of this carefully constructed gold standard during Mexico's recent unfortunate years of revolution does not fall within the province of this paper . . ."

By looking at the work of Alberto J. Pani on policy formulation in the midst of revolution, leading finally to the establishment of the Banco de México in 1925, we will see that the ability of Latin American economists to negotiate the difficulties of operating in an unstable peripheral state remained high.

Alberto Pani and economic analysis in the time of revolution

Alberto Pani was not formally trained as an economist, not surprisingly. He received his Civil Engineering degree from the Escuela Nacional de Ingenieros in 1902, a time when formal Economics faculties were few to non-existent in Latin America (Appendini, 1992). Nonetheless he played a central role in the post-revolution economic policy formulation. He served various governments in a variety of posts: Superintendent of Schools, Manager of Public Works, General Director of Railroads, Secretary of Industry and Minister of Foreign Relations. However, his major influence was as the Secretary of Treasury, a position he held at four different times, starting in 1923 under the Álvaro Obregón administration.

He was a colorful character, accused at one time of white slavery under the Mann Act in the US where he had gone to renegotiate debt agreements (Symes, 2005).[2] Nonetheless, his long stay in the Treasury was central to consolidating the Mexican Revolution and establishing a functioning economic system that transcended presidential administrations.

His signal accomplishment was the founding of the Banco de México in 1925 as a Sociedad Anónima. This was a different model from that pushed by the US, and it lasted until 1982. Discussions about a central bank had been ongoing since at least 1915. But Pani was instrumental in its formal creation in the first months of the Plutarco Elías Calles regime. He had continued as Treasury Secretary when the new administration began in November 1924, and thus was able to name a commission to draft the legislation and to put the bank in place by August, 1925. In addition, he had a major influence on the fiscal and monetary policy of the government under at least four presidents. He, and Calles, developed policies and approaches that were central to preserving the revolutionary governments and to providing the underlying economics structures and policies that launched the PRI on its long dominance of Mexico.

A measure of his activity in economic thinking in Latin America can be gained by noting the entries citing his writings in the 1936 bibliography of Latin American economics publications (Bureau for Economic Research in Latin America, 1936). Listed there are:

- Cuestiones Diversas. México, 1922: 414pp.
- La Política Hacendaria y la Revolución. México, 1926: 738pp.
- La Política Democrática Industrial. México, 1927: 21pp.

In addition he is cited for speeches on occasions such as the inauguration of the Museo Comercial de México. He was also instrumental in completing the Museo de Bellas Artes in the early 1930s.

Pani's own description of the challenges of moving from a revolutionary situation to consolidation of an economic system is an imposing treatment of the creativity and independence of economic thinking in Mexico (Pani, 1941). Its extensive political economic treatment of policy between 1910 when he became involved with the non-reelection movement to his final resignation from the Treasury Secretary in 1933 is an exceptional document of how the interplay of economic thinking and political forces turn the rhetoric of economics into actual economic policy. In Pani's case, he played a central role in consolidating the Mexican revolution and then in dealing with the early years of the world depression. His clear economic thinking in such times of turmoil has a contemporary ring in many cases. While the issues he dealt with are far too numerous to treat here, an overview of his policy stances can document the Mexican ability to chart an independent course for economic policy.

Pani took the Mexican Constitution of 1917 as his guide, and in particular Article 40 which guaranteed popular democracy, Article 27 that committed to equitable distribution of the country's riches, and Article 123 that guaranteed workers' rights (Pani, 1941, pp. 43–6). From them he developed certain economic principles that guided his policy work: inflation should be controlled because of its negative income distribution effects; fiscal policy should be designed to generate government resources necessary to facilitate redistribution of assets and capital investments to help the poorest; and protection should be limited to fiscal requirements, rather than used to protect domestic monopolies.

He took ever greater responsibility for economic policy between 1923 and 1933, which led to a number of significant policy accomplishments:

- Reform of the tax system in 1923: reformed toward direct and away from indirect taxes. This allowed the government deficit to become a surplus, which allowed Calles to begin to build a road network and undertake irrigation and other infrastructure projects (pp. 66–74).
- Rationalization of tariff system: in 1924–1926 he reformed the tariff system, designed for revenue, not protection, purposes. He used Ricardo and England's experience with free trade as his justification (pp. 82–8).
- Reorganization of the banking system: it had been in disarray since Huerta

allowed private money emission in 1913. The concession was removed in 1916 and the assets of the banks confiscated in 1918. Even before he became a Minister, Pani worked with the banks to reach an agreement that would restore some of their capital and allow them to function again. He was able to get an agreement on "re-regulation" of the banking system, a task facing many of our recently liberalizing governments. The linchpin of this reform was the creation of the Banco de México in 1925. It had a monopoly on monetary emission. In addition, the Bank could not lend to state governments and its loans to the central government were limited to a maximum of 10 percent of its capital. This should have given the bank independence in monetary policy, though this did not last long (pp. 88–104).

- Renegotiation of the international debt with the US: his predecessor as Treasury Secretary under Obregón, Adolfo de la Huerta, had signed a debt repayment agreement with Thomas Lamont, the President of the "International Committee of Bankers with Business in Mexico." Pani determined that the terms were quite onerous for Mexico and went to New York for two weeks in January 1925 to successfully renegotiate the terms of the agreement. He estimated that it reduced the debt burden on Mexico by over 50 percent. Debt payments were later suspended and Pani's successor, Luis Montes de Oca, signed another agreement with Lamont in July 1930. Pani criticized this agreement at length and showed how the payments agreed upon would lead to currency depreciation, since they were unlikely to attract added capital (pp. 135–44).

- Exchange rate management: this is most relevant to this chapter and is where Pani's importance was most realized. In 1925, the Banco de México was given control over foreign exchange transactions. It was committed to maintaining the gold exchange standard of 0.75 centigrams per peso. However, as international disarray grew in the later part of the 1920s, the silver that was the main tradable income source for the government decreased in price. Pani saw that the system would be unsustainable. Once again as Minister in 1931, he moved the country off that system into a pegged rate vis-à-vis the dollar in 1932. The pragmatic and far-sighted steps he took gave him a prominent place at the London World Monetary and Economic Conference in 1933. He and the US government were in agreement that the gold standard should not be reinstituted and so he received strong support from the Roosevelt administration. He was named to the Conference Steering Committee in recognition that Mexico had distinguished itself by implementing policies since 1925 that the conference agenda was suggesting for other countries in the world. The conference failed, but Pani's policies were successful through 1933. One other accomplishment was developing and signing an international price stabilization treaty for silver, which facilitated Mexico's international financial relations (pp. 144–91).

Pani's work underlines the basic claim of this chapter: that Latin American economic writing and thinking in the area of exchange rates showed independence and creativity. His role at the international monetary conference indicates that there was international recognition of Latin Americans' contributions.

Let us return now to the wider issue of exchange rate regimes and their analysis. In this case we want to examine the world context after the globalized world began to de-globalize in 1913 and to look at the role that Latin Americans played in international debates. This follows what we learned about Pani's international role.

Exchange rate regimes and analysis after 1915

While the Mexican Revolution amplified Mexico's turmoil, the war in Europe affected all of Latin America and its external economic relations. Rodríguez (1985, p. 118) described it well:

> World War I profoundly affected the financial system of the West. News of the outbreak of war sparked a worldwide financial panic. Individuals protected their wealth by converting paper currency into gold, thereby threatening the financial stability of banks as well as national currencies throughout the Western world. Governments enacted emergency legislation to protect their financial and banking systems; the belligerents and their trading partners either abandoned or relaxed the gold standard. They suspended specie payment, prohibited the export of gold, and took other emergency measures to protect national financial integrity. In Latin America the war forced Chile and Brazil, which were contemplating a return to the gold standard, to postpone it, while Ecuador, Argentina, and Bolivia, which based their currencies on the gold standard, instituted inconvertibility.

We can characterize this period as the "International Monetary Non-system, 1913–1930." McKinnon omits this period, though it was significant for Latin America.

As Europe dissolved in war, the United States became the dominant external player in Latin America. In Central America and the Caribbean, political and military control was often the preferred mechanism. US corporate and portfolio investment grew rapidly, supplanting British. In 1913, British capital totaled $5 billion while US investment was $1.6 billion, a fivefold increase since the turn of the century. The growth of U.S. investment continued, while European investment stagnated. This was reflected in changes in the direction of trade. In 1913, the volume of Europe's exports to Latin America was nearly three times the US's. By 1925, the US had surpassed Europe and would not fall behind again. Latin America's exports also shifted toward the US after 1913 (Glade 1969, Ch. 10). In value terms, Latin America's imports from the U.S. increased 2.6 times between 1913 and 1930, while exports to the US increased 2.1 times, far faster than overall trade (Drake, 1989, p. 12). Britain maintained some dominance only in Bolivia, Argentina and Uruguay (Drake, 1989, p. 10).

The US took a leading role in guiding how Latin America fit into the world monetary non-order. The pattern was set by US control of Cuba and the Philippines after the Spanish American War.[3] Economic advice combined with inflows of resources to stabilize the economies and their currencies. This model was later applied in Central America and the Caribbean, and prior to the Depression spawned the era of the "money doctors" (Drake, 1989, 1994). External advisors, financed initially by US private interests and later by public resources, had a common message for Latin America: if the countries modernized their economies, revamped their government, banking and trade systems, and put modern institutions in place, they would gain access to US capital and commodity markets. The most important steps were creation of a central bank and adoption of the gold standard. As Drake (1989, p. 14) wrote:

> The United States promoted worldwide adoption of the gold standard to guarantee order for its economic expansion, and sought to pull Latin American countries away from reliance on British sterling. Many of those nations even began having their money printed in the United States. U.S. business executives wanted predictable exchange rates. U.S. elites hoped that gold standards tied to the U.S. dollar and U.S. banks would increase U.S. exports and safeguard U.S. investments.

Among the most active money doctors was Edwin Kemmerer who undertook missions to seven Latin American countries, as well as to Germany, South Africa, Poland, China and Turkey. He convinced the Latin American countries to adopt his reforms. "His system, in turn, depended on foreign loans to help service previous external debts, to cover shortfalls in the balance of payments, and to convince Latin Americans of the value of exchange stability" (Drake, 1989, p. 14).[4]

Nonetheless, it would be very misleading to ascribe the consistent movement to strong central banks and the gold standard to Kemmerer alone. Latin American economists had positions on these issues and there was widespread concern with how to stabilize the currency and restore convertibility long before Kemmerer came on the scene. The Mexican case described above is an example.

One aspect that needs clarification is the role that was played by a number of international monetary congresses in the first decades of the century, under the auspices of the League of Nations (Traynor, 1949). These conferences were paralleled by efforts in the Americas to find a common "scientific" approach to issues, including economic issues. This was represented by the Second Pan American Scientific Congress in Washington in 1915–1916.

To illustrate why these conferences are likely to have played a role, let us look at the case of Ecuador. It is true that Kemmerer had his greatest influence in Ecuador. As Drake (1989, p. 3) writes: "In his most sweeping renovation he implanted twenty-six new laws and agencies in Ecuador, thoroughly revamping money, banking, government budgeting, taxation, customs, credit, public works, and railroads." However, there had been significant debates and policy development efforts long before Kemmerer's 1926–1927 mission to Ecuador. Rodríguez (1985, p. 128) wrote: "Ecuadorians had long considered the establishment of a central bank a prerequisite for modernizing and reforming the nation's finances. Indeed coastal bankers, as the individuals most concerned with monetary reform, had publicly discussed such a move since 1920." Almeida (1994) listed and summarized the formal proposals for a Central Bank that pre-dated Kemmerer's successful 1927 activity. She found eight proposals to create a Central Bank, the last being Kemmerer's (Table 4). The earliest was in 1922, a project developed by Deputy Dr Juan Cueva Garcia and that was approved in the House of Representatives. It never was passed by the Senate. The next project was developed by well-known Ecuadorian banker/economist, V. E. Estrada, and was published in 1925. Other Latin American countries exhibited the same pattern, including those that Kemmerer visited: the existence of a series of proposals to restore convertibility and to establish a Central Bank to control monetary emission and to maintain a stable relation between the domestic money and gold.

So the role of Kemmerer was to sell a program that had already been developed and in that way to break the political impasse that prevented adoption of these financial reforms. "A pattern emerged in the late nineteenth and early twentieth century: Ecuadorians would discuss intensely an issue and then invite foreign experts to propose solutions. Governments employed foreign advisers with known views who would recommend policies they favored (Rodríguez, 1985, p. 134). But why had these projects been developed and what had been the role of Latin American economists in their development? Let us examine the international context for possible clues to how these proposals had been formulated, well before Kemmerer or other international advisers arrived physically on the scene.

Latin American economists and international monetary conferences

We must examine the role of Latin Americans in two types of conferences. The first are the Pan American Conferences, which considered a broad variety of exchange rate regime questions. The second are the two main inter-war international monetary conferences, the first held in Brussels in 1920 and the second in Genoa in 1922. Both were under the auspices of the League of Nations. One of the recommendations of the Brussels Conference was establishment of Central Banks and removal of exchange controls. The Genoa Conference recommended "responsible government finance, balanced budgets, the freeing of central banks of issue from political controls, control of inflation, and a common standard of value based on a reestablished gold standard" (Seidel, 1972, p. 525). This was the package that Kemmerer proposed and that was also incorporated in most Latin American proposals for a Central Bank. So these conferences may provide a key to Latin American economic thinking on issues of exchange rate regime. An important question is the influence that the conferences had on Latin American economic thinking, and whether Latin Americans had any role in the conferences. This would require an entirely new paper and so only some initial suggestions can be made in this chapter.

The Pan American Conferences provide the starting point. The first Pan American Financial Conference was held in May of 1915 with delegations from all of Latin America, save Haiti and Mexico (Seidel, 1973, p. 74).[5] The main impetus came from the US Treasury, with the goal of beginning to replace European influence in Latin America. Delegations were composed of business and financial leaders, along with policy makers.

The primary concern was establishing uniform standards and legal stipulations for all elements of trade, including intellectual property. These were long-standing concerns, expressed at the Second Pan American Conference in 1902, dealt with specifically at a conference in New York in 1903, and then again in 1906 in Rio and 1910 in Buenos Aires at the Third and Fourth Pan American Conferences (Scott, 1916, vol. 7, p. 136).

In addition, there was agreement to pursue "establishment of a gold standard of value" (p. 88) and to establish an "International High Commission" to carry the work forward. By the time of the first Commission meeting in Buenos Aires in April 1916, it had become clear that few countries would reestablish the gold standard for their non-convertible currencies. Thus discussion shifted to the desirability of establishing central banks, along the lines of the newly established Federal Reserve, and the possibility of establishing an International Gold Clearance Fund. The latter would have allowed settling financial accounts without physically shipping gold. It would have come into being through a series of bilateral agreements with the US. Several South American countries ratified the treaty – Chile, Paraguay and Uruguay. However, the US never took action. Similarly, the proposal for Central Banks was never engaged and was caught up in internal US debates about establishing Federal Reserve Bank agencies in Latin America to clear financial transactions, deal in gold and make loans to finance trade (Seidel, 1972, p. 107). The Fed, led by Governor Benjamin Strong, opposed this step. By the Second Pan American Financial Conference in January, 1920, the US had turned to Europe, and so efforts to adopt reciprocal agreements and Pan American initiatives were abandoned (Seidel, 1972, p. 121). This led to the "privatization" of US external influence on Latin American economic policy and the resulting prominence of Kemmerer and other money doctors (Drake, 1989, p. xxvii).

Nonetheless, these steps initiated extensive debates in Latin America. For example, at the 1910 Buenos Aires conference, establishment of a Pan American money of account was considered. Though nothing came of it, the Argentines wished to adopt the European "Latin Union monetary unit," while the US defended use of its gold dollar.

This proposal was seriously examined at another Pan American Conference, the Second Pan American Scientific Congress held in Washington, DC during December 1915 and January 1916. The proceedings provide evidence of already existing Latin American economic analysis of exchange rate regimes. Specifically, there were four papers given that analyzed the possibility of a Pan American monetary unit. One was by Edwin Kemmerer, who suggested that such a unit should be established, based upon the US gold dollar (Kemmerer, 1917, p. 261). The three by Latin Americans were by Joaquin Casasús of Mexico, Guillermo Subercaseaux of Chile, and Pedro Cuadra of Nicaragua. In all three cases, they provided cogent critiques of Kemmerer's proposal, based both on theories of international monetary relations and on the experience in their individual country. They were joined in their critique by Victor González (1917) who had been involved in Peru's adoption of a gold exchange standard before emigrating to the United States. Thus once again, Latin American economists were active participants in the exchange rate debates at this time. Their work was one factor that led to the adoption of Article 46 of the Final Act of the Congress: "that the monetary systems of the American Republics be subjected to careful scientific study with a view to making the experience of each available to all" (Scott, 1916, vol. 7, p. 139).

The specific efforts to establish Pan American institutions were most active during World War I. At its end, US interest shifted back to Europe. This leads to the next chapter in the history of the development by Latin Americans of their approaches to exchange rate regimes and monetary authorities after World War I. For that we turn to the two international monetary conferences in Brussels in 1920 and Genoa in 1922.

Unfortunately, the link to the actual policy proposals must remain hypothetical. There is little information on Latin American participation at the Genoa Conference. And the documentation of Latin American involvement at Brussels is just that, with no indication that the conclusions reached were carried back to the home countries, with consequent influence on economic policy. Nonetheless, let us summarize the Latin American role in the Brussels Conference.

The Brussels Conference was initiated by members of the League of Nations in their second meeting in February 1920. The League intended to "convene an International Conference with a view to studying the financial crisis and to look for the means of remedying it and of mitigating the dangerous consequences arising from it" (League of Nations, 1920a, p. 73). This was in reaction to a letter sent to the League by a handful of European member countries and the US, calling for a financial assembly of the affected Allied and neutral European states, along with the exporting countries of South America. Invitations were sent to 25 member states including, Argentina, Brazil and Chile, along with an invitation to the United States (League of Nations, 1920a, p. 74).

In preparation for the conference, brief statistical reports were commissioned for the possible participating countries. Summaries of Chile's, Argentina's and Uruguay's currencies and banking system before the war and the effects of the war on their respective financial conditions were presented. The reports indicated that Argentina and Uruguay had some credit inflation from loaning to Allied powers. Argentina and Uruguay also had difficulties exporting surplus to Europe in the wake of insufficient exchange to pay for their exports (League of Nations, 1920b, p. 159).

The description of the pre-war banking system states that both Chile and Argentina had Central Banks very much along English lines, and that there was no change in the system after the war. Of the three countries in question, only Chile's bank notes were inconvertible internationally in 1920. Chile's economy, it was noted, was hardly affected by the war, with the exception of nitrate exports, which declined briefly at the onset of war, and again briefly after the armistice (League of Nations, 1920b, p. 173). This could be a possible explanation for why Chile chose not to send delegates to the conference, despite preparing the summary report.

After much debate on whether or not to address Germany's indebtedness, it was decided to forgo such talk for the conference and address other prevailing issues. In the end, 39 countries attended, four of which were from South America: Argentina, Brazil, Guatemala and Uruguay (League of Nations, 1920a, p. 226).[6] Documents noted that the special concerns of Latin America were an "immense unfulfilled demand for capital expenditure," and that the lack of capital in the world at the time impeded development in Latin America (League of Nations, 1920a, p. 229).

The conference divided into different committees in order to address the particular problems facing the international economy. The committees were: Public Finance, Currency and Exchange, International Trade and Commerce, and International Action with Special Reference to Credits (League of Nations, 1920a, p. 231). Julio Barbosa Carneiro played an important role in drafting recommendations for the International Trade committee under the direction of Arnold J. Toynbee, Chairman (Traynor, 1949, p. 52). Of the six resolutions of the International Trade committee, the most important was the recommendation for "restoration of free trade and the withdrawal of artificial restrictions, especially price discrimination" (League of Nations, 1920a, p. 60). This resolution was unanimously accepted by the general body of the conference (League of Nations, 1920a, p. 233)

Other resolutions passed that were relevant to issues of exchange rate regime and monetary policy included:

1   A call for taxation to meet deficit spending requirements.
2   The cessation of inflation by halting the artificial expansion of currency, and by a return to the gold standard as quickly as possible.
3   The need for an external credit organization where governments can draw funds to pay for essential imports. The states would pledge assets as collateral as a guaranty for the bonds issued.
4   Establishment of a Central Bank and categorization of attempts to limit fluctuations in exchange by imposing artificial control on exchange operations as "futile and mischievous . . . In so far as they are effective they falsify the market, tend to remove natural correctives to such fluctuations and interfere with free dealings in forward exchange which are so necessary to enable traders to eliminate from their calculations a margin to cover the risks of exchange, which would otherwise contribute to the rise in prices" (League of Nations, 1920a, pp. 231–6).

While all of these recommendations were unanimously accepted by the body of the conference, it must be noted that all attendees participated in an unofficial capacity; therefore the resolutions were non-binding. The need for an external credit organization was among the most significant ideas to come out of the conference. The Ter Meulen Plan, after the Dutch financier, was supported by the conference. Carneiro of Brazil was one of four signatories, along with Ter Meulen. Each provided a detailed outline of the possibility of an external credit organization (League of Nations, 1920a, p. 240). While never adopted, the Ter Meulen Plan and others presented the possibility of future international cooperation (Traynor, 1949, p. 65).

The Brussels conference was criticized for finding "no practical immediate solution to the many economic evils now restricting the resumption of international trading on pre-war volumes" (*Morning Post*, 28 October, 1920, in Siepman, 1920, p. 458). In the case of Latin America and the participating nations, it appears to have helped keep them moving in the same direction.

While we do not have evidence of a direct effect on Latin American economic policy in the 1920s, the commonality of approach suggests that Latin American participation in the Pan American and International Monetary conferences is likely to have contributed to the formulation of those policies. In any case, it is clear that Kemmerer and other external advisers entered into a situation that had seen widespread debates on the best economic policy. The adoption of their package of policy reforms was in part an outcome of that debate and in large measure a result of the rhetorical situation that they joined upon their arrival.

Conclusions

Latin American economists were present in the domestic and international debates surrounding exchange rate regimes and central banks from the turn of the twentieth century through the 1920s. This has shown that there was debate and that Latin American economists were writing on the issues around exchange rate regime choice in the first decades of the twentieth century. Their role in the debate clearly varied from country to country, but was significant. There are cases of economists guiding the direction of their own economy and confronting the growing dominance of the US to protect the direction that they had established in their own country. In particular cases, such as the Pan American Conferences, Latin Americans played an important role and took positions that were quite opposite those of US economists. The influence that US economists ultimately established in the 1920s was the outcome of a complex interaction that had more to do with economic and political power than with the power of economic ideas. That is part of a broader set of questions. The importance and independence of Latin American economists in these debates in the first decades of the last century should not be overlooked, however.

Notes

1 Gonzalez (1917) describes his role in this process and its domestic effects. By 1911 he had moved to the US and was the delegate of the US National Association of Manufacturers at the Second Pan American Scientific Congress.
2 Pani was featured in *Time* (1923) for his accusations against his predecessor for running a budget deficit and covering it by diverting funds destined to paying the foreign debt.
3 The significant role this experience had on US economists' thinking can be seen in Edwin Kemmerer's career. His earliest activity was as financial advisor to the US Philippine Commission in 1903 and then as chief of the division of currency of the Philippine Islands from 1904–1906 (Seidel, 1972, p. 521).
4 There are strong parallels with today's economic policy-making process. The main role is played by the IMF, which uses access to its funds and those that follow its lead to influence economic policy, including exchange rate policy. In addition, in some cases, such as official dollarization, the dynamic resembles the 1920s. Money doctors visit countries, usually at the invitation of export-oriented business groups desiring exchange rate stability. They use the media to recommend dollarization; any subsequent economic instability encourages governments to view dollarization as a guarantor of stability and growth. Ecuador is the best example of this pattern. There, dollarization gave access to external resources that had been completely unavailable: a $304 million IMF Standby Loan and access to up to an additional $2 billion from other multilaterals (Jameson 2003). Prior to dollarization, Ecuador had been a virtual pariah to the international financial community.
5 This section draws primarily on the Seidel study, particularly Chapter 2.
6 Latin American attendees were as follows: Argentina: Delegates of the Government, Alberto Blancas, Argentine minister to Belgium, and Carlos A Tornquist, of Messrs. Tornquist & Co.; adviser: Dr. Alejandro E. Shaw; secretary: A. C. Buenano; Brazil: Delegate of the Government: Julio Barbosa Carneiro, commercial attaché to the Brazilian Embassy; Guatemala: Delegates of the Government Guillermo Matos Pacheco, charge d'affaires of the Guatemalan legation at Paris, and Juan de Putte, consul of Guatemala at Ghent; Uruguay: Delegates of the Government M. Alberto Guani, Uruguayan minister to Belgium, and M. Abelardo Roy, consul-general of Uruguay in Belgium (League of Nations, 1920a, p. 249).

References

Almeida, Rebeca (1994) *Kemmerer en el Ecuador*, Quito: FLACSO.
Andrew, Piatt (1904) "The End of the Mexican Dollar," *Quarterly Journal of Economics* 18(3), pp. 321–56.
Appendini Vargas, Guadalupe (1992) "Aguascalientes: 46 Personajes en Su Historia," Aguascalientes, México.
Bureau for Economic Research in Latin American (1935, 1936) *The Economic Literature of Latin America*, 2 Vols, Cambridge, Mass.: Harvard University Press.
Casasús, Joaquín (n.d.) "La Moneda Internacional." In *Proceedings of the Second Pan American Scientific Congress. Volume 11*, Washington, DC: GPO, pp. 22–32.
Cerda, Luis (n.d.) "The 'Free Banking' Experience in Mexico: 1890–1925," mimeo, unpublished.
Crosby, Joseph T. (1915) *Latin American Monetary Systems and Exchange Conditions*, New York: NP.
Cuadra, Pedro J. (1917) "Unificación Monetaria." In *Proceedings of the Second Pan American Scientific Congress. Volume 11*, Washington, DC: GPO, pp. 271–5.

Drake, Paul (1989) *The Money Doctors in the Andes: The Kemmerer Missions, 1923–1933*, Durham, North Carolina: Duke University Press.

Drake, Paul, ed. (1994) *Money Doctors, Foreign Debts, and Economic Reforms in Latin America from the 1890s to the Present*, Wilmington, Del.: Scholarly Resources.

Fischer, Stanley (2001) "Distinguished Lecture on Economics in Government: Exchange Rate Regimes: Is the Bipolar View Correct?" *Journal of Economic Perspectives* 15(2), (Spring), pp. 3–24.

Glade, William P. (1969) *The Latin American Economies: A Study of Their Institutional Evolution*, New York: Van Nostrand.

Gonzalez, Victor (1917) "Comments." In *Proceedings of the Second Pan American Scientific Congress. Volume 11*, Washington, DC: GPO, pp. 269–70.

Hoogvelt, Ankie (1997) *Globalization and the Postcolonial World: The New Political Economy of Development*, Baltimore, Md: The Johns Hopkins University Press.

Jameson, Kenneth P. (2003) "Dollarization: Wave of the Future or Flight to the Past," *Journal of Economic Issues* 37(3), (September).

Kemmerer, Edwin Walter (1916) *Modern Currency Reforms: A History and Discussion of Recent Currency Reforms in India, Porto Rico, Philippine Islands, Straits Settlements and Mexico*, New York: The Macmillan Company.

Kemmerer, Edwin Walter (1917) "A Proposal for Pan American Monetary Unity," In *Proceedings of the Second Pan American Scientific Congress. Volume 11*, Washington, DC: GPO, pp. 254–62.

League of Nations (1920a) *Currencies After the War: A Survey of Conditions in Various Countries*, London.

League of Nations (1920b) "Report of the International Financial Conference," World Peace Foundation, Boston, Vol. 3.

McCloskey, Donald (1985) *The Rhetoric of Economics*, Madison, Wisconsin: The University of Wisconsin Press.

McKinnon, Ronald (1993) "The Rules of the Game: International Money in Historical Perspective," *Journal of Economic Literature* 31(1), March, pp. 1–44.

Ortiz, Guillermo (1982) "La Dolarización en México: Causas y Consecuencias," *Monetaria* 5(4), October–December, pp. 439–64.

Pani, Alberto J. (1941) *Tres Monografías*, México, D.F.: Editorial Atlante.

Seidel, R. (1972) "American Reformers Abroad: The Kemmerer Missions in South America, 1923–1931," *Journal of Economic History* 32(2), pp. 520–45.

Rodríguez, Linda Alexander (1985) *The Search for Public Policy: Regional Politics and Government Finances in Ecuador, 1830–1940*, Berkeley: University of California Press.

Rosenberg, Emily S. (1985) "Foundations of United States International Financial Power: Gold Standard Diplomacy, 1900–1905," *Business History Review* 59(2), (Summer), pp. 169–202.

Rosenberg, Emily S. (1999) *Financial Missionaries to the World: The Politics and Culture of Dollar Diplomacy, 1900–1930*, Cambridge, Mass.: Harvard University Press.

Rosenberg, Emily S. and Norman L. Rosenberg (1987) "From Colonialism to Professionalism: The Public-private Dynamic in United States Foreign Financial Advising, 1898–1929." Reprinted in *Money Doctors, Foreign Debts, and Economic Reforms in Latin America from the 1890s to the Present*, edited by Paul Drake, Wilmington, Del.: Scholarly Resources, 1994, pp. 59–83.

Scott, James Brown (1916) *Proceedings: Second Pan American Scientific Congress*, 12 vols, Washington, DC: GPO.

Seidel, Robert N. (1972) "American Reformers Abroad: The Kemmerer Missions in South America, 1923–1931," *Journal of Economic History* 32(2), June, pp. 520–45.

Seidel, Robert N. (1973) "Progressive Pan Americanism: Development and United States Policy toward South America, 1906–1931," PhD Thesis, Ithaca, New York: Cornell University.

Siepman, H. A. (1920) "The International Financial Conference at Brussels," *Economic Journal* 30(3), December, pp. 436–59.

Subercaseaux, Guillermo (1917) "A Common Monetary Unit for America." In *Proceedings of the Second Pan American Scientific Congress, Volume 11*, Washington, DC: GPO, pp. 295–304.

Symes, Peter (2005) "Two Mexican Women." Available at www.pjsymes.com.au/articles/MexicanWomen.htm (downloaded on 20 January, 2005).

Thorp, Rosemary (1998) *Progress, Poverty and Exclusion: An Economic History of Latin America in the 20th Century*, Washington, DC: The Johns Hopkins University Press.

Thorp, Rosemary and Geoffrey Bertram (1978) *Peru 1890–1977: Growth and Policy in an Open Economy*, New York: Columbia University Press.

Time (1923) "Latin America: Storm Threatening," (29 October), p. 12.

Traynor, Dean E. (1949) *International Monetary and Financial Conferences in the Interwar Period*, Washington, DC: The Catholic University of America Press.

Williamson, Jeffrey G. (2002) "Winners and Losers over Two Centuries of Globalization," *NBER Working Paper*, 9161 (September).

Williamson, John, ed. (1990) *Latin American Adjustment: How Much Has Happened?* Washington, DC: Institute for International Economics.

5 The Latin American theory of inflation and beyond

Julio López Gallardo and Ricardo Mansilla

Introduction

Fear of inflation was one of the initial reasons for abandoning expansionary demand policies in advanced capitalist economies. Both Keynes and Kalecki, the founding fathers of the principle of effective demand, anticipated that inflation would probably arise under full employment. However, high and accelerating inflation came to be seen as a real danger in those economies only after the oil shocks of the 1970s. During that period inflation in highly developed economies took on features that resembled those prevailing in Latin American economies; which had been plagued by high rates of inflation throughout most of the post-World War II period. Fortunately, the period of high inflation did not last long in industrialized countries, and from the mid-1980s onwards the growth rate of prices declined to low levels. Somewhat later in most Latin American economies inflation also fell, and nowadays it is within a relatively low, one-digit figure.

In most theories of inflation, the latter emerges as an effect of a demand shock. In models formulated with developed economies in mind, the shock reduces unemployment, improves workers' bargaining power, and thus lifts the target real wage. With greater bargaining power, workers demand and obtain a higher money wage. This brings about a further rise in costs and prices and inflation develops. This is the basic idea running through the literature at least since Phillips (1958) formalized this idea.

The main objective of this chapter is to explore two different and alternative routes to inflation. First, besides enhancing workers' bargaining power, high levels of economic activity are likely to weaken the current account balance. This may result in a currency depreciation. We explore here the effects of currency depreciation on the path of inflation. Second, we develop a model whereby inflation is built into the system, and does not need an exogenous shock to emerge.

In this chapter, we model inflation as a discrete dynamical system of equations. The trajectories of the system represent the dynamical paths followed by the vector of state variables. We use results of dynamical systems theory to analyze the behavior of these trajectories (Arrowsmith and Place, 1990).

Intellectual background

To start with reflection, it may be recalled that in his seminal and famous paper, Phillips (1958) took account of the impact of an autonomous rise in the international price of raw materials on domestic inflation. He did not discuss, however, the possible effects of an expansionary demand policy on the external deficit, on the exchange rate and on inflation. This last aspect has rarely been integrated into more recent models of inflation.[1]

In contrast with this outlook, the Latin American structuralist theory of inflation paid a lot of attention to external disequilibrium as a source of inflation.[2] Thus, in this theory structural disequilibria between demand and supply of particular sectors provoke inflation. Note, the term structural alludes not only to the long-lasting nature of the disequilibrium, but also implies that it will not be overcome by simply changing relative prices. In other words, the rise in the relative price and profitability of the laggard sector does not bring about an increase in the rate of expansion of its supply strong enough, which lags behind the rate of growth of demand.

Latin American authors identified two such typical disequilibria. One is between the rapid rate of growth of demand and the sluggish growth of supply of agricultural necessities (see also Kalecki, 1954). The second one arises because a rather slow rate of growth of the import capacity is confronted with a higher rate of growth of demand for foreign exchange. As Noyola, (1956 (1987, p. 74)) put it in his seminal paper

> the basic inflationary pressure in Mexico has ... arisen out of the incapability of exports to grow at the same rate as the domestic economy; balance of payment disequilibria have been thus created, which have brought about repeated currency depreciations, whose impact on the domestic price level has not been mitigated by exchange rate subsidies.

Noyola also advanced the proposition that monetary expansion was not the original cause of inflation, but rather a "propagation" mechanism which allowed the price rise to persist. In this context, he argued that money was endogenously created to satisfy the needs of trade. In his words, "With regards to credit expansion, it may be said ... that it has been the most passive of the propagation mechanisms; its role has been to provide the economy with enough liquidity in real terms to follow the rate of prices" (1978, p. 73).

The analysis of disequilibrium between supply and demand for agricultural output gave rise to a beautifully simple dynamical model almost four decades ago (Olivera, 1967). However, the impact of external disequilibrium on inflation has not been formalized to the same extend (but see Ros, 2001). In the next section we will formalize and further explore this intuition of the Latin American school.

A simple model of inertial inflation

The model of prices and inflation that follows assumes an industrial system where firms set their prices applying a mark-up to unit prime costs. The latter are made up, first, of wage costs, and also of imported raw materials costs.

The first equation says how prices are set. The variable p is the average price fixed by firms and w is the unit wage cost. d is the nominal exchange rate, which also represents the cost of imported raw materials. d thus changes over time according to, and in the same proportion as, the nominal exchange rate. a is the ratio of the price to the unit prime cost, i.e. Kalecki's "degree monopoly."

The second equation says that workers ask for, and obtain, a wage that varies over time. Nominal wages in time t depend on nominal wages in the previous period, and on the past evolution of prices. To stress the difference between this model and models based on the Phillips curve notion, we will not suppose that the target *real* wage rises with lower unemployment.

The third equation indicates how the exchange rate is determined. We assume that foreign exchange is a financial asset, whose price is set by the collective action of foreign exchange dealers (Schulmeister, 1988; Harvey, 1998–1999).[3]

We thus have:

$$p_t = a(w_t + d_t),\ a>1 \tag{5.1}$$

$$w_t = w_{t-1} \cdot \frac{p_{t-1}}{p_{t-2}} \tag{5.2}$$

$$d_t = d_{t-1} \cdot \frac{p_t}{p_{t-1}} \tag{5.3}$$

From (5.2) we know that $w_{t-1} = w_{t-2}\left(\dfrac{p_{t-2}}{p_{t-3}}\right)$ and from (5.3) we know that

$$d_{t-1} = d_{t-2}\left(\frac{p_{t-1}}{p_{t-2}}\right)$$

We use these conditions and we substitute (5.2) and (5.3) in (5.1) to get:

$$p_t = a\left[w_{t-2}\left(\frac{p_{t-2}}{p_{t-3}}\right) \cdot \left(\frac{p_{t-1}}{p_{t-2}}\right) + d_{t-2}\frac{p_{t-1}}{p_{t-2}} \cdot \frac{p_t}{p_{t-1}} \right]$$

$$= a\left[w_{t-2}\left(\frac{p_{t-1}}{p_{t-3}}\right) + d_{t-2}\frac{p_t}{p_{t-2}} \right]$$

$$= a\left[w_{t-3}\left(\frac{p_{t-3}}{p_{t-4}}\right)\left(\frac{p_{t-1}}{p_{t-3}}\right) + d_{t-3}\frac{p_{t-2}}{p_{t-3}}\frac{p_t}{p_{t-2}} \right]$$

Upon repeated substitutions we obtain:

$$p_t = a\left(w_1 \frac{p_{t-1}}{p_0} + d_1 \frac{p_t}{p_1} \right) \qquad \text{and} \tag{5.4}$$

$$p_t = \frac{\left[\dfrac{aw_1}{p_0}\right]}{\left[1 - \left(\dfrac{ad_1}{p_1}\right)\right]} \cdot p_{t-1} \tag{5.5}$$

Let:

$$A \equiv \frac{\left[\dfrac{aw_1}{p_0}\right]}{\left[1 - \left(\dfrac{ad_1}{p_1}\right)\right]}$$

So that:

$$p_t = A \cdot p_{t-1} \tag{5.6}$$

And the rate of inflation is:

$$\hat{p}_t = \frac{p_t - p_{t-1}}{p_{t-1}} = \frac{p_t}{p_{t-1}} - 1 = A - 1 \tag{5.7}$$

Equation (5.6) has an exact solution, namely:

$$p_t = A^t \cdot p_0 \tag{5.8}$$

The solution of (5.6) thus depends on the value of A, which is a constant. Now, from (5.1) we know:

$$p_t = aw_t + ad_t \Rightarrow \left(1 - \frac{ad_t}{p_t}\right) = \frac{aw_t}{p_t}$$

Accordingly, upon simplification:

$$A = \frac{\left[\dfrac{aw_1}{p_0}\right]}{\left[1 - \left(\dfrac{ad_1}{p_1}\right)\right]} = \frac{p_1}{p_0} \tag{5.9}$$

Note that while the equilibrium position for the price level is dynamically unstable, the rate of inflation, namely the ratio

$$\frac{p_t - p_{t-1}}{p_{t-1}}$$

is a constant. Thus, forexample, if $A > 1$, a positive demand shock will make prices persistently rise. However, the rate of inflation will be a positive constant.

That is, prices will persistently rise but at a constant rate. According to (5.9), this is given by the initial rate of inflation

$$\frac{p_1 - p_0}{p_0},$$

following the shock.

Equations (5.1) through (5.9) are behind the so-called theory of inertial inflation. This was developed in Latin America (especially in Argentina and Brazil) during the 1970s and the 1980s (Frenkel, 1979; Fanelli and Frenkel, 1990; Carvalho, 1993; Rego, 1986, Bresser-Pereira and Nakano, 1987). In this theory, owing to an initial shock inflation arises, and owing to further shocks it escalates until it reaches a high plateau.

The story can be told assuming that up to period 0 prices have been stable, and that in period 1 an expansionary demand policy is put into effect. This brings about a currency depreciation. In other words, the nominal exchange rate adjusts immediately upwards. Since workers have not had an inflationary experience, wages do not immediately react.

Indeed, when a (positive) demand shock brings about a current account deficit, a discrepancy arises between the actual real exchange rate and what the foreign exchange dealers consider should be the new equilibrium real exchange rate.[4] We define here the equilibrium real exchange rate as the real exchange rate which is required in order to ensure current account balance at a given level of aggregate domestic and external demand. After the demand shock takes place a currency depreciation thus occurs. This aims to restore external equilibrium by raising the nominal exchange rate in order to improve the real exchange rate and competitiveness. Unit prime costs and prices thus rise. But workers do not accept a fall in their real wage and claim and obtain a higher nominal wage. This brings about a new round of cost and price inflation. The price hike nullifies the previous rise in the real exchange rate and if aggregate demand does not fall the whole process starts again. Accordingly:

$$D_1 = \frac{d_1}{p_1} = \frac{d_0}{p_0}(1 + g) \Rightarrow d_1 = d_0 \cdot \frac{p_1}{p_0} \cdot (1 + g), g > 0 \tag{5.10}$$

Condition (5.10) alludes to the demand shock and the ensuing current account deficit that takes place in period 1. The latter makes the equilibrium real exchange rate exceed the actual real exchange rate of the previous period (g is the requisite rate of change of the real exchange rate). Thus, we are assuming that the real exchange rate immediately adjusts to its new, higher value.

Moreover, we can see from (5.6) that the value of A will be higher, the higher the ratio d_1/p_1, i.e. the higher the new real exchange rate following a given deterioration of the external balance. In other words, the higher the impact of the demand shock on what foreign exchange dealers perceive as the equilibrium real exchange rate, the higher the inflation rate will tend to be.

Now, the model proposed has the important feature that wages are adjusted looking purely backwards. Closely related to the above, workers accept a fall in real wages. Lastly, the real exchange rate stabilizes at its new level. We will first deal with the last assumption.

Our assumption that the real exchange rate stabilizes at its new level, d_1/p_1, was based upon the assumption of a one-off expansionary demand policy. Let us now broaden our perspective to investigate the effect of a long-lasting expansionary demand policy. In other words, consider a demand policy whereby the country grows permanently at a higher rate than is warranted by its normal export capacity. Let M be the demand for and X the supply of foreign exchange. As before, d is the nominal exchange rate and p the price (index) of the domestic production. D is the relative price of the foreign exchange, i.e. $D = d/p$. Further, let ε and η be the elasticity of supply of and demand for foreign exchange with respect to its relative price D. Last, let us assume that the autonomous rate of expansion of the demand for and the supply of foreign exchange, at a given relative price of the foreign exchange, are π and σ respectively. It may be assumed that the autonomous demand for foreign exchange is given by the rate of growth of domestic output, while the autonomous rate of growth of the supply of foreign exchange is given by the rate of growth of exports, which in its turn depends upon the rate of growth of world output. We see now how prices evolve when $\pi > \sigma$.

Under equilibrium conditions we have (Olivera, 1967):

$$X(D,t) = M(D,t) \tag{5.11}$$

Where as always t is time.

$$\frac{\delta X}{\delta D} \frac{\delta D}{\delta t} + \frac{\delta X}{\delta t} = \frac{\delta M}{\delta D} \frac{\delta D}{\delta t} + \frac{\delta M}{\delta t} \tag{5.12}$$

In terms of the elasticities involved, and given that in equilibrium $X = M$

$$\frac{1}{D} \frac{\delta D}{\delta t} (\varepsilon + \eta) = \frac{\left(\dfrac{\delta M}{\delta t} - \dfrac{\delta X}{\delta t}\right)}{X} = \frac{1}{M} \frac{\delta M}{\delta t} - \frac{1}{X} \frac{\delta X}{\delta t} = \pi - \sigma \tag{5.13}$$

And then:

$$\hat{d}_t - \hat{p}_t = \hat{D}_t = \frac{\pi - \sigma}{\eta + \varepsilon} \tag{5.14}$$

Thus:

$$\hat{d}_t = \hat{p}_t + \frac{\pi - \sigma}{\eta + \varepsilon} \tag{5.14a}$$

Accordingly, when $\pi > \sigma$ the relative, and absolute price of the exchange tends to grow. But the higher price of exchange *d* in turn brings about higher unit costs, and accordingly translates into higher price *p*, which brings about a wage rise. Our dynamical system now becomes:

$$p_t = a(w_t + d_t), \ a > 1 \tag{5.1}$$

$$w_t = w_{t-1} \cdot \frac{p_{t-1}}{p_{t-2}} \tag{5.2}$$

$$\hat{d}_t = \hat{p}_t + \frac{\pi - \sigma}{\eta + \varepsilon} \tag{5.14}$$

This is a dynamical system which does not have an analytical solution. However, we can simulate the time-path of p assuming some initial values. This is done in Figure 5.1. The values of the parameters in Figure 5.1 are $\sigma = 1$, $\varepsilon = 1.5$, $\eta = 2$. The different graphs are related with different values for π. Ordered from smaller to greater: $\pi = 2$, $\pi = 2.1$, $\pi = 2.3$, $\pi = 2.7$.

It can be seen that the price *p* follows an upward seesaw-shaped path. Moreover, as was to be expected, the rate of growth of prices is positively related to

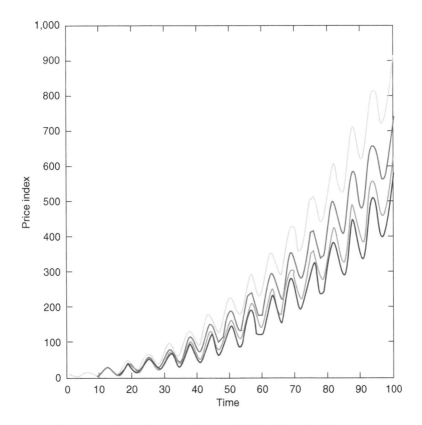

Figure 5.1 Evolution of the price index for model (5.1), (5.2) and (5.14a).

the difference between the autonomous rate of expansion of the demand for, and of the supply of foreign exchange, π and σ respectively.

Now, one peculiarity of the model (5.1), (5.2), (5.14a), is that prices, and with them nominal wages, can fall. This may seem somewhat unrealistic. To see if things turn out to be qualitatively different if we exclude that possibility, we may substitute equation (5.2) by:

$$w_t = \max\left(w_{t-1} \cdot \frac{p_{t-1}}{p_{t-2}}, w_{t-1}\right) \tag{5.2a}$$

Admitting or not condition (5.2a) causes that the dynamics of prices vary somewhat. This can be appraised in the following figures.[5] Figure 5.2 shows the model under the assumption that prices and wages are allowed to decrease. The values of the parameters are $\sigma = 1$, $\varepsilon = 1.5$, $\eta = 2$ and $\pi = 2$. Figure 5.3 shows the model under the assumption that prices could not decrease. The values of the parameters are $\sigma = 1$, $\varepsilon = 1.5$, $\eta = 2$ and $\pi = 2$.

On the other hand, if we do not take into account the restriction involved in (5.2a), that is to say, if we allow wages to diminish, prices grow exponentially but slower than if we admit such condition. However, in both cases a similar behavior for the rate of increase of prices obtains. Namely, the rate of inflation starts at a high level, and then it decreases slowly and tends asymptotically toward a low level, as shown in the Figure 5.4.

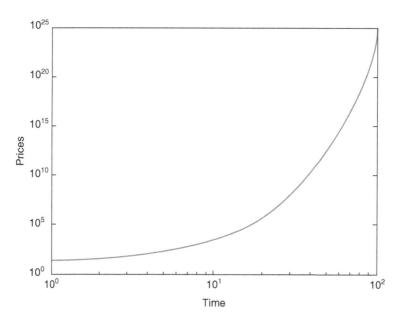

Figure 5.2 Evolution of prices in model (5.1), (5.2) and (5.14a).

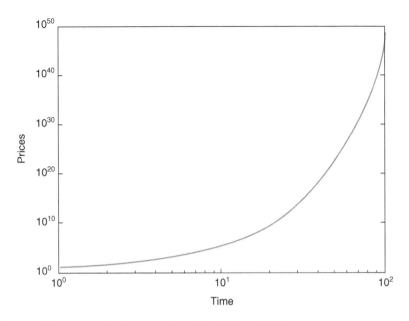

Figure 5.3 Evolution of prices in model (5.1), (5.2a) and (5.14a).

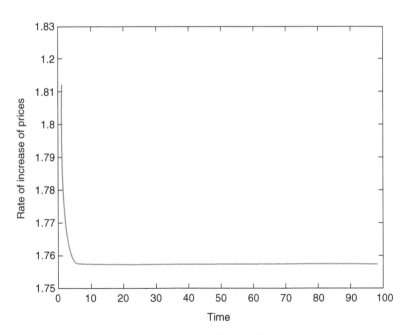

Figure 5.4 Rate of increase of prices in model (5.1), (5.2) and (5.14a).

Endogenous inflation

An important consequence of the previous model is that real wages have to fall. This can be shown to be the case if we solve the model for w_t. We can express w_t as:

$$w_t = w_1 \frac{p_{t-1}}{p_0} \tag{5.15}$$

Or, equivalently:

$$\frac{w_t}{p_t} = \frac{w_1}{p_0} \cdot \frac{p_{t-1}}{p_t} \tag{5.15a}$$

Given the delay in the reaction of wages, we know:

$$\frac{w_1}{p_0} = \frac{w_0}{p_0}$$

Thus, if prices were constant, the real wage would also be constant. However, we already found that prices are rising, i.e.:

$$\frac{p_{t-1}}{p_t} < 1$$

Thus,

$$\frac{w_t}{p_t} = \frac{w_1}{p_0} \cdot \frac{p_{t-1}}{p_t} = \frac{w_0}{p_0} \cdot \frac{p_{t-1}}{p_t} < \frac{w_0}{p_0}$$

i.e. the real wage has fallen compared with its value at the beginning of the process. It also follows that, in tandem with stabilization of the inflation rate (p_{t-1}/p_t is a constant), real wages also stabilize.

We may safely assume that this situation is not likely to be sustainable, except if the fall in real wages is small; i.e. except when the inflationary shock is insignificant. But if the inflationary shock is significant, workers will bargain a nominal wage giving more weight to expected price, and less weight to past-period prices.

In order to take account of this situation, we will now assume that when they bargain next period's wage, workers have a certain expectation for prices for that period. More precisely, following Chiarella *et al.* (2000) we assume the existence of two groups of workers. Members of the first group are endowed with rational expectations and can perfectly anticipate next period's price. The second group simply bargains according to past inflation. α is the relative share of wage earners in the first group, and $1 - \alpha$ the share in the second group. We discuss below the specification for α.

We thus posit:

$$p_t = a(w_t + d_t), \quad a > 1 \tag{5.1}$$

$$w_t = \left[\frac{\alpha_t p_t + (1 - \alpha_t) p_{t-1}}{\alpha_{t-1} p_{t-1} + (1 - \alpha_{t-1}) p_{t-2}} \right], \quad 1 > \alpha > 0 \tag{5.2b}$$

$$d_t = d_{t-1} \cdot \frac{p_t}{p_{t-1}} \tag{5.3}$$

The factor α, which plays an important role in our model through its impact on the wage bargain, takes on values ranging from 0 to 1, but has to be lower than 1. More precisely, we assume that the relative weight of the two groups endogenously changes, according to how high inflation has been in the past. This can be rationalized with the idea that an effort is required in order to anticipate inflation. The higher the inflation rate, the larger will be the loss for incorrectly anticipating it. Therefore, the greater will be the number of workers making that effort. Accordingly, we assume α changes as a function of past inflation; i.e. the rate p_{t-1}/p_{t-2}. We thus specify the following functional form for α:

$$\alpha t = \frac{k_0 e^{\,\delta\, \frac{p_{t-1}}{p_{t-2}}}}{1 - k_0 + k_0 e^{\,\delta\, \frac{p_{t-1}}{p_{t-2}}}} \quad 0 < k_0 <<< 1 \tag{5.16}$$

The functional form in (5.16) has been selected to convey the idea previously advanced. α_t depends on how prices behaved in the recent past. If the rate of inflation (p_t/p_{t-1}) has been high then the share of workers who consider it worthwhile to make an effort to anticipate future prices correctly, will tend to be high and a low proportion of workers will simply react to past prices; and the opposite. Note, the constant k_0 should be close to, but always higher than zero. We explore below the evolution of system (5.1), (5.2b), (5.3), with condition (5.16).

We can substitute in (5.1) the expressions for d_t and w_t to get:

$$p_t = a \left\{ w_{t-1} \left[\frac{\alpha_t p_t + (1 - \alpha_t) p_{t-1}}{\alpha_{t-1} p_{t-1} + (1 - \alpha_{t-1}) p_{t-2}} \right] + d_{t-1} \left[\frac{p_t}{p_{t-1}} \right] \right\} \tag{5.17}$$

And after successive substitutions we will have:

$$p_t = a \left\{ w_{t-r} \left[\frac{\alpha_t p_t + (1 - \alpha_t) p_{t-1}}{\alpha_{t-r} p_{t-r} + (1 - \alpha_{t-r}) p_{t-r-1}} \right] + d_{t-r} \left[\frac{p_t}{p_{t-r}} \right] \right. \tag{5.18}$$

In particular, for $r = t - 1$ we get:

$$p_t = a \left\{ w_1 \left[\frac{\alpha_t p_t + (1 - \alpha_t) p_{t-1}}{\alpha_1 p_1 + (1 - \alpha_1) p_0} \right] + d_1 \left[\frac{p_t}{p_1} \right] \right. \tag{5.19}$$

Let us introduce the following notation:

$$c_1 \equiv \frac{aw_1}{\alpha_1 p_1 + (1 - \alpha_1) p_0}, \quad c_2 \equiv a \frac{d_1}{p_1}$$

We then have:

$$p_t = c_1 \{\alpha_t p_t + (1 - \alpha_t) p_{t-1}\} + c_2 p_t \tag{5.20}$$

from which we get:

$$p_t = \frac{c_1 (1 - \alpha_t) p_{t-1}}{1 - c_1 \alpha_t - c_2} \tag{5.21}$$

And finally:

$$p_t = \frac{(1 - k_0) c_1 p_{t-1}}{(1 - c_2)(1 - k_0) + 1 - c_1 - 1 - c_2) k_0 e^{\alpha \left(\frac{p_{t-1}}{p_{t-2}}\right)}} \tag{5.22}$$

Now let:

$$J \equiv (1 - k_0)c_1; \quad R \equiv (1 - c_2)(1 - k_0); \quad Z \equiv (1 - c_1 - c_2)k_0$$

We can then write:

$$p_t = \frac{J p_{t-1}}{R + Z e^{\alpha \left(\frac{p_{t-1}}{p_{t-2}}\right)}} \tag{5.23}$$

We introduce now the following change of variable:

$$\begin{bmatrix} u_t \\ v_t \end{bmatrix} = \begin{bmatrix} p_t \\ p_{t-1} \end{bmatrix}$$

We then have the following system of equations:

$$\begin{bmatrix} u_t \\ v_t \end{bmatrix} = \begin{bmatrix} \dfrac{J u_{t-1}}{R + Z (\exp) \alpha \left(\dfrac{u_{t-1}}{v_{t-1}}\right)} \end{bmatrix} \tag{5.24}$$

We will prove the above model has no isolated equilibrium point. In fact, let us suppose that (u^*, v^*) is an equilibrium point. Then, the following relations should hold:

$$u^* = \frac{Ju^*}{R + Z\,(\exp)\,\alpha\left(\frac{u_{t-1}}{v_{t-1}}\right)}$$

$$v^* = u^*$$

The above equations only hold if:

$$1 = \frac{J}{R + Ze^{\delta}}$$

Note that, in the case such constants exist, every point in the plane (u, v) would be an equilibrium position. Therefore, the dynamical systems theory cannot be applied to this pathological case. It can be proved that any equilibrium position for this system would be unstable. Moreover, it can also be proved that solutions of system (5.24), or equivalently, solutions of equation (5.23) grow at exponential (constant) rate.

We can now explore the behavior of the model simulating the time path of prices under hypothetical values of the parameters. Figure 5.5 shows the system with condition (5.16), and the values of the parameters are: $a = 2$, $k_0 = 0.001$, $\delta = 1.17$, $w_0 = 11$, $d_0 = 1.65$. The model described by equations (5.1), (5.2b), (5.3), with condition (5.16) results in an average exponential (constant) rate of growth of prices. Note, this last result would not change if we were to assume that nominal wages cannot fall. That is, if we substitute equation (5.2b) by the following one[6].

$$w_t = \max\left\{ w_{t-1}\left[\frac{\alpha_t p_t + (1 - \alpha_t)p_{t-1}}{\alpha_{t-1}p_{t-1} + (1 - \alpha_{t-1})p_{t-2}} \right], w_{t-1}\right\}, \quad 1 > \alpha > 0 \qquad (5.2c)$$

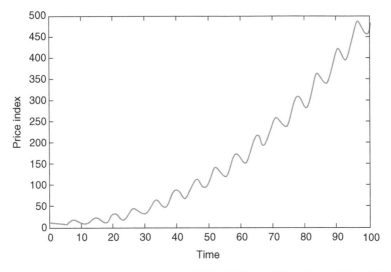

Figure 5.5 Evolution of price index in model (5.1), (5.2b) and (5.3), with condition (5.16).

To complete our discussion, we want to mention that in spite of its simplicity, the model (5.1), (5.2b), (5.3), with condition (5.16) has an interesting mathematical property. Namely, it is endowed with a point of bifurcation in one of the parameters, d_0, which we have managed to identify with high exactitude:

$$d_0 = 1.659876791066502765836787602893305$$

We show below the evolution of the growth rate of prices for values of d_0 slightly below and slightly above the bifurcation value. We use the growth rate of prices rather than their absolute level because in the former case the differences appear more noticeable. The values of the remaining parameters are the same as in figure 5.1, except for δ, which is set to 1.5 for a similar reason.

The values of the parameters in Figure 5.6 are: $a = 2$, $k_0 = 0.001$, $\delta = 1.5$, $w_0 = 11$. Figure 5.6 shows the growth rate of prices for the values of the initial exchange rate a little smaller than the value of bifurcation. If we slightly increase the value of the constant d_0 over the value of bifurcation to $d_0 = 1.659876791066502765836787602893399$, we obtain a behavior like the one in the following Figure 5.7. The values of the parameters in Figure 5.7 are $a = 2$, $k_0 = 0.001$, $\delta = 1.5$, $w_0 = 11$. Note that the pattern of variation of the prices growth rate changes with respect to the previous case. It is important to indicate that in both cases the general tendency in the (average) growth of prices is exponential.

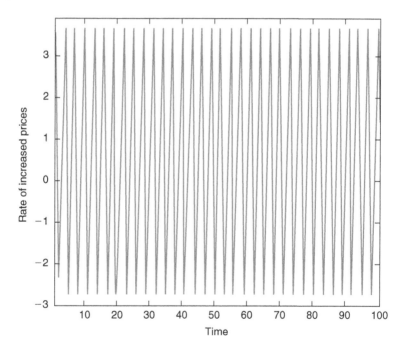

Figure 5.6 Rate of growth of prices in model (5.1)–(5.4).

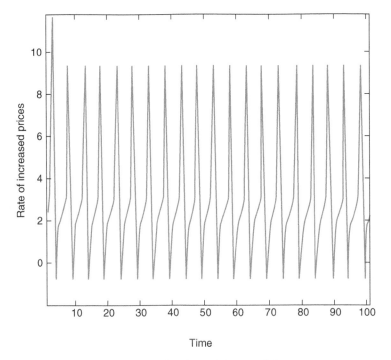

Figure 5.7 Rate of growth of prices in model (5.1)–(5.4).

The existence of a bifurcation point creates a serious problem in the dynamics of prices, because if tiny variations in one of the parameters can generate patterns of different behaviors, then the intrinsic non-linearity of the system makes practically impossible any price prediction. In fact, this would be a case,[7] where rational expectations could not apply because the agent could not know the "true" value of the variable to be forecasted.

Conclusions

In this chapter, we have explored two different routes to inflation. Starting with a structural model of inflation, as proposed by the Latin American structuralist school, we moved on to an endogenous model of inflation, where the price rise comes about due to the pattern of the wage bargain and price determination.

Regarding our structural model, we found that the initial price hike plays a crucial role as regards the rate of inflation. More precisely, suppose an expansionary policy which provokes a current account deficit. This brings about a currency depreciation. Now, the future rate of inflation is entirely determined by the extent of the initial currency depreciation. We would argue that this point helps to understand the different inflationary experiences of advanced vis-à-vis developing economies.

The reason has to do with the following. In developed economies, the domestic currency enjoys a certain reputation (Yotopoulos, 1996). When an expansionary policy brings about current account deficit, the exchange rate does not immediately devalue, or does not devalue by much. The economy is thus endowed with a certain breathing space. Since an economic expansion is associated with rising labor productivity (Okun, 1981), unit labor costs may fall, and the current account disequilibrium tends to correct itself, or is much milder than it would have been otherwise. By contrast, in developing economies, where the domestic currency has no reputation (or has a very bad one), any current account deficit tends to be immediately followed by an exchange rate devaluation, which has a negative impact on future growth and on the dynamics of labor productivity.

Second, hyperinflation does not take place in either of the two models we developed.[8] Now, experience shows that not only a moderate, but even a high but constant rate of inflation, need not disrupt the functioning of an economy, because mechanisms and institutions can be created that can accommodate that type of situation (Carvalho, 1993). It would then appear that inflation should not be such a great cause of concern, because in spite of its persistence, the rate of inflation tends to stabilize. However, this conclusion is too optimistic, because when inflation is high, changes in income distribution tend to become dramatic, and the whole social fabric is disrupted. This is probably the most important reason why high inflation should always be a cause of concern.

Notes

1 But see Carlin and Soskice (1992) and Layard *et al.* (1991), and the bibliography therein cited.
2 The Latin American structuralist school is by and large linked with the name of Raúl Prebisch, who headed the Economic Commission for Latin America and the Caribbean (ECLAC) from its inception until 1963. Most members of that school were associated with ECLAC. This was the case in particular of Juan F. Noyola, who was the original creator of the structuralist theory of inflation. The original paper by Noyola was firstly published in 1956, and was reprinted in 1987. See Canavese (1982), for a comparison between the Latin American and the Scandinavian theories of inflation, and Danby (2005) for a much broader view of Noyola's economics.
3 The results would not be different if we assumed, more in line with the conventional view, that the real exchange rate cannot vary too greatly from its "long-run equilibrium" value, and that foreign exchange dealers are endowed with rational expectations.
4 As mentioned, for the purpose of our reasoning the results would not change if we assumed that foreign exchange dealers are endowed with rational expectations. Note, we define the real exchange rate D as $D = d.(p^x/p)$. d is the nominal exchange rate, p^x is the index of international prices and p is the index of domestic prices. Without loss of generality p^x will be set as 1 throughout the paper and so $D = d/p$.
5 Note, the scales in Figures 5.2 and 5.3 are different. With a different scale the seesaw-shaped path would be more visible in Figure 5.2, while it would be apparent that prices discontinuously rise in Figure 5.3.
6 In the case when (5.2b) is substituted by (5.2c) the time path of prices would not be seesaw-shaped but prices would discontinuously rise.
7 There are many more, see for example Bhaduri (2002).
8 This is in contrast with the model originally proposed by Olivera (1967).

References

Arrowsmith, D.K. and C.M. Place (1990) *An Introduction to Dynamical Systems*, Cambridge: Cambridge University Press.

Bhaduri, Amit (2002) "Chaotic implications of the natural rate of unemployment," *Structural Change and Economic Dynamics* 13(3), pp. 357–66.

Bresser-Pereira, Luiz Carlos and Yoshiaki Nakano (1987) *The Theory of Inertial Inflation. The Foundation of Economic Reform in Brazil and Argentina*, Boulder, Co: Lynne Rienner Publishers.

Canavese, Alfredo (1982) "The Structuralist Explanation in the Theory of Inflation," *World Development* 10(7), pp. 523–9.

Carlin, Wendy and David Soskice (1992) *Macroeconomics and the Wage Bargain*, Oxford: Oxford University Press.

Carvalho, Fernando Cardim de (1993) "Strato-inflation and High Inflation: the Brazilian Experience," *Cambridge Journal of Economics* 17(1), pp. 63–79.

Chiarella, Carl; Peter Flaschel, Gangolf Groh and Willi Semmler (2000) *Disequilibrium, Growth and Labor Market Dynamics*, Berlin: Springer-Verlag.

Danby, Colin (2005) "Noyola's Institutional Approach to Inflation," *Journal of the History of Economic Thought* 27(2), pp. 161–78.

Fanelli, José Maria and Roberto Frenkel (1990), *Hiper-inflación en Argentina*, Buenos Aires: Editorial Tesis.

Frenkel, Roberto (1979) "Decisiones de Precio en Alta Inflación," *Estudios CEDES*, Vol. 2 No. 1, Buenos Aires.

Harvey, John (1998–1999) "The Nature of Expectations in the Foreign Exchange Market," *Journal of Post Keynesian Economics* 21(2), pp. 181–200.

Kalecki, Michal (1954) "The Problem of Financing Economic Development." In *Collected Works of Michal Kalecki, Vol. V*, edited by Jerzy Osiatynsky, Oxford: Oxford University Press, 1993.

Layard, Richard, Stephen Nickell and Richard Jackman (1991) *Unemployment. Macroeconomic Performance and the Labour Market*, Cambridge: Cambridge University Press.

Noyola, Juan (1956) "El Desarrollo Económico y la Inflación en México y otros Países Latinoamericanos," *Materiales, Investigación Económica*, Facultad de Economía UNAM, México, 1987.

Okun, Arthur (1981) *Prices and Quantities: A Macroeconomic Analysis*, Washington, DC: Brookings Institution.

Olivera, Julio H. G. (1967) "Aspectos Dinámicos de la Inflación Estructural," *Desarrollo Económico* 17(7), pp. 261–6.

Phillips, A. William (1958), "The Relationship between Unemployment and the rate of Change of Money Wage Rates in the United Kingdom, 1861–1957," *Economica* 25, November, pp. 283–99.

Rego, José Marcio (ed.) (1986) *Inflação Inercial, Teorias sobre Inflação e o Plano Cruzado*, São Paulo: Paz e Terra.

Ros, Jaime (2001) *Development Theory and the Economics of Growth*, Ann Arbor: University of Michigan Press.

Schulmeister, St. (1988) "Currency Speculation and Dollar Fluctuations," *Banca Nazionale del Lavoro Quarterly Review* 167, pp. 343–65.

Yotopoulos, Pan (1996) *Exchange Rate Parity for Trade and Development*, Cambridge: Cambridge University Press.

6   The unfamiliar Raúl Prebisch

Carlos Mallorquín[1]

Prebisch was a very well known figure amongst the intellectual and political elite of most Latin American countries in the early 1940s. Yet there is a sense in which, before his arrival to the Economic Commission for Latin America (ECLAC), he was relatively unknown. This chapter tries to describe what I consider an exceptional period in his intellectual life: the years that follow his dismissal as the Director of the Argentinean Central Bank in 1943 up to a few days before he departs from México City on his way to Santiago de Chile to report to ECLAC in 1949, that is, right before the formulation of his development manifesto (*Economic Development and Its Main Problems*),[2] Indeed Prebisch himself said it on various occasions that this was an exceptional period in his intellectual life.[3]

Prebisch's ideas in the Manifesto (first draft from May 1949) and the theoretical considerations which from there on give expression to the notion of peripheral economy, and to the very notion of cycle, were not predetermined in his previous intellectual work. However, the notion of development and the importance of planning (Toye and Toye, 2004a) were questions that he had already been tackling and there we do not observe a very radical change in theoretical vocabulary as in other aspects which we will mention later.

Prebisch assumed the position of Executive Secretary of ECLAC and tried to give intellectual leadership to the process of development and industrialization. The process of industrialization was already in motion in Latin American, and that seemed like one of the goals that many countries in the region had set for themselves.

Prebisch had always been a much more complex theorist than what the paternity of the thesis of deterioration of peripheral countries terms of trade would suggest. For that reason, we do not deal with the question of paternity of the terms of the trade thesis.[4] For the period we are discussing the central point is the strategy and policies that they were going to promote in countries such as Argentina, in an environment dominated by the international stabilization plans by Keynes and White and dollar scarcity. Even more noteworthy is that for Prebisch the explanation for the different elasticities of demand among distinct nations was not important, since he was interested in economic theory in general. Although, he had earlier reported the issue of primary prices deterioration he did not have a theory or explanation for the mechanism more than the classic theory of the cyclical variation of prices (e.g. Prebisch, 1991b, pp. 566–9).[5]

It would appear that my reading of Prebisch of this period might find some uncompleted theoretical developments but it is very difficult to transform them into "confusion" as Toye and Toye (2004a, p. 116) put it, unless one reads his previous reflections in terms of the so-called Manifesto (1949). My argument is that his period in ECLAC marks a new turn in Prebisch's thoughts and ideas: on the one hand he goes in depth into economic development policies, and on the other hand, he leaves aside his most critical ideas about capitalism and economic thought. Thus the period in discussion presents a theoretical transition in which his ideas were frozen when he assumed his responsibilities at ECLAC. Then, Prebisch initiated a strategic change in the vocabulary he used, which can be explained by the environment of prudence demanded by international organizations, especially ECLAC which would be hounded by the United States of America without much success.

On 18 October 1943 Prebisch was sacked from the Central Bank, it was "the most painful experience of his life" (Dosman, 2001, p. 89). Prebisch mentions this event on various occasions (Magariños, 1991; Pollock *et al.*, 2001; González del Solar, 2006). By December 1943, Prebisch had already taken an important decision: to find finance and support for the investigation and writing of a book entitled "Money and Economic Activity." The Argentinean editors rejected his proposal, but Prebisch continued his plan to write the book while teaching at the University (Dosman, 2001, p. 94).[6] The texts and reflections of the following year such as his talk at the Bank of Mexico (Prebisch, 1944a), and the paper titled "Currency and Economic Cycles in Argentina," (1944b)[7] suggest, given their content (even though the latter would not be published),[8] that he still planned to publish the book.

In general, the theoretical caution in terms of economic policy presented in both texts is explained as a result of Prebisch's deep critical analysis of the economic theory. The objective of his critical analysis of economic theory was to develop new instruments to improve "collective well-being" and to reduce the severe costs to the "main" groups in society.

During the second part of the 1940s Prebisch's discourse becomes more radical politically and theoretically. Meanwhile, in his writings after 1944, it is fascinating to observe the moderation with which he hints that one should stay away from the conventional wisdom, without providing an alternative. His well thought considerations regarding economic policy and his speculations on how to transform the dominant views about peripheral countries offered by "classical" doctrines show that Prebisch thought that conventional wisdom was frankly limited. To encapsulate this period, in political and existential terms, we can mention his decision to allow the translation from English and publication of a conference given in Australia in 1924 where he clearly portrays himself as an anti-oligarchic thinker (Prebisch, 1945a).

His vision on economic policies that in general should be pursued by the state remains relatively immune to the evolution of his critical views of capitalism and of economic thought. His ideas on how to grow and improve "the standard of living of large masses of (the) population" (Prebisch, 1944b, p. 211) are accompanied by a reflection on the importance of industrialization, a problematic that had been debated since the 1920s, Alejandro Bunge being its first "apostle" (Prebisch, 2006).

Before continuing it is important to mention some aspects that would limit his theoretical horizons and the political alternatives. Ten years before, the debate about the creation of the central bank in the House of Representatives and the Senate provides a degree of variety of theoretical views (for example: 1944a in 1972: 1063–352), unusual in Latin America for the time, that precedes the so-called "infamous decade" of the 1930s.

The intellectual and professional formation of Prebisch was marked deeply by two eminent figures who were his teachers: Luis Roque Gondra (1881–1947),[9] and Alejandro E. Bunge (1880–1943).[10] These two figures developed the main set of ideas with which Prebisch always confronted his own views. Bunge and the fight for Argentinean industrialization generated the "desarrollistas" or "mercadointernistas" of many colors, both Peronist and anti-Peronist.

During this period, a theoretical and political discussion on economic growth had been developing in Argentina, that Prebisch could not avoid, and in which he, in fact, had participation since he was involved in projects that bore fruit only later on, paradoxically in the hands of those who originally defeated the Pinedo Plan.[11]

In a reference to Bunge and his group Prebisch says:

> It is usually believed among us that the industrial growth of the country makes us more vulnerable to the action of these international factors of disruption. The belief is not totally supported. I am going to show (. . .) that industrial growth would make us less vulnerable but if Argentina were to go on operating under classical gold standard, industrial growth would make us more vulnerable than before.
>
> (Prebisch, 1991c, p. 279)

Prebisch adds that industrialization would reduce external vulnerability provided aspects of monetary and economic policy were incorporated, taking into account the negative aspects of the automatic system of the gold standard (Prebisch, 1991c, pp. 309–10). In particular it was necessary to control foreign exchange, something that the international plans did not consider.

On the other hand, Gondra can be considered as one of the most renowned driving forces of the Lausanne School in the world, the most important "geometrician" of neoclassical economics in Latin America. With Gondra the mathematization of economics was based on the hegemonic currents of mathematics of the time, in particular, the influential views of Vito Volterra (Weintraub, 2002). Part of this work was carried out by Ugo Broggi (another professor of Prebisch), who, perhaps in his younger years, Prebisch heard him say that he was trying, long before Gerard Debreu, to prove the existence of general equilibrium.[12]

There were always open and undercover dialogues between Bunge, Gondra, their followers and Prebisch over several decades. For that reason, Prebisch could not radicalize his theoretical positions or his economic policy views without before clarifying the conceptual development of his ideas. Gondra was one of the bitterest critics of the creation of the Central Bank, and constantly referred negatively to the "advisors of the executive," that is to say to Prebisch and its team in the Central Bank (e.g. Gondra, 1937a, p. 100). Nevertheless, during the 1940s, Gondra moderated his criticism, became a lot more understanding of the economic difficulties faced in the 1930s, and adapted to a world where "free trade theory" had "the value of a purely theoretical concept" (Gondra, 1943, p. 31), and even began to distance from the sacred principles of the Paretian utility:

> The ministerial resolutions of November 28, 1933, on control of foreign exchange, basic prices of grain and the regulating institutions related to those, are typical of induced or forced redistributions, and they can be seen as a lesser evil, and be justified in exceptional cases.
>
> (Gondra, 1943, p. 31)

In contradistinction, Prebisch begins to use a metaphor utilized a year before by Gondra[13] to criticize American economic policies:

> In synthesis I believe that the attitude of the United States in the years since the world crisis was simply that of the horticulturist's dog,[14] that did not eat neither allowed others to eat; the United States neither traded nor allowed others to trade. The United States does not trade because it does not contribute to increase persistently world commerce in the necessary measure to stimulate other countries.
>
> (Prebisch, 1993, p. 93)

"Nearly at the end of his life, Gondra publishes an article on Argentinean economic thought and Prebisch is the only one mentioned by name." Though Prebisch has said that his dismissal from the Central Bank became a "true theoretical liberation" (Prebisch, 1949b, p. 412; 1946, pp. 242–3; 1944b), we should not forget the "bitter grapes," like the fox of the fable said after not being able to reach them.

Prebisch always considered autarchy as well as free trade extremes as absurd (Prebisch 1944a, pp. 454–5). Prebisch argued that economic policy problems should not be dealt with in purely abstract terms (Prebisch, 1944a, p. 456). Therefore, it was important to differentiate a policy of import restrictions that resulted from the collapse of the gold standard or currency depreciation from one that is carried out in a deliberate way in a regime with exchange controls without protectionist interest "but regulates imports" (Prebisch, 1944a, p. 453).

Prebisch argued that

> It would be an error to produce at exorbitant costs the machineries that a country requires (. . .) if they can be bought at a lower cost abroad (. . .) the

great problem of economic policy that consists of determining how much should production, elaboration or local extraction of those goods and essential articles be promoted to protect the economy of external fluctuations and contingencies.

(Prebisch, 1944a, p. 455)

It is interesting to indicate that Prebisch (1944a) is inhibited from speaking about economic policy in general, about internal production or importing, clarifying that it will always depend on something meditated (technical aptitudes, amplitude of the market), questions that are not of a static nature, but they evolve as the country grows and the efficiency of the labor force increases. For him:

The problem of the economic policy is, therefore, very complex and, by the same token, should be studied carefully; it would be so senseless to believe that the critical experiences that we have had in this generation are going to disappear, as to fall in the autarkic tendencies that would carry to severely unfavorable extremes.

(Prebisch, 1944a, p. 460)

Prebisch assumed that the country would continue to face certain external restrictions given the decline of exports, and he does not have any inhibition in suggesting that the country must grow "internally" (Prebisch, 1944a, p. 461), which implies undertaking the internal production of the instrumental goods, even though that would suppose that the possibilities "of demographic and economic development of the country (. . .) would be lower to the ones that there would be in the [case] of growing exports" (ibid.). Another case would be that of the hypothesis of substituting foreign investments for growing exports, if it is done "in accordance with a program where resources are invested in essentially productive and beneficial applications from the collective point of view," (ibid.). In addition, Prebisch searches for a factor of "growth analogous to the one that land has had in last century" (Prebisch, 1944a, p. 462).

For Prebisch, economic policy is concerned with the problem of protective rights and the stimulus to the domestic production of essential materials, and the foreign exchange policy has an important function in that strategy. Prebisch insists that without any doubt "the advantages that free markets offer outweigh all their small disadvantages" regarding foreign exchange policies, but those depend on the existence of financial resources to carry out the remittances (Prebisch, 1944a, pp. 468–70). Therefore, he argues that:

To make a decision we have to ask whether we should take advantage of the country's technical possibilities without passing the point at which production becomes uneconomical or socially inconvenient. (. . .) But before forcing high cost production of basic materials in cases of extreme emergency, it would be convenient, perhaps, to examine in our country, if there are more economic solutions from the collective point of view, and that permit to maintain low costs of production.

(Prebisch 1944a in 1972, pp. 456–7 and 458)

Prebisch emphasizes the importance of differentiating the operation and responsibilities of monetary and exchange rate policies, on the one hand, and economic policy, on the other (Prebisch, 1944a, p. 405). Communication flow between the Central Bank and the administration was important to coordinate policies. A well designed economic policy, supported by an adequate monetary policy, is required, especially because since the post-war period the most important economic agents are the "large commercial and industrial corporations, so that if Argentina does not outline its policies, they will be decided by outsiders" (Prebisch, 1944a, p. 571).

The problem was how to devise expansionary policies given the different rhythms and cyclical patterns of Argentina and the large industrial centers. Also, it was possible that the expenses of the state in public works and to buy crop surpluses were considerably higher than what fiscal mechanisms could cover, in other words, the "financial policies of the state [not] always obeys to cyclical considerations" (Prebisch, 1944a, p. 490).

Therefore, even though the business cycle cannot be predicted, Prebisch argues that its existence must be taken seriously and that the boom phases are not indefinite. Only then, he argued, the administration would be able to develop an anti-cyclic policy, adapting the plans of cyclic expenses that should be elastic. This implies the necessity to differentiate between nonessential and essential imports as well as the necessity of providing permission for foreign exchange remittances. Foreign exchange policy should be articulated to monetary policy, because the former allows the restriction of some imports and facilitates the importing of some essential goods and the latter provides "the purchasing power so that the current level of economic activity is not restricted" (Prebisch, 1944a, p. 481).

The problem was how to devise expansionary policies given the different rhythms and cyclical patterns of Argentina and the large industrial centers. Also, it was possible that the expenses of the state in public works and to buy crop surpluses were considerably higher than what fiscal mechanisms could cover, in other words, the "financial policies of the state [not] always obeys to cyclical considerations" (Prebisch, 1944a, p. 490).

All depends on how the state behaves in the ascending or descending phase of the cycle. If the financial policies are governed by political considerations, promoting growth would be more complicated. Prebisch's idea was to maintain expansionary policies without the disruptions of the gold standard or depreciated currency. Therefore the relation between the Central Bank's policies and economic policies should be clearly laid out. Monetary expansion was required in the boom phase and contracted in the recessive phase of the cycle. Prebisch already believed it was possible to return the dynamism of growth, that in the past originated in the external sector, through industrial growth. Yet industrial growth should be excluded when the circumstances dictate it; he recommended against the promotion of "the heavy industry," and suggested that it was better to develop the "transforming industries." He believed that it was simple to select "a sector of the economy of sufficient importance and amplitude that it would influence other sectors" (Prebisch, 1944a, p. 505). And this policy would be sustainable "provided the exports permit to pay for the growing imports of commodities, of essential articles for the industry, of capital goods and durable and other essential goods" (Prebisch 1944a, p. 507).

More interesting, is it to observe how Prebisch's conceptual vocabulary and theoretical views, after 1944, evolve, in particular the radicalization of his criticism classical economics. Prebisch was free of institutional responsibilities, including academic institutions, and could radicalize his positions towards the principles of economics.

Correlatively to his vision of growth, Prebisch (1944a) was already marking the limits to his criticism of the accepted monetary doctrine, and also delineates what would be a series of theoretical tasks to carry out in the near future. On the relevance of said doctrine for the country, he expresses his doubts that it "corresponds faithfully to the structure of the Argentinean economy." He questioned whether it would be better "to seek our own principles, given that the same traditional principles are suffering a severe critical revision process" (Prebisch, 1944a, p. 255).

Under the gold standard, external equilibrium was achieved through outflows of gold and the monetary restriction at home (Prebisch, 1944a, p. 493). This adjusting mechanism produces internal equilibrium by restricting economic activity and producing serious economic consequences. These external disruptions are the ones that Prebisch regarded as relevant. As we have seen, Prebisch suggested different alternatives to produce some products internally, in other words alternatives for reducing the import coefficient. Prebisch believed that it was possible that active monetary and fiscal policies could reduce the vicissitudes of the gold standard system. But that is exactly the problem. In the midst of the discussions of the Keynes and White Plans, Prebisch worried about the freedom to establish foreign exchange controls and the ability to set the value of its currency, since initially the White Plan seemed to be willing to "crucify" peripheral countries on a "cross of gold" (Cole, 1945, p. 318).

For Prebisch conventional wisdom presented deficiencies since:

> Within the strict gold standard regime, there was an intrinsic failure in the system, namely: during the boom period bank's reserves grow and this induces them to lend more money as normal competition among them implies, creating greater quantity of purchasing power than the one that is obtained by virtue of the balance of payments. This creation of purchasing power magnifies the effects of the boom phase and forces a more violent contraction in the recessive phase.
>
> (Prebisch, 1944a, p. 385)

Months later, Prebisch (1944b) presented these ideas again with some changes and important additions with respect to some aspects of economic policy; in particular he provided specific proposals in terms of the growth strategies for Argentina. Even though several propositions of the latter work appeared in his previous writings, Prebisch (1944b)[15] provided more fundamental critical positions about economic theory, that perhaps Prebisch already had been entertaining, but that he had not yet elaborated conceptually, and, therefore, refrained from presenting in México.

Prebisch indicated time and again the failures and deficiencies of the gold standard system (1944a, 1944d), and that with that system, apparently automatic, the situation in the economies of the periphery gets worse and therefore it was important to be prepared before the eventual cyclical oscillations of the capitalism system.[16] He argued in favor of devising "our own ideas and adjusting them to the development of a national monetary policy" (Prebisch, 1944d, p. 229).

Nevertheless, after his return to Argentina, Prebisch provided more elaborate theoretical explanations on the cyclical aspects and their consequences for the countries of the periphery. Prebisch criticized not only conventional doctrines and the gold standard by discussing alternative monetary and economic policies and the interrelation that should exist among them.

Prebisch (1944b) tried to formulate a "rigorously scientific (. . .) national monetary policy." Prebisch maintained that "economic theory" was indispensable "to clarify the problem and to understand it" (ibid.), without disregarding the facts of practical life that give support to new hypotheses and practical solutions. In this manner one would be able to discern and to disagree with the explanations of the cycle that were developed for countries of different "magnitude and structure." Common elements exist between the cycle in central and peripheral countries, "but differ in other." In this period, Prebisch did not believe that national monetary and economic policies were contra-posed to "effective cooperation in international plans" (Prebisch, 1944b), but in the absence of adequate monetary policies subjugation by external forces would be imminent.

Prebisch supposed that the form to analyze the economic phenomenon should privilege the examination of money, as he said clearly money is the "technical method to measure values" (Prebisch, 1944b), and it has an importance that is "fundamental in the life of the community" and in "collective welfare" (ibid).

A great part of the dissertation of the introduction was to indicate the serious consequences of the gold standard in Argentina. Furthermore, Prebisch says that in 75 years the gold standard only functioned reasonably well during 25 years (ibid.). But Prebisch clarified that "it is not a matter of ditching the gold standard as monetary regime in our country, but to seek the form of adapting its operation to our needs, to our monetary and economic reality" (ibid.).

Therefore, "monetary incontinence" is not the cause of the economic problems, but the rules of the international commercial regime are instead. Prebisch clarified, also, that he did not stand for a mercantilist policy of restrictions, but an exchange rate policy that avoided the administrative complications of restructuring imports within "a vast plan of national economic policy" (ibid.).

The idea of Prebisch (1944a) and (1944d) was "to perfect," "to correct," "not to destroy" the gold standard in "our countries" (Prebisch, 1944d, p. 233). In the latter work as opposed to the earlier some theoretical positions were developed. He assumed that the gold standard behaved in a diverse way depending on the existence or absence of full occupation in the "main countries of the world," a thesis that was already glimpsed in his discussion about the international plans in his earlier paper and his critical reply to Kindleberger's position on the differences of income-elasticity of demand of different countries. This explains why in his classes his arguments against the position of Kindleberger disappeared, not because he assumed the one that Kindleberger proposed, but due to the fact that he was devising and exposing, for "first time here" (Prebisch, 1944b, p. 286), an additional theoretical explanation, beyond the one related to the adverse consequences of any automatically adjusted system. He regarded himself closer to the "classical" tradition, that observed reality without repeating known formulas and then interpreting it scientifically (Prebisch, 1944b, p. 286).

Prebisch (1944b) developed a series of examples, under different hypotheses (growing imports or their reduction, internal expansion of income, etc), of the evolution of the economy and the consequences of the process of income circulation and the reproduction of the economy, indicating the interdependency of the various sectors, supposing in each case a different velocity of generation and reproduction of income. Depending on the phases of the cyclical process, whether it is the upturn or the downturn, Prebisch insisted that the "external or internal influences cause expansionary and contractionary phenomena bigger in their amplitude than the initial impulse that originates them" (Prebisch, 1944b, p. 250). In each one of the hypothetical models Prebisch indicated the deficiencies of the classical theory (Prebisch, 1944b, pp. 274–5). Prebisch wanted to introduce the time factor into his models. The time in which the productive sectors of diverse productive sectors generate new income implies the interval that is required to expand productive activities (Prebisch, 1944b, p. 280).

To the question of the time, or of the velocity of circulation and reproduction of income, Prebisch added the thesis that income increases of diverse countries are a function of the size of their profits; in other words, that would explain the reason they have remained with the gold that crossed their borders.

The retention of gold in different countries was not related to their degree of openness or interrelation with the international market, it followed instead the distribution of total revenues between internal activity and foreign trade (Prebisch, 1944b, p. 290). Prebisch presented these results using numerical models of countries with similar productive structures and models with countries with different import coefficients.

Therefore, as gold was distributed among countries of the world according to their income and not according to their foreign trade, countries that were in a considerably more vulnerable position to face the fluctuations of foreign trade and of their balance of payments were those countries that had a smaller revenue and a higher import coefficient, and this is of particular importance, in the national and international monetary policies (Prebisch, 1944b, p. 296).

To the extent that the governments of the "countries that are not central" tried to counteract the downturn phase of the cycle with some expansionary policy and/or import controls, in order to minimize the most harmful effects on the internal level of economic activity, or the sterilization of the gold flows during the upturn phase, they would be able to reduce the effects of a continuous drainage of their gold reserves, but not to hold them back totally, especially if the government follows the rules "of the gold standard regime."

Due to the fact that the classical theory of the gold standard "is not universal," diverse countries enter the system in different ways. According to Prebisch the regime represents the "experience of the center," that of the "industrial and creditor" countries, "but not the experience of the countries of the periphery" (Prebisch, 1944b, p. 19).

In contrast to central countries, the gold standard was "an automatic system for the countries of the periphery" and their cycles were the reflection from those of the center. The system would eventually lead to the concentration of gold reserves which contradicted the idea that the gold was only a vehicle to carry out transfers and to support foreign trade. Prebisch supported theoretically the existing asymmetry through the notion of the "coefficient of expansion," that according to his view was different than the concept of the Keynesian "multiplier." The reason is that both "rest on a substantially different theory" (Prebisch, 1944b, p. 350). While for Keynes the multiplier was the constant that indicated the total by which the original investment increased, Prebisch maintained that the idea of the "coefficient of expansion" had "limits" and these were not related to the total "savings" as in Keynes's theory (Prebisch, 1944b, p. 365), but were related to the "time" that elapses to generate new income, which, in turn, was determined by two elements: "the number of times that the money changes hands to produce such income" (that is to say the velocity of circulation of the money), and by the "quantity of money that is lost in each exchange as a result of the payment of imports" (Prebisch, 1944b, p. 358).

It was exactly this time factor that explained the asymmetry: economies with low coefficients of importing that at the same time delay their reincorporation to the international market concentrate gold reserves within their borders, which as a result of cyclical cumulative processes increases their "metallic retention." Thus, Prebisch explained that it was the relation of total revenues, the velocity of its generation, with respect to foreign trade that explains the process. If one accepted that in "the upturn phase" of the cycle "exports grew more quickly than imports and the balance of payments had a positive balance, while in the downturn phase exports decreased more quickly than imports" (Prebisch, 1944b, pp. 320–1), then the different velocities of circulation of income explained the cumulative circular process.

Prebisch proposed a theory, an explanation, about the operation of world capitalism and even though he was concerned with the international monetary plans, he insisted that these plans could be articulated to well-designed national policies. Without doubt this was the first time[17] that Prebisch proposed a significant explanation for the evolution of the cycle, which he had been already elaborating for some time,[18] but based on a "system of communicating vessels;" a certain notion of asymmetries among different economies finally appears.

For Argentina it was necessary to take anti-cyclical measures for more obvious and important reasons that the ones that Prebisch (1944b) proposed and discussed. In the first place, the United States was the new financial center, pushing Great Britain "toward the periphery," precisely the economy with whom Argentina had been articulated economically for more than a century. In the second place, the United States did not have the managerial skill to control the international financial system and a very reduced import coefficient, a country that at the same time elevated its import tariffs and was not willing to devise policies of full employment, thus inhibiting a greater demand of imports from the rest of the world (Prebisch, 1944b, pp. 84–5 and 329).

Prebisch started to put more emphasis on well-designed monetary policies and anti-cyclical economic policies, as well as policies that transformed the economy. Given the theory of the relation "greater revenue, greater quantity of gold" (Prebisch, 1944b, p. 20) (as already noted before in allusion to Bunge), Prebisch doubted the effectiveness of the industrialization policy *per se* to face the oscillations brought by the gold standard. But any policies were still more complicated if it was taken into account that "the elevation of the standard of living of the masses" was "the capital objective of social policies" (Prebisch, 1944b, p. 399).

Therefore, having developed alternative theories in Prebisch (1944b), his next writings present some synthesis of his previous work, and obviously the attitude toward economic thought was already modified. In his "Introduction to the Political Economy Course" (Prebisch, 1945a) and "Preliminary Concepts on Income Circulation" (Prebisch, 1945b)[19] he reiterated his theoretical evolution and, in contrast with the previous year's writings, he argued that it was insufficient to indicate "the failures of the gold standard."

On this occasion Prebisch (1945a) reiterated the limitations of the traditional doctrine, but the criticism was done through the metaphor of the geographical charts, that is, the traditional doctrines (protectionism, free trade, free but regulated competition) should be thought as "old maps" (Prebisch, 1945a, p. 443), whose deficiencies should be improved by introducing "real" aspects, requiring, therefore, "a revision task" that accentuates "its large successes" and amends "its many errors," (Prebisch, 1945a, p. 444).

With respect to Prebisch (1944b), he declared that he had advanced and that no one must seek "two types of theories," a cycle in the periphery and another in the industrial center, since it is a matter:

> of two phases, of two different aspects from the same international phenomenon. But it is not admissible to apply the interpretation of a phase to the events that happen in the other phase, obverse instead of reverse, (. . .) internal and international economic activity [that] manifests itself in a continuous process of income circulation.
>
> (Prebisch, 1945a, p. 446)

Under capitalism this is reflected in the absence of full employment and productive waste.

In contrast with his (1944b) paper, in his subsequent text, Prebisch (1945b), no longer did any reference to the quantitative theory of the money appear. Perhaps still more significant than the continuous process of theoretical elaboration is the fact that he did not mention his concept of coefficient of expansion in contrast to Keynes's multiplier, and that at the same time, as we will see further on, he transformed it into the concept of "exit coefficient" (Prebisch, 1949b, p. 464). It was obvious that Prebisch was not yet totally comfortable with his theoretical stance since the evolution did not stop there. After a year, in 1946, in the *First Meeting of Technicians on Central Banking Problems of the American Continent*, he said in a more radical vein: "I find myself disturbed by the thesis that the free competition leads to general equilibrium and to the most adequate distribution of the resources and income within the community. I do not see any correspondence between these abstract propositions and the reality of the economic world" (Prebisch, 1946, p. 227).

But by then he already perceives that the ontological characteristic of capitalism was essentially stochastic:

> I have found but wave motions, a succession of ascendant and descendant wave motions. (...) The cycle (...), in the center as much as in the periphery, is the characteristic form in which the economy grows – the capitalist economy has not had another form of growing than the cyclical form.
>
> (Prebisch, 1946, pp. 226–7)

The theoretical work in the following years was dedicated to the "dynamic exam of the economy" which was at that time still "in its beginnings" (Prebisch, 1946, p. 227). Between August 1946 and early 1947 Prebisch dedicated himself to the analysis of the classical work of Keynes: *The General Theory of Employment, Interest and Money* (1936), and it was during this period that he carried out the final step of his theoretical evolution.

Even though the "practical solutions" proposed by Keynes were unquestionable, it did not imply necessarily that Prebisch agreed with his criticism of political economy (Prebisch, 1948, pp. 505–6) and even less with the "dogma" that was elaborated by Keynes's followers from which, in turn, they devise "new theoretical constructions that are increasingly disconnected from reality, and, in my view from Keynes's own construction" (Prebisch, 1948, p. 504). He insisted that anti-cyclical economic policies should be supported by a different theoretical perspective. In fact Prebisch widened, when he was able, his differences with respect to Keynes. He wrote a series of articles where he analyzed the basic, elementary concepts of Keynes that later would become the book *Introduction to Keynes* (Prebisch, 1947f), which was really a glossary of Keynes. In the presentation of Keynes's ideas, Prebisch did not intercept his own critical ideas. Two criticisms appeared in the original papers, and he excluded from the book the strongest critique[20] leaving the following question: "What is the relation of these theoretical thoughts with reality? It cannot be said that Keynes's book presents a systematic analysis of facts that can verify his theories," (Prebisch, 1947e, p. 258 and 1947f, p. 86).

Nevertheless, his critique of classical thought in general and particularly of Keynes's ideas was already formulated:

> To explain the phenomenon of continuous imbalances of real economies, Keynes dedicates some pages at the end of his work – the so-called notes on the cycle – in which he does not use the results developed in his theoretical discussion. He seeks the explanation of the cycle in another vague form. (. . .) That is to say that, as much as in the classics, his fundamental theory is unsuited to explain the cyclical reality.
>
> (Prebisch, 1948, p. 506)[21]

In the middle of 1948, in his *Notes on Political Economy* (Prebisch, 1948), right after finishing his book on Keynes, Prebisch presented an important evolution of his conceptual vocabulary. He proposed the reconstruction of "classical economics" or "traditional economics." To the initially timid vocabulary of the course ("to see the things through our own mind" and "to be disconnected from certain foreign theories") (Prebisch, 1948, p. 495), a frontal attack to the whole apparatus of the discipline follows. He emphasized emphatically that only "a deep revision of the classical theory and devising a new theory and not an appended theory to be added on top (. . .), we would be able to find the theoretical elements to guide us with efficacy and success in the practical action" (Prebisch, 1948, pp. 325–6). The economy as a discipline, Prebisch argued, even from the moral point of view, was in a "serious crisis" given its excessive "exaltation of the individual interest as the supreme regulator of economic activity" (Prebisch, 1948, p. 496). As a "scientific discipline" it was "incipient" and "undecided." In the same vein as in previous periods, this critical situation should be surpassed through a "complete effort to renew it from its roots," since economic theory was not able "to explain rationally" the form "in which the economic movement occurs, the form in which the phenomena of the economy are produced, the reason of how things are the way they are" (Prebisch, 1948, p. 96).

Two different steps explained the path of the theoretical strategy adopted. The first one, as "mere foretaste" (Prebisch, 1948, p. 328) devised a history and explanation of the different breaks in the history of economic thought, and showed the theoretical inconsistencies of the "classical" authors (that includes Keynes, since Prebisch utilizes, as much as Keynes, the term "classical" for the ideas of the old classical political economy and the modern neoclassical ideas). The second step, synthesized his theory of the capitalist cycle, as in fact his own evaluation of the discipline required it: an "absolutely endogenous theory of the cycle, in which this is repeated systematically by work of the same inherent factors of the system" (Prebisch, 1949b, p. 42 and 1993, p. 458).[22]

As we will see further on, he argued that the "general theory of the cycle" should be devised without "the false sense of universality that up to now the main theories of the cycle suffer, that cycle theories have exclusively dealt with the phenomena of the center, ignoring what occurs in the periphery and foreclosing, thus, one of the most fertile fields of investigation" (Prebisch, 1949b, p. 4 and 1993, p. 414). But Prebisch was hopeful that:

[T]he theory of the cycle will become the *only* dynamic theory of the economy, or better said, in the *only* theory of the overall movements of the economy. I do not believe that the overall movements of the economy can be the object of a static theory that pursues equilibrium positions.

(Prebisch, 1949b, p. 4 and 1993, p. 415; italics added).

Prebisch argued that there cannot be a "production optimum" when the recessive and expansive phases are systematic; the system approaches, but never arrives to "full employment," there is, in fact, waste of "productive forces." Instability cannot be reconciled with the body of doctrines of classical economics and even less with the form in which it explains the "distribution of income" (Prebisch, 1948, p. 500).

This does not imply that the classical doctrine ignored the phenomena indicated above, but the crisis stems from the inability of classical authors to act "scientifically," since they did not reject the theories that did not explain "reality satisfactorily" (ibid.). As a matter of fact, they adopted certain "attitudes" when faced with phenomena like unemployment, indicating the "inflexibilities" or "rigidities" of reality, like the downward rigidity of wages and not the logical failure of their "premises;" even Keynes, in spite of his "efforts" to get rid of classical doctrines, presented "a type of essentially classical explanation," in this case another inflexibility: "the interest rate" that is not sufficiently low to counteract "the fall in the marginal efficiency of the capital." According to Prebisch, both the classical and Keynes's explanations of unemployment are mistaken because "in reality phenomena of that form are not present" (Prebisch, 1948, p. 501). Another theoretical position assumed by the classics was to indicate the "excesses" and depressions of the cyclical process caused by the "abuses of the monetary system" (ibid.) and, therefore, resulting from the intervention of the state.

Also, a last theoretical strategy among the defenders of classical postulates existed, and was not particularly congruent: they accepted the postulates of the classical doctrine but they explained reality on the basis of different assumptions. Prebisch indicates Alvin Hansen[23] as an example of that behavior, which should not be a surprise if we recall that Prebisch was not very "respectful" with Keynes.[24]

The absence of the element of time can be seen in the notions of capital and savings in the Keynesian and classical doctrines, because it is through the device of the interest rate that time is dealt with theoretically.[25] The interest rate then is the mechanism through which the savings that the "community is willing to offer" equilibrates with the demand of the capitalists to form capital: depending on the demand for savings the interest rate will rise or fall and, therefore, the businessmen's required savings will materialize. But Prebisch maintained that for a given interval, production requires a certain time to reach the market, and therefore there should exist in the process higher revenues than the value of the production of final consumption. This would obviously not be explained by the famous Say's Law according to which supply creates its own demand, because then at the end of the productive cycle there would be a demand exceeding supply. Nevertheless, in classical doctrines this imbalance is explained as a result of the savings that the community carries out based on the interest rate. The interest rate is the device that facilitates or limits the amount of total savings that would be utilized for the production in a certain given interval: the total amount of income that would be generated at the end of the process. The excess would be explained through the existence of the respective savings, complying with the famous Say's Law.

Keynes, on the other hand, deals with the problem of time in several ways (Prebisch, 1948, p. 275). Prebisch argued that as the rate of interest falls, Keynes follows the classical authors, but once the marginal efficiency of capital gets disconnected from the rate of interest (as a result of liquidity preference), then Keynes departs from the classics. Savings remain in liquid form, they are not invested and a shortage of the demand arises. Nevertheless, according to Prebisch, Keynes remained "inside the logical game," of the classics: on the one hand he recognizes the time factor, but utilizes the device of the interest rate to handle it; on the other hand, this device has limits after a certain point (liquidity preference). In contrast with this position, in the multiplier theory, Keynes denies the role to the interest rate that the classical doctrines assign to it and dispenses with the time; and the savings are a totally different phenomenon than the one discussed by the classics.

In this case, the supposed simultaneity of savings and investment was not taken into account, and it was simply accepted that savings would come out of income that would multiply the initial investments (Prebisch, 1948, p. 276). The multiplication of income, product of the initial investment, will itself produce a certain level of savings. Savings are a function of the rhythm of growth of income. However, Prebisch indicated that for investment to produce income a certain amount of time was required, otherwise one would be confusing the present with the future, and that according to Prebisch is the problem of the Keynesian multiplier. This logical weakness nullifies the Keynesian theory (Prebisch, 1948, p. 277) and sets it totally apart from the classical school.

In addition, Prebisch briefly described the history of humanity as a process in which "dominant groups and classes" utilized diverse instruments to shift income distribution in their favor, the monetary instrument being the privileged one under capitalism. The fact that the process might be different under a collectivist system did not guarantee necessarily, in his view, that inequalities would be suppressed. All the regimes utilize certain instruments "to favor to the dominant groups" (Prebisch, 1948, p. 303).

Still, Prebisch would accept the proposition advanced by the classical theories on the way in which capitalism transfers the fruits of the technical progress: whether through wage increases or decrease in prices but: "the process by which that transfer has occurred, the time that it has taken and the amounts are, in my judgment, different to those assumed by the classical theory" (Prebisch, 1948, p. 311).

Given the centrality of money and its creation in Prebisch's plan to understand the cycle and capitalism, it is the Keynes of the *Treatise on Money* who presents useful tools for his own theoretical evolution, and he also emphasized the importance of Wicksell.[26]

If we look back to the *Treatise on Money*, we will find that its reasoning on the economic process and on the cycle, are fundamentally Wicksellian. (. . .) I would not be able to explain (. . .) the reasons of this abrupt change in Keynes's thought when moves after some years from *Treatise on Money* to the *General Theory*, forgetting everything that he had said about Wicksellian theory and about the economic cycle.

(Prebisch, 1948, p. 326)

In his anti-equilibrium dynamic theory, Prebisch proposed to integrate the monetary theory with the theory of production. He presented the deficiencies of the classical theory of money showing that an increase of money supply (under the assumption that the economy is at equilibrium) is followed by an increase in prices, and that was explained on the basis of the thesis that a "proportional relation between the movement of prices and the quantity of money" exists (Prebisch, 1948, p. 327), which means a new "position of equilibrium." As a result of the assumption of "full utilization of resources," in classical theory "prices rise or fall" without affecting production. But a disruption of the assumption of full capacity "leads to variation in the *quantity* of the benefits of the businessmen and makes them increase and contract production moving the economy away from the position of equilibrium assumed by the classical theory" (Prebisch, 1948, p. 328).

The "intimate relation" between the monetary and the productive sphere could be visualized, according to Prebisch, in the "cycle's upturn;" there it could be seen that the "increase of money supply tends to expand production and, at the same time, prices (or avoids the fall in prices to the extent that, in a state of free competition, they would fall because of the reduction of costs, due to the technical innovations). This process generates profits for the businessmen and to the sequence of actions and reactions" (ibid.) that had been mentioned as a characteristic of the capitalist cycle.

The nuclear center of Prebisch's explanation implies understanding the variations and the *quantity* of the profit. Profit is the consequence of the successive processes of money creation used during different periods to form or to cover the costs of capital formation, and that is different from the uses of savings. If we exclude the phenomenon of the increments of money that are filtered toward other economic spaces, the function of money that remains in certain space is that of "absorbing" the "increase of production finished consumption goods" (Prebisch, 1948, p. 332).

This is crucial to understand the capitalist cycle – according to Prebisch – this "excessive (. . .) money increase" with respect to output growth, in fact determines its characteristic: prices rise generating an increase in productivity when competition exists. Then the origin and reason of the amount of the "profits of the businessmen" result from the "increase in money which leads to the profits of the businessmen and causes changes in its quantity with very important repercussions on the economic process" (ibid.).

Thus Prebisch denied that the mechanism of "the supply and demand of savings," assumed in the Keynesian and classical theories, was so important. In fact, he employed "money increase" instead of "savings" because in the lower point of the cycle, the businessmen have relatively "large quantities" of money "inactive in their bank accounts" (ibid.) and they do not need the savings of the market "forcing the interest rates" up. A paradoxical phenomenon in the lower point of the cycle exists then: savings become scarce, "but money is abundant; a very important distinction indeed, with no savings money abounds, money is used instead of savings to finance investment" (Prebisch, 1948, p. 333).

When the net increment of money decreases or its rhythm of expansion is reduced and is "insufficient to absorb the increment of production, to current prices" (Prebisch, 1948, p. 335), the "decrease of prices" is not automatic, "obstacles" exist, otherwise classical ideas would prevail. The situation where profits would be eliminated completely is never reached, as a result that in the capitalist economy profits are "irreversible" (Prebisch, 1948, p. 336), that is to say, cannot be reduced. This becomes clearer when he argued that profit did not "flourish" in the last phase of production and sale of the product in question, but that it was being generated through several productive phases among diverse businessmen while its culmination in the final consumer approached; that is to say, that in terms of the metaphor of Marx on "the mortal leap" of the commodities, that event already happened before the commodity arrived at the market, the profit is materialized in the prices of the products.[27]

Therefore, what stops the continuation of the expansive phase of the cycle is insufficient demand caused by the *reduction in the rhythm* of money supply increases with respect to the increment of the production. As profits – "accumulated by businessmen" – would not be "validated" the economy contracts and typical phenomena of the "downturn phase of the economic cycle" take place (Prebisch, 1948, p. 338). If the net increment of money is insufficient to cover the increment of production, according to the supply value, the revenue could not be returned: it is an irreversible phenomenon.

At the same time, the growing accumulation of inventories indicates that one must reduce production, leading to the cyclical downturn.[28] Nevertheless, if in the classical theories profits (resulting from cost reductions) diminish with competition, for Prebisch competition did not have "any influence on the general amount of profits in the economy as a whole," since profits were determined "*exclusively* by the difference between the increment of production and that part of the increments of money that remain in the economic system" (Prebisch, 1948, p. 355, italics added).

All this does not imply that competition was not important for Prebisch, but that it suggests for him the function of competition was not that of "reducing the amount of *total* profits that is given by other factors but to establish the form in which profits are distributed among businessmen" (ibid.). The amount of profits is determined by two factors: the productive and the monetary activities, competition does not alter the "*amount* neither the variations" but the *distribution* "within the businessmen group" (ibid.).

Prebisch underlines that though capitalism requires a "compulsive" mechanism to guarantee savings in the "cyclical expansion," his concept of "forced savings" should not be seen in terms of a "redistribution" in which some are forced to "give to others" (Prebisch, 1948, pp. 357–8). He argued that profits could be nil, and businessmen are the ones who "begin to use increments of money that lead to rising prices and cause the transfer of consumer goods of some sectors to others generating profits," by which, "what the businessmen receive is, exactly, what would correspond to them, since the businessmen were working without profits and now [that] the increment of money generates it (. . .) the incentive that should stimulate them to introduce innovations and to increase production is generated" (Prebisch, 1948, p. 361).

If one assumes that the economic spaces are always connected by entry and exit income channels, another mechanism by which income is filtered appears, reducing the "net increment" of money in one of the spaces. It is the thesis of the "doctrinaire economists" (Prebisch, 1948, p. 367) that, supported on the "brilliant" "theorem of comparative costs of Ricardo," demonstrates what should be imported and/or exported between countries and what to produce locally. Prebisch maintained, nevertheless, that "this reasoning is only valid from a static point of view," that is to say, when: "it is shown (. . .) that the protection of B is an economic heresy: [since] it would employ more labor and the rent of the land would be lost by the intention to produce directly what can be obtained indirectly in better conditions" (ibid.).

But in dynamic terms certain levels of protection between countries A and B can cause important changes. A certain "net loss from A" can be a "net profit for B," (Prebisch, 1948, p. 368), but not always since it would depend on how B reduces its "Ricardian loss" (ibid.). If one also considers that B has been "subjected to the cyclical fluctuations engendered in A, the achievement of a more stable production, although at a greater cost, implies enlarging B's net profit," (Prebisch, 1948, p. 369). At this point, Prebisch already speculated that B represents a "group of countries" (Prebisch, 1948, p. 368)[29] that try a process of industrialization, indicating that the position of presenting to "the classical theory of international trade," as the "United States of North America" does it (Prebisch, 1948, p. 373) is unjustifiable and unsustainable; that is, to limit protectionist policies in the B countries when in fact the "rules of the game" are violated systematically by the A countries.

It is in this context that Prebisch gave a qualitative theoretical leap, developing the theory center–periphery that he discussed in a series of conferences in Mexico eight months after his *Notes on Political Economy* course (Prebisch, 1948) titled *Theory of Economic Dynamics: with Special Application to the Latin-American Economies* (1949b). There is a very clear division of functions between center and periphery. For him, "the theory should explain the operation of the economy between the center and the periphery and the intimate connection between both" (Prebisch, 1949b, p. 413).

The notion of "the laws of motion" forced Prebisch to define his conception of time and the reason of the "cyclical motion." The cycle is defined as the result of certain time lags and not as he had done previously simply by the business profit impulse, even though without that impulse there would be no movement. Prebisch argued:

> A time disparity, a disparity between the time of the productive process and the time of the circulation process, is generated in the process itself. The disparity of both times is what generates the cyclical movement with its prosperity and depression phases. Even with the more perfect free competition and the total lack of state intervention in the economy the mere disparity of times would produce the cyclical phenomenon.
>
> (Prebisch, 1949b, p. 416)

If we accept Prebisch's hypothesis that the revenues that were paid in one day surpass those of the production finished the same day, then what was emphasized was the asynchrony between the productive and the circulation processes, asynchrony between the creation of liquid resources in the market and the products. This asynchrony impedes that there could be a "perfect equilibrium between the total global demand of revenues and profits and the global supply (value of finished goods)" because then one would have to assume an "equality between the time of the process of circulation of the revenues and profits and the time that the integral process of the production takes" (Prebisch, 1949b, p. 418).

It can be said that money or final demand today arrives at the market long before the production in process in the course of the same day; there is, in Armando Di Filippo's words an "asynchrony" (Di Filippo, 1981, p. 54). Therefore, "there is no automatic mechanism in the economy even if there is perfect competition, that assures the perfect correlation between the time of formation of the values and the time of the circulation of the income generated in the productive process" (Prebisch, 1949b, p. 419).

Starting from the above-mentioned asynchrony Prebisch presented the model of the world economy divided between the periphery and the center, which at the same time led him to explain the expansionary and contractionary phases of the cycle, or in other words, the reason for the changing rhythms of the world economy. If the cycle is presented from the perspective of the origins of the revenues or of demand, center and/or periphery, and their respective production, we see that in contrast with the periphery, the demand curve of the center always exceeds production or the supply of final goods, that is to say, in the periphery the demand curve always presents a shortage with respect to the supply of final goods. The excess in the center is the corresponding part of the peripheral shortage. If it is observed from the center, the "point of conjunction" that can be seen in the cycle in its expansionary phase indicates that the above-mentioned "excess" of the demand disappears and the supply curve surpasses it, since it continues moving up while the demand curve falls (Prebisch, 1949b, p. 456).

This phenomenon would never take place between the demand and supply in the periphery, since the shortage represents a series of revenues that always fall short of the supply of final goods curve. Prebisch assumed that in the expansionary phase of the cycle the revenues of the entrepreneurs are always above that of the finished production (the "demand curve exceeds the supply curve"), a situation that inverted after the point of inflection. Demand exceeds supply, because "the time of return of the revenues paid to the businessmen is smaller than the time it takes to produce output and, therefore, before the production is finished the flow of income exceeds it" (Prebisch, 1949b, p. 420).

The division between center and periphery was fundamental to understand "our [economic] processes." The origin of demand and the place of production of certain goods had, in Prebisch's view, different effects due to the diverse amplitudes and velocities that were present in each economic space. The center would always have excess of demand that would diminish slowly, as a result of the amplitude and velocity of return of the revenue. It should be noted that I emphasize Prebisch's use of the term velocity, when, in fact, Prebisch (1949b) eluded the use of the term systematically. In a way then, the velocity of return of income was greater in the center than in the periphery. That is to say, a disparity between the period of production and that of circulation exists, and the return of the income originates in the "cyclical center" (Prebisch, 1949b, p. 422).

For Prebisch the cycle was, as noted before, a consequence of the disparity between production and circulation periods. In the upward phase there was an accumulation of circulating capital, because there was production in process and finished production; in the downward phase, the circulating capital was liquidated. Investment and disinvestment followed each other. As much as in the boom the revenues were lower than income disbursements, during the recession "the return on income" is superior to the "payment of income by the entrepreneurs" (Prebisch, 1949b, p. 425).

Then, as the different productive phases took place, profit was incorporated in the final goods, and the rigidity that those values brought with it was what would induce the cyclical contraction "when the demand, after the point of inflection, is insufficient to absorb the supply" (Prebisch, 1949b, p. 433). Then it was the "disparity of revenues and income and the affluence of the production" (ibid.) that produced the "imbalance between demand and supply" during the upward phase of the cycle.

Even under the idyllic idea of the perfect market without rigidities, it would be the time factor, in particular the time it takes for agents to produce certain output, which would define the existence of profits and would explain their total amount. As in the periphery the process of production, or the reaction to a certain stimulus, was slower than in the center, the amount of the "profits that corresponds to the periphery will be smaller that the one that corresponds to cyclical center" (Prebisch, 1949b, p. 440).[30] This results from the fact that in terms of the total amounts in question, for the center and the periphery, smaller unit profits are not at odds necessarily with a greater amount of total profits.

Since the dynamic element stems from the decrease or not of inventories, forcing the businessmen to invest or to disinvest, "the idea of equilibrium with the possibility of an increase or a systematic decrease of inventories [was unsustainable]. They are two conditions that repel themselves" (Prebisch, 1949b, p. 462).

Therefore, the mechanism of adjustment of the "center and periphery phenomena" would not change, independently of the variable you considered, and those were exactly the phenomena that impeded the achievement of any "equilibrium." When he described the depressive phase of the cycle, after the point of inflection, demand did not exceed supply and therefore "the circulating capital that is accumulated turns out to be excessive," (Prebisch, 1949b, p. 485). The problem of liquidating stocks comes then, and stocks generally surpass the necessary levels required by "demand at the inflection point" (ibid.), and it is "at this moment when the reactions of the businessmen take over, their reaction carries the economy again to recovery, since, while the businessmen accumulate idle stocks, it is natural that they try to contract production" (Prebisch, 1949b, p. 486).

The idea that this process would stop only because the economy reached "full occupation," was for Prebisch a theoretical delirium, simply because while the inflationary process continues fast and furious, businessmen will continue investing and receiving the respective profits that arise from higher prices. Circulating capital would continue to grow, requiring, as in all expansionary processes, sums of money to expand the circulating capital stocks; but also they would have to utilize their profits for purchase and investment in the periphery, which implies that "excess demand of cyclical origin" would be reduced, which would, in turn, reduce the "demand shortage of peripheral origin" (Prebisch, 1949b, p. 488), producing "fatally" a point of "inflection later after which the contraction of the system would come" (ibid.).

Here I have tried to describe a period of Prebisch's reflection and criticism about economics. Due to the fact that some followers and critics of his work distorted what he said, including during his life time, I adopted the strategy of presenting his ideas using his own reflections as much as possible. The evolution and conclusion of his ideas on the world economic cycle during this period were not carried out without before leaving aside certain ideas that he had defended initially. His political radicalization was the other face of his theoretical revisionism. I ignore it if those dedicated to the history of Latin American economic thought have examined this intellectual period of evolution in Prebisch's ideas, but his ascent to fame after the meeting of CEPAL in Havana, changed the course of his reflections. Nevertheless, those ideas were not completely forgotten, in the mid-1970s, Prebisch recovered his manuscripts, modified them in part, and produced *Peripheral Capitalism: Crisis and Transformation* (Prebisch 1981).

Notes

1 Universidad de Puebla, México. Translated by Marcia von Pressentin, technical revision by Matías Vernengo.
2 The first draft of the Manifesto (E/CN.12/89; 14 de mayo de 1949), does not include the term "some."
3 Magariños (1991, pp. 130–1), Pollock *et al.* (2001, p. 11), and Prebisch (1984, pp. 175–6).
4 I deal with the subject in Mallorquín (2005); Love (1996, pp. 118, 136 and note number 87, p. 271); Toye and Toye (2004b) chapter 5; Shaw (2002) chapter 7; Furtado (1985, pp. 85–6).

5 Further, in 1933, in the International Financial meeting in London Prebisch presented a project to reduce wheat production quotas.

6 Dosman sent me a copy, a text of ten pages.

7 Dr. Washington Ashwell sent me a copy of the manuscript.

8 Only two articles were published in 1944: Prebisch (1944c and 1944d).

9 See Gondra (1932), (1933), (1934), (1937a), (1937b) and (1943).

10 See Molteni (2003), Luchini *et al.* (2000), Imaz (1974) and Bollo (1999).

11 See Piñeiro (2003), Llach (1984 and 1985) and Pugliese (1939).

12 See Fernández López (2000).

13 "The horticulturist's dog, when it becomes protectionist, does not eat the cabbage nor allows the owner to eat it," Gondra (1943, p. 244).

14 Translator note: "El Perro del Hortelano" is one the comedies of Lope de Vega Carpio, and a classic of the Spanish Golden Age.

15 Prebisch's (1944a) occupies two-thirds of the third part of Prebisch's (1944b) paper.

16 "The Gold Standard, as it has worked, does not respond to our necessities," (Prebisch, 1944d, p. 246).

17 Prebisch clarifies that this is "a hypothesis that must be tested," that is, "the disposition of this process of income circulation from the monetary center to the peripheral countries explains by itself, without further motives, the generation of a global cycle, which does not mean that other motives should be discarded as irrelevant," (Prebisch, 1944b, p. 30).

18 See Fernández (2000).

19 Both texts appeared in the *Revista de Ciencias Económicas*, second series, 33rd year, number 288, 1945.

20 "That is categorically affirmed by [Keynes], even though he does not offer arguments to support what he briefly mentioned" (Prebisch, 1947b, p. 476). See the last part of the first paragraph in page 57 in the book *Introduction to Keynes* (1947f). It is not casual the place for this outburst, since he is discussing the multiplier. Prebisch's criticism of Keynes is associated with the fact that "his general theory of employment seems to take place in a independent plane from cyclical movements" (Prebisch, 1947e, p. 89).

21 For Ralph W. Souter equilibrium implies "the conception of a continual attempted adaptation towards real equilibrium which is continually thwarted in some degree by the inequality of time-coefficients *plus* the constant emergence of new evolutionary changes" (Souter, 1930, p. 82).

22 For a more elaborate discussion see Mallorquín (2005a).

23 "The same economist that writes about the typical equilibrium dedicated time (. . .) to the study of the economic cycle, and goes from one to the other without any theoretical scruple. (. . .) In the first part he digresses with great doctrinaire rigor his equilibrium theory, and in the following he presents the theory of disequilibrium without explaining how to combine the two fundamentally different theories" (Prebisch, 1948, pp. 502–3). A very good discussion of the topic can be found in Mirowski (1985).

24 In another context Prebisch argued for a "respectful revision of classical theories," (Prebisch, 1948, p. 325).

25 "I refer to the interest rate as a logical device created by classical authors to deal with the element of time, because after observing the facts, and reflecting, I am convinced that the interest rate does not play the regulating role in production and distribution attributed to it by the classical authors. (. . .) Capital formation in society plays a completely different role and only to a minimal extent does the rate of interest play the regulating role that the classical school attributes to it" (Prebisch, 1948, p. 278).

26 Gottfried Haberler (*see* Pribram, 1983, p. 323) said "the process of monetary expansion by way of reciprocal stimulation of consumption and investment – the so-called Wicksellian process."

27 "But there is a fundamental difference between the value of the products created in

each phase of the process and the respective revenues. The value that is created in each phase is not the value of a good that can be consumed immediately. (. . .) Therefore, they are a series of value added phases, but the final product is available for consumption at the end of the productive process" (Prebisch, 1948, pp. 417–18)

28 "If profits were reversible or only appeared at the end of the productive process with final sales, it would be conceivable that investment could fall with generating severe complications, since prices and profits would fall when the increase in money that had led to the increase of both would be reabsorbed" (Prebisch, 1948, p. 339).

29 For a presentation of Prebisch-like arguments in modern guise see Cypher and Dietz (1998).

30 It should be noted that these are lectures that were not revised by Prebisch. He says right after the above-mentioned quote that "it is obvious, on the other hand, that if the increase in demand did not change, remained fixed, and for some reason the time that it takes to the entrepreneur in the periphery is now inferior to that taken by entrepreneurs in the center, the amount of profits in the periphery would fall and remain the same in the center: total unit profits would be, then, smaller than in the precedent case" (ibid.).

References

Bollo, Hernán G. (1999) "La Formación Intelectual de entre Guerras, el Caso del Ingeniero Alejandro E. Bunge." In *Décimo Congreso Nacional y Regional de Historia Argentina,* editorial, Buenos Aires: Academia Nacional de Historia.

Cole, G. D. H. (1945) *Money, Its Present and Future,* London: Cassell and Company Ltd.

Cypher, James and James Dietz (1998) "Static and Dynamic Comparative Advantage: A Multi-Period Analysis with Declining Terms of Trade," *Journal of Economic Issues* 32(2), June.

Di Filippo, Armando (1981) *Desarrollo y Desigualdad Social en América Latina,* México: Fondo de Cultura Económica.

Dosman, Edgar (2001) "Los Mercados y el Estado *en la Evolución del* Manifiesto de Prebisch," *Revista de la CEPAL,* No. 75, diciembre, pp. 89–109.

Fernández López, Manuel (2000) "Ugo Broggi, a Neglected Precursor in Modern Mathematical Economics," www.aaep.org.ar/espa/anales/pdf_00/fernandez-lopez.pdf

Furtado, Celso (1985) "El declive de la influencia de los intelectuales: entrevista a Celso Furtado." In *Ideas e Historia en Torno al Pensamiento Económico Latinoamericano,* edited by Carlos Mallorquín, Mexico: Plaza y Valdés.

Gondra, Luís Roque (1932) *La Circulación Monetaria en la República Argentina,* Buenos Aires: La Vanguardia.

—— (1933) *Elementos de Economía Política,* Buenos Aires: La Facultad.

—— (1934) *Problemas Sociales y Económicos del Momento,* Buenos Aires: La Facultad.

—— (1937a) *Teorías antiguas y Recientes sobre la Moneda, el Crédito y los Ciclos Económicos,* Buenos Aires: Tomás Palumbo.

—— (1937b) *El radicalismo y la Política del Momento Motivos de Crítica y Polémica,* Buenos Aires: La Facultad.

—— (1943) *Ensayo sobre una Teoría General de las Fluctuaciones Económicas Elementos de Dinámica Económica,* Buenos Aires: Imprenta de la Universidad.

González del Solar, Julio (2006) "Conversaciones con Raúl Prebisch," *Cinta de Moebio,* No. 24, diciembre.

Haberler, Gottfried (1937) *Prosperity and Depression,* Geneva: League of Nations.

Imaz, José Luis de (1974) "Alejandro E. Bunge, Economista y Sociólogo," *Desarrollo Económico* 55(14), oct.-dic.

Keynes, John M. (1936) *Teoría general de la Ocupación, el Interés y el Dinero*, México: Fondo de Cultura Económica, 1965.

Kindleberger, Charles P. (1943) "International Monetary Stabilization." In *Postwar Economic Problems*, edited by Seymour E. Harris, London: McGraw-Hill, pp. 375–95.

Llach, Juan José (1984) "El Plan Pinedo de 1940, su Significado Histórico y los Orígenes de la Economía Política del Peronismo," *Desarrollo Económico*, vol 23, enero-marzo.

—— (1985) *La Argentina que no Fue*, Buenos Aires: Ediciones del IDES.

Love, Joseph (1996) *Crafting the Third World. Theorizing Underdevelopment in Rumania and Brazil*, California: Stanford University Press.

Lucchini, María Cristina, Teodoro Blanco and Ángel Cerra (2000) "El Pensamiento Industrialista Argentino en el Período de Entreguerras – el Estudio de un Caso: la Influencia de List en Bunge," *Estudios Interdisciplinarios de América Latina y el Caribe* 11(2), julio–diciembre.

Magariños, Mateo (1991) *Diálogos con Raúl Prebisch*, México: Fondo de Cultura Económica.

Mallorquín, Carlos (2005a) "Raúl Prebisch Before The Ice Age." In *Prebisch and Globalization*, edited by Edgar Dosman, Washington: INTAL.

Molteni, Gabriel R. (2003) "Structural Change in Argentina: Economic Ideas, Economic Policy and Institutional Constraints during the Inter-War Period. The Case of Alejandro E. Bunge," *Cuestiones Sociales y Económicas* 1(2), sept.

Piñeiro Iñiguez, Carlos (2003) *Herejías Periféricas. Raúl Prebisch. Vigencia de su pensamiento*, Buenos Aires: Grupo Editor Latinoamericano.

Pollock, David, Daniel Kerner and Joseph Love (2001) "Entrevista Inédita a Prebisch: Logros y Deficiencias de la CEPAL," *Revista de la CEPAL*, No. 75, Santiago de Chile, dic.

Prebisch, Raúl (1944a) "Conversaciones en el Banco de México S.A.," In *La Creación del Banco Central y la Experiencia Monetaria Argentina entre los Años 1935–1945*, Buenos Aires: Banco Central de la Republica Argentina, 1972.

—— (1944b) *La Moneda y los ciclos económicos en la Argentina.* In *Raúl Prebisch. Obras 1919–1948, vol. III;* Buenos Aires: Fundación Raúl Prebisch, 1991c.

—— (1944c) "Observaciones sobre los Planes Monetarios Internacionales," *El Trimestre Económico* 11(2), julio–sept.

—— (1944d) "El Patrón Oro y la Vulnerabilidad Económica de nuestros Países," *Jornadas*, El Colegio de México, marzo. In *Raúl Prebisch. Obras 1919–1948, vol. III*, Buenos Aires: Fundación Raúl Prebisch, 1991c.

—— (1945a) "Introducción al Curso de Economía Política." In *Raúl Prebisch. Obras 1919–1948, vol. III*, Buenos Aires: Fundación Raúl Prebisch, 1991c.

—— (1945b) "Concepto Preliminar de la Circulación de Ingresos." In *Raúl Prebisch. Obras 1919–1948, vol. IV*, Buenos Aires: Fundación Raúl Prebisch, 1993.

—— (1946) "Panorama General de los Problemas de Regulación Monetaria y Crediticia en el Continente Americano: América Latina." In *Raúl Prebisch. Obras 1919–1948, vol. IV*, Buenos Aires: Fundación Raúl Prebisch, 1993.

—— (1947b) "La Propensión a Consumir y la Teoría Keynesiana del Multiplicador." In *Raúl Prebisch. Obras 1919–1948, vol. III*, Buenos Aires: Fundación Raúl Prebisch, 1991c.

—— (1947e) "La Conjunción del Ahorro y las Inversiones en la Teoría Keynesiana." In

Raúl Prebisch. Obras 1919–1948, vol. IV, Buenos Aires: Fundación Raúl Prebisch, 1993.

—— (1947f) *Introducción a Keynes*, México: Fondo de Cultura Económica.

—— (1948) *Apuntes de Economía Política (Dinámica Económica)*. In *Raúl Prebisch. Obras 1919–1948, vol. IV*, Buenos Aires: Fundación Raúl Prebisch, 1993.

—— (1949a) *El desarrollo económico de la América Latina y sus principales problemas*, E/CN.12/89, Santiago de Chile, 14 de mayo de 1949a.

—— (1949b) *Teoría Dinámica de la Economía (con Especial Aplicación a las Economías Latinoamericanas)*. In *Raúl Prebisch. Obras 1919–1948, vol. IV*, Buenos Aires: Fundación Raúl Prebisch, 1993.

—— (1972) *La Creación del Banco Central y la experiencia monetaria argentina entre los Años 1935–1945*, Buenos Aires: Banco Central de la Republica Argentina.

—— (1981) *Capitalismo Periférico: Crisis y Transformación*, México: Fondo de Cultura Económica.

—— (1984) "Five Stages of my Thinking on Development." In *Pioneers In Development*, edited by Gerald H. Meier and Dudley Seers, Washington, DC: The World Bank, Oxford University Press.

—— (1991b) *Raúl Prebisch. Obras 1919–1948, vol. II*, Buenos Aires: Fundación Raúl Prebisch.

—— (1991c) *Raúl Prebisch. Obras 1919–1948, vol. III*, Buenos Aires: Fundación Raúl Prebisch.

—— (1993) *Raúl Prebisch. Obras 1919–1948, vol. IV.*, Buenos Aires: Fundación Raúl Prebisch.

—— (2006) "Conversaciones con Raúl Prebisch," *Cinta de Moebio*, No. 25, marzo.

Pribram, Karl (1983) *A History of Economic Reasoning*, Baltimore: The Johns Hopkins University Press.

Pugliese, Mario (1939) "Nacionalismo Económico, Comercio Internacional Bilateral, e Industrialización de los Países Agrícolas, desde el Punto de Vista de la Economía Argentina," *Revista de Ciencias Económicas* 27(2), No. 219, octubre.

Shaw John D. (2002) *Sir Hans Singer*, New York: Palgrave Macmillan.

Souter R. W. (1930) "Equilibrium Economics and Business-Cycle Theory: a commentary," *Quarterly Journal of Economics* 45(1), November.

Toye John and Richard Toye (2004a) *The UN and Global Political Economy*, Bloomington Indiana: Indiana University Press.

—— (2004b) "Raúl Prebisch y los límites de la industrialización." In *La economía entre/vista*, edited by Carlos Mallorquín, México: Editorial Universidad de la Ciudad de México.

Weintraub, Roy E. (2002) *How Economics became a Mathematical Science*, Durham: Duke University Press.

7 Mexico's market reforms in historical perspective

Juan Carlos Moreno-Brid and Jaime Ros[1]

Introduction

This chapter looks at Mexico's development policies and problems from a historical perspective.[2] It reviews long term trends in the Mexican economy, and examines in particular some past episodes of radical shifts in development strategy and in the role of markets and the state. The shift of the last twenty years is given particular attention. A major theme is that the real obstacles to economic development have often been misperceived in the past and that the same may be happening at present. The chapter is organized as follows. The second section, after this brief introduction, reviews the debates on the causes of Mexico's long period of economic stagnation experienced during most of the nineteenth century. The third section examines the long expansion of the Mexican economy that began in the Porfiriato – in the late nineteenth century – and ended with the collapse of a short-lived oil boom in 1981. The fourth section focuses on the economic and policy adjustments to the external shocks of the 1980s and discusses the Mexican economy's prospects under the radical shift in development strategy implemented since the mid-1980s. The chapter ends with some thoughts on the challenges of the Mexican economy now, when after more than fifteen years of economic reform it is – for the first time in its modern history – experiencing successive years of absolute decline in its real GDP per capita.

Market reforms in the nineteenth century

By the end of the eighteenth century Mexico was probably one of the most prosperous regions in the world. It was surely one of the wealthiest Spanish colonies in America, with an economy whose productivity was possibly higher than that of Spain herself. Output per capita (in 1800) was around half that of the US, and Mexico's economy was less agricultural, with an advanced mining industry and a significant manufacturing sector. The value of exports was similar to that of Mexico's northern neighbor, even though total output produced was around half (Coatsworth, 1978). Several of the conditions for rapid capitalist development were in place. The creation of an industrial labor force – that "most difficult and protracted process" by which the population's ties to the land are broken (Gerschenkron, 1952) – although far from complete, was probably more advanced

Table 7.1 Gross domestic product per capita and by sector, 1800–1910

	1800	1845	1860	1877	1895	1910
Per capita GDP at constant 1900 prices (index 1800=100)	100.1	78.4	70.9	85.0	128.8	190.2
% of GDP						
Agriculture[a]	44.4	48.1	42.1	42.2	38.2	33.7
Mining	8.2	6.2	9.7	10.4	6.3	8.4
Manufacturing	22.3	18.3	21.6	16.2	12.8	14.9
Construction	0.6	0.6	0.6	0.6	0.6	0.8
Transportation	2.5	2.5	2.5	2.5	3.3	2.7
Commerce	16.7	16.9	16.7	16.9	16.8	19.3
Government	4.2[b]	7.4	6.8	11.2	8.9	7.2
Other	1.1	–	–	–	13.1	12.9

Source: Coatsworth (1989), tables 4 and 5.

Notes
a Includes livestock, forestry and fishing
b Excludes net fiscal remittances to the Spanish Treasury. Total government revenues, including these remittances, amounted to 7.8 percent of colonial income.

than in many European countries (especially in Central and Eastern Europe). The relatively high share of manufacturing in total output in 1800 (22.3 percent, see Table 7.1) also speaks about the presence of a critical mass of native industrial entrepreneurs.

Mexico's century of decline (1780–1870): obstacles to economic development

Yet between 1800 and approximately 1860 – at the time when the US and other now developed economies were recording unprecedented rates of economic growth – total production fell by 5 percent and per capita incomes declined by as much as 30 percent. Between 1820 and 1870, Mexico's income per capita had fallen from 60 to 28 percent of that of the US, and has since then fluctuated between 24 and –33 percent (Table 7.2). Whether this decline had already started in the later decades of the colonial period or not, everybody agrees that independence did nothing to prevent the economy's stagnation during the half century that followed it. Why did independence and the emergence of a nation-state not stimulate economic development?

Independence eliminated the fiscal burden on gold and silver extracted from the colony. This had been a substantial burden – estimated by Coatsworth at 7.2 percent of total output around 1800 – much higher, for example, than the burden of British colonialism on its North American colonies. Yet the end of Spanish rule also brought some unexpected costs for the mining sector that partly offset the removal of this burden. Not only were the direct effects of the independence wars on mining production highly disruptive, but they also involved the loss of low cost and guaranteed supplies of mercury (essential for processing low-grade

Table 7.2 Total and per capita GDP and population, 1820–1998

	1820	1870	1913	1950	1973	1990	1998
Per capita GDPa	759	674	1732	2365	4845	6097	6655
GDP gap (Mexico/United States)	0.60	0.28	0.33	0.25	0.25	0.26	0.24

	1820–1870	1870–1913	1913–1950	1950–1973	1973–1998
Per capita GDP growth rates (%)	–0.2	2.2	0.9	3.2	1.3
Total GDP growth rates (%)	0.4	3.4	2.6	6.4	3.5
Population growth rates (%)	0.7	1.1	1.8	3.1	2.2

Source: Maddison (2001).

Note
a Dollars at 1990 international prices.

ores) that Spain had provided from its large state-owned mine at Almaden. As a consequence of this disruption, silver production fell to less than one-fifth from 1812 to 1822, and the mining sector did not recover its pre-independence level of production until the 1860s (Cárdenas, 1985). The depression of silver production had, in turn, other important consequences for the economy. Besides the contraction of all the activities linked to the mining sector, it implied a reduction in the volume of international trade and a decrease in the means of payment available in the domestic economy (Cárdenas, 1985). The latter aggravated the consequences of capital flight brought about by the exodus of Spanish miners and merchants, and thus the general lack of financial capital, which characterized this period up to the 1860s when the first commercial banks were founded.

The abolition of restrictions to foreign trade also turned out to be a mixed blessing. While generally regarded by economic historians as beneficial to the Mexican economy, the end of trade restrictions accelerated the diversion of Mexican foreign trade away from Spain and towards the emerging industrializing powers in the North Atlantic, a trend which had very harmful effects on domestic manufacturing and, therefore, on the major activity that could have compensated for the decline of the mining sector. Several studies have documented how exposure to US and British competition led to the collapse of the wool textile industry at the turn of the century and to the prolonged decline of cotton textiles throughout the first half of the nineteenth century. Trade opening towards the Atlantic economy and foreign competition – which in fact started in the period of "*comercio libre*" and "*comercio neutral*" introduced by the Bourbon reforms – also appears to have deepened the fragmentation of local markets and the cleavage between, on the one hand, a mining and agricultural north trading with the rest of the world and, on the other, a manufacturing center and agricultural south plunged into economic depression (Thomson, 1986).

In addition, little progress was made in other areas. The colony had been one of the regions in the world with the sharpest social and regional disparities; a caste society, in fact, where access to employment as well as geographical and occupational mobility were restricted on the basis of ethnic distinctions, and where a number of institutional arrangements tended to increase, rather than reduce, the gap between the private and social benefits of economic activity. Although some changes did take place with independence,[3] many of these had little effect on a backward social and political order. The ultimate reason is probably the nature of the foundational act of the post-independence state: the fact that having begun and been defeated as a popular insurrection – feared by both the Spanish and Creole conservative elites – independence came eventually to Mexico through "a virtual *coup d'état* by the colony's Creole elite, carried out largely to separate Mexico from the liberalizing process under way in the mother country" (Coatsworth, 1978).

This had several consequences. Institutional modernization was de facto and sometimes *de jure* slow. A new civil code was only produced in 1870 – almost 50 years after independence – and even then nothing replaced a repudiated commercial code. The mining colonial code remained almost intact until 1877. Modern banking and patent laws were non-existent. In spite of constitutional dispositions, taxes and restrictions on domestic trade remained.

The system of government preserved the arbitrary nature of political power in colonial times. Economic success or failure strictly depended on the relationship between enterprise and political authorities; or as Coatsworth (1978, p. 94) puts it:

> Every enterprise, urban or rural, [was forced] to operate in a highly politicized manner, using kinship networks, political influence, and family prestige to gain privileged access to subsidized credit, to aid various stratagems for recruiting labor, to collect debts or enforce contracts, to evade taxes or circumvent the courts, and to defend or assert titles to land. ... The chief obstacle was the nature of the state itself, its operating principles, the basis for all its acts. Mexico's economic organization could not have been made more efficient without a revolution in the relationship between the state and economic activity."

Most importantly, repeated efforts to preserve or recreate the arbitrary centralism of the colonial state plunged the country into a prolonged period of political instability and continuous struggle opposing the conservative and liberal factions.[4] Half a century of political, social and international wars annihilated the potentially beneficial effects of independence, while at the same time curtailing the resources needed for the state and the private sector to support the recovery of the mining sector and improve the transport infrastructure in a country where the lack of natural communications and the resulting high transport costs had highly adverse effects on the division of labor and regional specialization (Coatsworth, 1990).

In sum, while economic activity had remained "state-centered," in the sense that "every enterprise was forced to operate in a highly politicized manner," the state, compared with colonial times, had in fact been weakened and was unable to remove the obstacles to economic development resulting from the decline of mining activity, foreign competition, and the lack of transport infrastructure and financial capital. Economic and industrial stagnation followed, then, as a consequence of a persistent lack of markets and their fragmentation.

Liberal misperceptions in the mid-nineteenth century?

This list of obstacles to economic development in nineteenth-century Mexico is equally significant for what it excludes. Revisionism by economic historians suggests, indeed, that two of the traditional culprits, the land tenure system and the economic power of the Church, were not in fact among the major causes of economic stagnation during this period.

The system of land tenure and agricultural production had been organized since the seventeenth century into large estates called "haciendas." While highly inequitable and thus, socially and macroeconomically inefficient, the hacienda system was far from a semi-feudal organization, promoting waste and resource misallocation. Recent research has produced a new image of the hacienda as one of a capitalistic and technologically dynamic undertaking with an economic rationality comparable with that of a modern agricultural enterprise, and one which largely exploited its comparative advantages – economies of scale, and access to external credit and information on new technologies and distant markets (see, among others, Van Young, 1981 and 1986). A "division of labor" had, in fact, been established through time between the hacienda and other forms of agricultural production – small landowners, tenant farmers or Indian villagers – by which each of them had specialized in those products and crops where they enjoyed a competitive advantage: cattle, sheep, wool, food grains, pulque, sugar and sisal in the haciendas, and fruits, tomatoes, chiles, silk, and small animals such as pigs and chickens by the villages and small-scale producers.

Similar revisionism applies to the Church as an economic institution. By the middle of the nineteenth century, the Church had become the country's single major landowner and an important lender in the emerging financial markets. With respect to its first role, according to Coatsworth (1978, 1990), several studies suggest that Church haciendas were at least as well managed as private haciendas; and, in any case, after independence most of these estates were rented to private farmers and *hacendados* so that their efficiency did not depend on Church administration. On the other hand, the Church appropriated the tithe (*diezmo*), a 10 percent tax on gross output and charged mainly on agricultural and livestock production. As any other tax, the tithe reduced the profitability of agricultural production and probably discouraged it (although some authors have doubts about this).[5] More important, however, is the use to which these revenues were put. Far from financing wholly "unproductive" expenditures, the Church invested a considerable portion of its revenues (including also private donations and net income from its various properties) in loans to private entrepreneurs with no legal or practical restrictions to prevent recipients from investing in factories rather than haciendas or other activities. It did this by lending at below market interest rates – usually at a 6 percent rate on the security on real property. Because it dominated the mortgage-lending market, this probably had the effect, in turn, of bringing market interest rates down. As Coatsworth (1978) has put it, the Church acted like a modern development bank raising the rate of capital accumulation above what it would have been in the absence of the tithe.

If this revisionism by economic historians is correct, then some of the main elements of the liberal economic program – free trade, the privatization of corporate and public property, and the liberalization of the land market – were largely misdirected from a strictly (and admittedly narrow) economic development perspective. The first, free trade, probably gave further stimulus to the decline of local manufacturing – and to the "ruralization" of the labor force – as the expansion of railways in the late nineteenth century sharply reduced the natural protection provided by traditionally high transport costs. The second, the privatization of corporate property, had the effect of destroying the major, and for a long time practically the only, banking institution in the economy; while the third, the liberalization of the land market, was to contribute to further land concentration and, eventually, to the social explosion of 1910.

The conservative faction was, of course, no better. Although some of its members, Lucas Alamán in particular, pioneered the first, and short-lived, industrialization efforts in the 1830s – through industrial protection and the creation of the first public development bank (*Banco de Avío*) to finance the development of the textile industry[6] – the social and political forces that supported them tended to perpetuate the very arbitrary centralism of political power that had had such harmful effects on economic development since colonial times.

As a result, the coalition that could forge a developmental state did not emerge; and in its absence, some of the major obstacles to economic development remained in place. The politically liberal who could and were willing to carry out the country's political and social modernization were also furiously anti-statist in economic terms; while the only ones that favored an economic modernization through an interventionist state were the politically conservative, strongly opposed to political and social modernization. It would take a social explosion and a popular revolution in the early twentieth century to bring these two requirements for economic development into a less conflictive relationship.

The traumatic emergence of a Gershenkronian developmental state

The Porfiriato: political stability and the emergence of a unified national market

Modern economic growth began, in fact, in the late nineteenth century.[7] In 1895, 72 percent of the population lived in rural areas and more than 80 percent of those aged ten and above could not read or write (Table 7.3). In 1877, when Por-

Table 7.3 Population and social indicators, 1895–2000

Year	Total population (millions)	Rural population (%)	Life expectancy at birth (years)	Literacy[a] (per cent)	Average years of schooling[b]
1895	12.6	72	30	17.9[c]	–
1910	15.2	–	–	27.7	–
1930	16.6	66.5	33.9	38.5	–
1940	19.7	64.9	38.8	41.8	2.6
1980	68.3	33.7	66.2	83.0[c]	4.6
1990	81.2	28.7	70.8	87.4	6.6
1995	91.2	26.5	73.6	89.4	7.2
2000	97.0	25.4	75.3	90.3[b]	7.6

Sources: Maddison (1989) and INEGI (various years).

Notes
a Population age ten or above.
b Age 15 or above.
c Age six or above.

firio Díaz seized power, 42 percent of Mexico's GDP was generated by rural activities and only 16 percent by manufacturing (Table 7.1). In the following two decades, a turnaround in Mexico's long-term decline was becoming evident. The barriers to economic recovery had been brought down by the transformation of the international economic environment and by domestic changes in Mexico's political and economic structure that took place under the dictatorship of Porfirio Díaz, a 33-year period of political stability (1877–1910), aptly named 'the Porfiriato' by Mexican historians.

Melding a liberal political background with conservative economic goals, the Porfiriato's ideology is summarized in the positivist lemma of "Order and Progress." Order was considered a sine qua non for economic growth. The end of the military and political struggles that had plagued Mexico since its independence were seen as an essential pre-condition for business confidence and the recovery of private investment. Strengthening of the central government was efficiently pursued, and combining the use of force and alliances with relevant groups brought Díaz full hold of the political structure.

Progress meant transforming Mexico into an industrialized nation by effectively addressing some of the traditional barriers to economic recovery, such as the lack of transport infrastructure and financial capital.[8] To foster expansion of the railway network, the state awarded concessions and financial incentives. Subsidies granted on railway construction amounted to 50 percent of their total cost. The railway system expansion enormously amplified the market's size, brought down local and regional trade barriers and intensified competition.[9] This effect was reinforced by the significant increase in road travel safety that the Díaz regime achieved.

Foreign investment was another key aspect of Díaz's development strategy, and was actively sought through various incentives. These inducements and the profitable investment opportunities led to the inflow of foreign capital. From 1880, US capital flowed in, later followed by European investments

(Coatsworth, 1989). This flow increased continuously for the next 15 years, and boomed in the first decade of the 1900s (King, 1970). More generally, state policies were geared to promote private investment and guarantee the best conditions for its operation. The legal framework for the conduct of private business was soon transformed. In 1883 new legal codes for trade and mining were adopted to improve conditions for foreign investment. Regional tariffs on domestic trade were abolished. Trade policy combined focused tariff protection consistent with supporting industrialization in consumer goods sectors, with declining average tariffs that enhanced manufacturers' access to low-cost capital and intermediate goods (Beatty, 2002; Kuntz Ficker, 2002).

Foreign investment meant access to world markets, and between 1870 and 1913 Mexico's exports as a share of GDP increased threefold. The expansion of foreign trade helped also to increase government funds, as taxes on foreign trade provided more than half of public revenues. Greatly helped by the depreciation of silver at the end of the nineteenth century,[10] the export sector became an engine of growth, as it had done previously in colonial times. This time the export basket became considerably more diversified than in the colonial period as it included, besides silver, other minerals – industrial metals such as copper, lead and zinc, whose demand from the industrial centers of the world economy was expanding rapidly – as well as a number of agricultural products (coffee, livestock and others which were added to those already with some importance in the composition of exports, such as henequen, furs and wood).

Accompanying these policy changes and responses was a more propitious external economic environment. By 1870 the second industrial revolution in the industrialized countries had spurred demand for minerals and other raw materials. In addition, there was a notable expansion of international investment to several less developed countries: between 1870 and 1900 this flow doubled the value of the outstanding capital stock held by foreign investors (Maddison, 1989). Combined with the end of political instability, the new environment helped to restore international creditworthiness.[11]

What was the overall development outcome of this strategy? Economic growth and modernization was felt in many areas, reversing a century of decline, and from 1877 to 1910 Mexico's GDP per capita increased at an annual average growth rate of 2.1 percent (Bortz and Haber, 2002, see also Table 7.2). The railroad boom benefited some old activities – such as mining[12] – and simultaneously helped in the creation of new activities whose production scales and capital intensity had made them unprofitable in the absence of a unified national market. Indeed, underlying this modernization was Mexico's first wave of large-scale industrialization. Through import substitution in textiles, beer, papermaking, cement and steel, manufacturing output increased at an average rate of 3.6 percent per annum from 1877 to 1910 (Coatsworth, 1989). Manufacturing changed from being an artisans' activity, carried out in small handicraft firms, to a productive process done in large-scale plants. The rural areas were also deeply transformed in their social and economic structure. Based on a diagnosis of the rural sector as unproductive, with most agricultural output distributed through non-market channels, the Díaz administration pushed an accelerated redistribution of federal and communal land to private development companies and wealthy individuals. Privatization would promote large-scale commercial cultivation. By 1890, 20 percent of Mexico's total area was held by less than 50 individuals or companies. By the early 1900s, 95 percent of all arable land was in the hands of 835 families (Manzanilla Schaffer, 1963).

By the early 1900s, this pattern of development started to show symptoms of exhaustion. From 1903, real wages began to decrease in a systematic and persistent way. Droughts in 1907 reduced output of food products, and furthermore increased their prices. By 1910, the cumulative decline in real wages was 26 percent relative to 1903. If hunger was not evident, poverty was most common, especially in the rural areas.[13] At the same time, recourse to force to repress labor and suppress political opposition became more frequent and eventually unsuccessful. By 1910, the system's unequal distribution of benefits and access to power reached its limit. The emerging middle classes excluded from political decisions, and the workers and peasants marginalized from the benefits of economic growth, were successful in developing a triumphant coalition under the banners of political democracy, agrarian reform and labor rights.

What had gone wrong? Clearly, the Porfiriato's "primary contradiction" was in its results: the growing imbalance between rapid economic growth, on the one hand, and the slow pace of political and social progress on the other. Porfirio Díaz had set out to make of Mexico a modern industrial nation. But, by 1910 only 28 percent of Mexicans could read and write, and life expectancy at birth was not above 37 years (Table 7.3). With two-thirds of its population still living in rural areas, Mexico was still a fundamentally backward economy and, overall, a backward society.

There were also shortcomings in the design of the development strategy. Three of these turned out to be particularly relevant. First, rather than increasing labor mobility, the enclosure system implemented in the Porfiriato strengthened labor's links of dependency with the rural areas. Deprived of land plots, the great majority of the population was forced to work permanently as indebted labor in the haciendas. Thus, at the same time that the expansion of the railway system was creating a national market, huge contingents of the population were cut out from the possibility of entering it.

A second aspect concerns the sources of finance for development. The existing banking system was simply a source of short-term loans, most suitable for purely commercial needs. By 1897 no bank had legal authorization to give loans for a period longer than a year. By 1910, some banks were legally allowed to give such loans, but the great majority of them were provided for investments in real estate. Besides foreign investors, Mexico's first wave of industrialization was carried out by the merchant elite who financed it through the reinvestment of their accumulated profits.[14] At the end of the Porfiriato, Mexico still faced the urgent need to create banking institutions capable of financing its long-term investment needs.

The third is related to the role of the state in the quest for development in backward economies. For the Porfiriato's elite, the role of the state, besides ensuring social peace, was to guarantee the best conditions for private investment without intervening directly in the productive sphere. Public investment never amounted to more than 5 percent of total investment, and only 7 percent of public expenditure was directed at capital formation purposes. While the emergence of a national market had broken through some of the barriers of stagnation, this limited role of the state proved insufficient to overcome the still enormous obstacles to economic development.

Revolution and the consolidation of a developmental state

In 1910 the *Pax Porfiriana* drew to a dramatic close with the Mexican Revolution. Once more, the absence of social consensus became the fundamental obstacle for Mexico's development. The construction of a stable social pact would be fully achieved only three decades later.

The most violent stages of the Mexican Revolution ended with the adoption of a new Constitution in 1917. Political unrest continued for the next ten years – marked by the killings of important figures such as Zapata, Carranza and Obregón, and numerous uprisings – but the scale of armed struggle diminished significantly. The 1917 Constitution redefined the legal framework for land property and labor relations. It placed the nation over and above private property on matters regarding land, water and subsoil resources; established the right to form trade unions, a system of minimum wages, eight-hour workdays within a six-day workweek, and equal pay for equal work; and included an agrarian reform through the expropriation of large land holdings and their allocation to "ejidos," a land tenure system combining collective ownership with private exploitation of the land.

A fundamental move towards the consolidation of social peace and political stability was the creation of the Partido Nacional Revolucionario (PNR) in 1929.[15] Renamed Partido de la Revolución Mexicana (PRM) in 1938 and Partido Revolucionario Institucional (PRI) in 1946, the official party encompassed all relevant social forces of the Mexican Revolution and soon became a functional vehicle for political control and the only legitimate arena in which to settle political differences. By 1940, the government party had formed solid alliances with labor through the Confederación de Trabajadores Mexicanos (CTM) and the Federación de Sindicatos de Trabajadores al Servicio del Estado (FSTSE), and controlled peasants' organizations through the Confederación Nacional Campesina (CNC). The private sector, although not formally included in the official party, was recognized and taken into account by the political system through a number of business organizations and chambers. In addition, by the 1940s the military had been professionalized, divested of its political role. The age of Caudillos was over, and Mexico's particular form of institutionalized authoritarian control had begun.

The process of consolidation of political power after the Revolution had been accompanied by an expansion in policy instruments available to the government.[16] Under the Cárdenas presidency (1936–1940), the public sector expanded further with several developments of financial entities. Most important, the oil industry was nationalized and agrarian reform began to be implemented on a massive scale. Fiscal policy became counter-cyclical and budget deficits were run to boost productive and social investment. Public expenditure was reoriented away from military and administrative spending. The highway system increased sevenfold, covering 9,900 km by 1940. In addition, temporary flotation of the exchange rate led to a depreciation of the peso in real terms.

With the turnaround in the conduct of government policies and the extraordinary recovery in the terms of trade of silver and oil (the country's main exports), Mexico resumed growth in 1933–1934. The first new round of investment since the Porfiriato began in manufacturing and concentrated on new textile activities. Manufacturing became the economy's most dynamic sector.

The Post-war Golden Age of industrialization (1940–1980)

In the process of achieving hegemony, the Mexican state arrived at the strong conviction that it should play an active role in investment and production if Mexico was to develop. By the late 1940s, it controlled fundamental resources and had increased the number of its policy instruments significantly. Public investment expanded systematically (Table 7.4) and was oriented to urban and industrial development. Additional incentives such as tax concessions were used to promote manufacturing activities. Investment in education and welfare held their share in federal expenditure. The industrialization drive also came hand in hand with a deepening of trade protection.[17] By 1947 protectionism had been officially adopted as a government intermediate objective (Mosk, 1950).

A complete overhaul of the economy and society took place from 1940 to 1980. Mexico's economy grew at a sustained pace of 6.4 percent per annum in real terms and GDP per capita at 3.2 percent per annum. Manufacturing became the engine of growth, with rates of growth of production of 7.4 percent per annum from 1940 to 1955 and accelerated its pace of development in 1957 to

Table 7.4 Investment rates, 1900–1980

Year	Total investment (% of GDP)	Public investment (% of GDP)
1900	10.1	0.5[a]
1910	10.1	0.4
1921	10.1	–
1930	9.4	2.2
1940	9.3	3.5
1960	17.2	5.2
1980	24.8	11.4

Sources: ECLAC and INEGI.

Note
a 1895.

1970 expanding at annual rates of 8.9 percent per annum with the dynamic domestic market as its major source of demand. The country was transformed from an agrarian into an urban, semi-industrial society. From 1940 to 1980, the output share of manufacturing rose from 15.4 to 24.9 percent (Table 7.5) and the share of the population living in urban areas soared from 35 to 66 percent at a time when the total population increased from 20 to 70 million people (Table 7.3). Literacy rates nearly doubled, reaching 83 percent in 1980. The average number of years of schooling of the adult population jumped from 2.6 to 7.1, and life expectancy at birth increased 24 years to 65 (Table 7.3). Despite these improvements, the benefits of growth were far from being evenly distributed. By the end of this period, 20 percent of the population accrued more than 50 percent of total disposable income while 58 percent of Mexicans were still in poverty (less conservative estimates put this figure as high as 63 percent, see Hernández Laos, 1989). Thus, at the end of Mexico's Golden Age, poverty and inequality were still major problems to be solved.

The macroeconomic performance from 1940 to 1970 was undoubtedly impressive. The strategy on which it was based tackled important obstacles on the road to Mexico's development. However, it ignored or underestimated the magnitude of other obstacles.

The first obstacle arose from the neglect of agriculture, which, after 1965, faced serious difficulties in expanding production. Its rate of growth in the second half of the 1960s fell below the pace of demographic expansion. Among the factors explaining this decline were the dual character of the sector, the adverse trend in the prices of agricultural goods relative to manufacturing goods (as urban consumption was subsidized), and the continuous decline of its share in public investment after the 1950s. All these elements contributed to an increase in poverty, a contraction of the potential domestic market, and a loss of social cohesion, which led to emergent social instability.

Second, while trade protection proved a valuable instrument in promoting growth and import substitution in many sectors, there was no explicit policy, either from the private or the public sector, to strengthen over time the economy's export potential. Neither was it clear whether the policy as it stood could complete the most difficult phase of import substitution involving high-technology capital goods.

Finally, tax reforms were systematically aborted, and public finances became increasingly dependent on external debt.[18] So too did the balance of payments, which became more and more vulnerable to short-term capital flows, with their potentially destabilizing influence. As long as the Golden Age of world economic growth continued, misperceptions regarding the potential relevance of these issues could remain. Unfortunately, this Golden Age was coming to an end.

"Shared development," the oil boom and the debt crisis

To the extent that the administrations of the 1970s did not solve these obstacles, they could, and did, become painfully costly. The new Echeverría administration

Table 7.5 Structure of GDP, 1895–2002

	1885	1910	1926	1932	1940	1955	1970	1970	1980	1980	1990	2000–2002
	(based on 1960 prices)							(based on 1980 prices)		(based on 1993 prices)		
Agriculture[a]	29.1	24.0	19.7	24.1	19.4	18.3	11.6	12.2	9.0	7.1	6.7	7.6
Mining	3.0	4.9	9.3	7.2	6.4	4.8	4.8	2.5	3.3	1.4	1.5	2.1
Industry	9.0	12.3	14.7	13.3	18.7	22.1	29.7	30.1	31.9	25.0	24.1	27.0
(Manufacturing)	(7.9)	(10.7)	(11.6)	(10.2)	(15.4)	(17.5)	(23.3)	(23.7)	(24.9)	(19.2)	(19.6)	(21)
Services	58.9	58.7	56.3	55.4	55.5	54.7	53.9	55.2	55.8	66.5	67.6	63.3
Total	100	100	100	100	100	100	100	100	100	100	100	100

Sources: Banco de México and INEGI.

Note

a Includes livestock, forestry and fishing.

taking office in late 1970 had as a central point of its political platform the claim that the "stabilizing development" strategy of the period between 1956 and 1970 had failed to address the fundamental problem of inequality. A new strategy of "shared development" was thus proposed in which the benefits from economic growth would be more evenly distributed. In practice, however, the policies adopted would fail to fulfill these objectives.

Temporarily, the strategy did have the intended impact on the functional distribution of income. Gil Díaz (1987) shows that the share of labor in net national product went from 40 percent in 1970 to 43 percent in 1972–1974, and reached 49 percent in 1976. In addition, GDP achieved an average rate of growth of 6.1 percent per annum. Unfortunately, these achievements were accompanied by the emergence of severe macroeconomic imbalances. A number of reasons accounted for this. On the external front, the collapse of the world's Golden Age had its toll on the Mexican economy. The first oil price shock found Mexico as a net importer of oil and, together with the decline in external demand, tightened the balance of payments' constraints on growth. Moreover, the increase in domestic inflation rates to the 20 percent range, the expansion of public investment, and a fixed exchange rate, tripled the trade deficit from 1970 to 1975. The model of industrialization also began to show some signs of exhaustion. Investment was carried out to modernize plants in old sectors already conquered by foreign competition, but failed both to increase exports significantly and to deepen import substitution in the capital goods sector.

The limitations of capital goods manufacturing were evident, for example, in the fact that during 1974–1975 they accounted for less than 8 percent of manufacturing output, while at the same time they represented more than 50 percent of total imports. As a share of GDP, overall exports declined, largely as a result of stagnating agricultural supplies and productivity. Manufacturing export coefficients increased but remained at low levels, and the share of imports in the domestic market started to climb as the investment process failed to diversify into new activities.

To the extent that tax reform was not addressed, public revenues lagged behind. The fiscal deficit climbed from 2.5 percent of GDP to 9.9 percent between 1971 and 1976, and was increasingly covered through monetary expansion and external debt (which increased at an average annual rate of 40 percent from 1973 to 1976).[19] In addition, private enterprise did not find a fertile ground in the "shared development" rhetoric, and soon public spending was exclusively driving the economy's expansion. Eventually, the situation worsened significantly as a result of capital flight. Notwithstanding the increase in import controls and tariffs, balance of payment pressures forced the government to depreciate by nearly 100 percent in 1976, thus abandoning the exchange rate parity that had remained fixed for more than 20 years.

Despite the severity of the 1976 crisis, in a year or so the economy's prospects were fully turned around with the announcement of Mexico's vast oil resources. Their exploitation and sale in the international market would bring a swift and strong recovery. The trade deficit was under control again, averaging

1.5 percent as a share of GDP. The term profile of foreign debt was restructured and, for a while, new indebtedness did not grow in a noticeable way. An ambitious industrialization plan was launched on the assumption of a sustained long-term increase in the price of oil. Manufacturing investment soared, boosted by public and private entrepreneurship, and GDP reached rates of 8 to 9 percent per annum from 1978 to 1981. A major tax reform was also carried out in this period, and these changes reduced some of the inequities of the Mexican tax system.[20]

However, with the benefit of hindsight, some signs were already worrying by the late 1970s. The inflation rate had reached a plateau of around 18 percent and did not seem to be decreasing. Interest payments were increasing as nominal rates in the international credit markets floated upwards in an unprecedented way. Few investments were directed to the export sector, although two exceptions are worth noting: the motor-vehicle industry – where a new generation of plants was being built with state-of-the-art technology, explicitly designed to compete in the world markets – and the petrochemicals sector, where the public sector was investing heavily.

The whole strategy had been based on: (1) the premise of a long-term foreign exchange and fiscal abundance from oil exports (and the 1979–1980 oil price hike had only confirmed expectations that the era of high real oil prices had come to stay); and (2) the notion that the external debt problem was over, given the low real interest rates that had so far prevailed. Thus when the oil market started to crumble and foreign interest rates drastically jumped upwards in 1981, both of these shocks were taken to be transitory, and thus to be dealt with by additional external finance. Short-term external indebtedness was accelerated in an effort to sustain economic expansion. The increase in foreign indebtedness in 1981 was equivalent to 10 percent of GDP and by the end of that year the account deficit reached 12.5 million dollars, half of it due to interest payments, while capital flight was soaring. Indeed, the whole international economic environment that made the oil boom possible had been tragically misperceived (by the government, foreign banks and international financial institutions alike) and when this became clear Mexico suddenly became a highly indebted country, that is, an over-indebted borrower given the new levels of interest rates and export revenues with which the old debt had to be serviced. In 1982, the oil boom was over.

The shift in the market–state balance since the mid-1980s

The Mexican economy was subject to two major external shocks during the 1980s: the 1982 debt crisis, which increased debt service and curtailed new external finance, and the 1986 oil price shock, which dramatically cut off a major part of the country's main source of foreign exchange and fiscal revenues. These external shocks created imbalances in both the balance of payments and the fiscal accounts.

The strategies adopted to restore domestic and external balance and the adjustments that followed can be briefly summarized as follows. In the wake of the 1982 debt crisis, a very orthodox, stabilization-first strategy was adopted, with the aim of rapidly restoring price and balance-of-payments stability. This was to be followed by a gradualist approach to structural adjustment, which would promote an incremental process of resource reallocation in a stable and growth-oriented macroeconomic framework. This strategy – which prevailed as a policy stance during 1984 and part of 1985 – was soon to be abandoned in favor of an increasing radicalization of market reform measures which, contrary to conventional wisdom and advice, took place within the highly adverse macroeconomic environment created by the 1986 oil price shock. At the same time, and after the failure of successive orthodox attempts at inflation control, macroeconomic policy shifted in late 1987 to a rather heterodox approach to stabilization – the "Economic Solidarity Pact" – aiming at rapid disinflation through the combination of wage and price controls, an exchange rate freeze, and tight fiscal and monetary policy. From then, market reform measures, especially in the areas of trade policy and privatization, underwent a radical acceleration.

By the early 1990s the foreign exchange and fiscal gaps that were opened by the debt crisis and the oil shock had been closed. But the legacy of these external shocks – the collapse of public and private investments in the wake of the debt crisis and the loss of foreign exchange and fiscal revenues after the 1986 oil shock – had been harsh. Together with the stagnation of productive activity and the contraction of the population real incomes that followed, these shocks adversely affected the economy's growth potential by reducing the domestic savings rate and producing an aging of the capital stock and lower overall economic efficiency.[21] The economy emerged weaker, rather than stronger, from the years of crisis and adjustment.

At the same time, a "great transformation" had been taking place, if we may appropriate Polanyi's expression for events of a different scale. Balance of payments liberalization and the North American Free Trade Agreement (NAFTA) have closely integrated the economy with that of the US, both in terms of trade and capital flows. Foreign participation in the economy has increased through direct investments in new plants, as well as mergers and acquisitions, following the elimination of restrictions on foreign ownership. State banks and public enterprises have, with few exceptions, been turned into private hands. Privatization revenues, together with debt relief (under the 1989 Brady Plan) and fiscal adjustment allowed the government to reduce its debt, as a proportion of GDP, to rather low levels by international standards. A market-oriented rural economy emerged following far reaching changes in the land tenure system, price policies, and the privatization or elimination of state enterprises and its substitution by a combination of subsidies and public programs. In sum, a massive reform process occurred with a view to giving a larger economic role to the private sector and greater scope to market forces, and to accelerating integration into the international economy.[22]

Some policy reforms – especially those affecting the domestic regulatory framework – were long overdue (as exemplified most strikingly by the regulations in road transportation) and, overall, were clearly desirable on both efficiency and equity grounds.[23] Their adverse impacts have been rather limited or even absent, and the benefits of regulatory changes in many areas have by and large exceeded the costs. These have not been, however, the most radical reforms, nor the most beneficial. In what follows we focus on the most import- ant of these reforms – privatization and state reform, trade, investment and financial liberalization – and on an evaluation of their effects.

Privatization and economic efficiency

The case for greater selectivity in state participation in the economy and, indeed, for state disengagement in a number of productive activities, has been based on macroeconomic grounds: a government rationed in credit markets, pressing social needs to be met, and a private sector with ample financial resources abroad ready to be invested in previously state-dominated activities which do not have a high social priority.[24] The case is certainly extremely powerful; but this is so for macroeconomic reasons related to the special conditions of the 1980s. It has less significance for the long-term growth potential of the economy, beyond the promise (which so far largely remains just that) of a con- siderable expansion in human capital investments that huge privatization rev- enues make possible.

There is also, of course, the more traditional microeconomic case for privati- zation based on the notion that greater participation of the private sector will bring about improvements in the overall efficiency of investment. If the latter is a positive function of the share of private investment in overall investment, then part, if not all, of the drop in the overall rate of accumulation could be compen- sated for by the shift in the composition of investment. And as shown in Table 7.6, there has indeed been a dramatic shift in the composition of investment during the 1980s: from 56 percent in 1980–1981, the share of the private sector in total fixed investment rose to 77 percent ten years later and then to 84 percent by the late 1990s.

The first point to be made in addressing this issue is to recognize that the effi- ciency of overall investment does not depend only on its private/public sector composition, but also on the rate of investment itself, which affects investment efficiency through its consequences on the age distribution and the structure of the capital stock (residential/non-residential, net investment/depreciation). Now, as clearly shown also in Table 7.6, the shift in the private/public composition of investment was a result of the absolute decline in the rate of public investment, rather than of an absolute increase in private investment: the latter, as a fraction of GDP, was in the early 1990s at approximately the same levels as ten years earlier and only 3 to 4 percentage points higher in 2001–2002. Thus, if the share of private investment in overall investment increased, this was only because of the collapse of public investment rates. Unless the productivity of public invest- ment was actually negative – and nobody to our knowledge has argued this – the efficiency losses resulting from the absolute fall in the overall rate of investment are bound to outweigh any efficiency gains brought about by the shift in its

Table 7.6 Structure of gross fixed capital

	Investment								
	Total			Public			Private		
	GDP	Billions	% of GDP	Billions	% of total investment	% of GDP	Billions	% of total investment	% of GDP
1980	948.6	206.3	21.8	88.8	43.0	9.4	117.5	57.0	12.4
1981	1,029.5	239.8	23.3	108.8	45.4	10.6	131.1	54.6	12.7
1982	1,024.1	199.6	19.5	88.3	44.2	8.6	111.3	55.8	10.9
1983	988.4	143.1	14.5	56.5	39.5	5.7	86.6	60.5	8.8
1984	1,022.1	152.3	14.9	58.8	38.6	5.8	93.5	61.4	9.1
1985	1,044.5	164.3	15.7	59.3	36.1	5.7	105.0	63.9	10.0
1986	1,012.3	144.9	14.3	50.9	35.1	5.0	94.0	64.9	9.3
1987	1,029.8	144.7	14.1	44.6	30.8	4.3	100.1	69.2	9.7
1988	1,043.0	162.5	15.6	40.6	25.0	3.9	121.9	75.0	11.7
1989	1,085.8	171.9	15.8	43.5	25.3	4.0	128.4	74.7	11.8
1990	1,142.0	194.5	17.0	48.4	24.9	4.2	146.1	75.1	12.8
1991	1,190.1	215.8	18.1	48.7	22.6	4.1	167.2	77.4	14.0
1992	1,232.3	239.2	19.4	47.1	19.7	3.8	192.2	80.3	15.6
1993	1,256.2	233.2	18.6	47.3	20.3	3.8	185.9	79.7	14.8
1994	1,312.2	252.7	19.3	64.9	25.7	4.9	187.9	74.3	14.3
1995	1,230.6	179.4	14.6	44.6	24.8	3.6	134.9	75.2	11.0
1996	1,293.9	208.9	16.1	38.0	18.2	2.9	170.9	81.8	13.2
1997	1,381.5	252.8	18.3	41.8	16.5	3.0	211.0	83.5	15.3
1998	1,449.3	278.8	19.2	38.7	13.9	2.7	240.1	86.1	16.6
1999	1,503.5	300.3	20.0	42.9	14.3	2.9	257.4	85.7	17.1
2000	1,602.3	334.4	20.9	54.5	16.3	3.4	279.9	83.7	17.5
2001	1,597.2	314.9	19.7	47.5	15.1	3.0	267.5	84.9	16.7
2002[a]	1,611.7	310.9	19.3	50.9	16.4	3.2	260.0	83.6	16.1

Sources: ECLAC and INEGI.

Note
a Preliminary figures.

composition. The rise in the capital-output ratio since 1982 is fully consistent with this conclusion.

In addition, the relationship between the efficiency and the composition of overall investment is surely more complex than generally assumed. It is likely to have the shape of a Laffer curve with low efficiency levels being consistent with both too high and too low shares of public investment. This is so because public investment itself, as much recent empirical research suggests,[25] affects positively the productivity of private investment, and thus at low levels of public investment, further reductions can bring about losses rather than gains in overall efficiency. Given the sharp contraction of public investments during the 1980s, and the fact that the microeconomic efficiency gains and performance improvements of the newly privatized enterprises are yet to be seen in most cases, the question arises as to whether the economy moved to the wrong side of the Laffer-type curve. In such circumstances, an increase in public investment in areas with high social returns and high positive externalities for the productivity of private investment is the best way of addressing the problem of investment efficiency.

Trade liberalization, productivity and growth

The results of trade policy reform are also controversial. Let us look first at the static efficiency gains expected by classical trade theory.[26] One of the striking features of the Mexican transition towards a liberalized trade regime is the smoothness of the microeconomic processes of resource reallocation. The absence of massive reallocation processes is revealed by the fact that current trends in the trade pattern and industrial structure are largely an extrapolation of the past. Beyond a few exceptions – such as the accelerated expansion of labor-intensive maquiladora exports in the 1990s – the reallocation processes have witnessed an extrapolation of past trends in the trade and industrial patterns marked by the increasing importance of heavy intermediates, consumer durables and capital goods. The counterpart of this smoothness and of the lack of reversal in the direction of structural change in manufacturing is, however, that the classic efficiency gains expected from trade liberalization cannot possibly be very important. For those expecting a large, painful but greatly beneficial reallocation of resources in favor of traditional exportable goods (labor- and natural resource-intensive), the experience with trade liberalization to date should have been, in fact, greatly disappointing.

In our view, two major factors explain these developments. First, and perhaps paradoxically, the adjustment to the debt crisis and declining terms of trade in the 1980s, and then later the adjustment to the 1994–1995 financial crisis, forced macroeconomic policy to provide unprecedented levels of "exchange rate protection," which facilitated the adjustment of industrial firms to a more open economy. The second is simply Mexico's successful import-substitution experience in the past and the advanced stage that intra-industry (and intra-firm) processes of specialization and trade had already reached by 1980, including in those capital-intensive, large-scale manufacturing industries which have been

Table 7.7 Employment, working hours and labor productivity

	1950	1973	1990	1998
GDP per person employed[a]	7,685	18,399	20,747	20,810
Labour productivity[b]	3.6	8.9	10.1	10.0
Employment, as a percentage of the population	30.8	26.3	29.4	32.0
	1950–1973	1973–1998	1973–1990	1900 1998
Growth of GDP per hour worked	4.1	0.5	0.7	−0.04

Source: Maddison (2001).

Notes
a In 1990 international dollars.
b GDP per hour worked (1990 international dollars per hour).
c Annual average compound growth rate.

partly responsible for the export boom of the last two decades. The industrial policy reforms of the late 1970s, especially in the automobile industry, gave further impulse to those processes. The incentives provided later by a very attractive exchange rate and by the mid-1980s trade reforms fell thus on an already fertile ground. The outstanding export performance of Mexico's manufacturing is thus, to a large degree, a legacy of the import substitution period and highlights in a very real sense its success: it led, indeed, to an irreversible change in the economy's structure of comparative advantages.

What can be said now about the dynamic effects of trade liberalization on productivity and growth performance?[27] In the economy as a whole, labor productivity has stagnated since the early 1980s (compared with a trend growth of the order of 4 percent per annum in 1950–1973; see Table 7.7), and this applies to the periods both before and after the 1985 trade reform. At the same time, growth in manufacturing productivity shows a recovery in the post-trade liberalization period since 1985 compared with the first half of the decade. Although difficult to disentangle from other effects, including those of privatizations, industrial policy and a declining real exchange rate from 1988 to 1994, trade liberalization's contribution to productivity growth appears to have been positive in a number of manufacturing industries.[28] In those sectors producing capital goods and heavy intermediates, it has facilitated a greater degree of intra-industry (and intra-firm) specialization in foreign trade, as suggested by the rapid and simultaneous expansion of both exports and imports in some of these industries. In some light manufacturing industries – such as food processing and segments of the textile industry – it has shaken out less efficient local producers or forced them to modernize, as conveyed by the fact that the recovery of productivity growth has taken place in the midst of a slowdown of output growth partly explained by the high rates of import penetration in these sectors. However, the benefits of import penetration, in terms of productivity performance, become much more doubtful when we look at other manufacturing sectors – such as the wood industry and other manufacturing – which also show a rapid displacement of local producers resulting from increased exposure to foreign competition. Here, the result of import penetration has been a worsening of both output and productivity performance whether compared with historical trends or to the period immediately preceding trade liberalization.

The surge in imports that followed the 1987–1988 acceleration of the trade-liberalization program had other impacts of doubtful value. Import trends from 1988 to 1994 – by which imports at current dollars grew at an annual rate of over 30 percent – left the country's current account balance in a very vulnerable position. These developments are also partly explained by the real appreciation of the peso during the period, the decline of the domestic savings rate, and the eventual recovery of aggregate demand and private investment. But the fact that the import boom was clearly linked to the trade liberalization measures of late 1987 provides a strong indication that trade liberalization since 1987 contributed to the worsening of the trade-off between growth and the current account of the balance of payments that preceded the 1994–1995 crisis.

Thus, while trade and foreign investment liberalization have resulted in fast export and labor productivity growth in a limited number of sectors, overall economic growth has remained problematic. GDP growth finally resumed at relatively fast rates from 1996 to 2000, but it did so in an exceptionally favorable international environment. The recovery turned out, indeed, to be short lived. The renewed appreciation of the peso eventually slowed down the export boom and the US recession starting in 2001 put an end to the short period of export-led growth. Since 2001 the economy has stagnated and income per capita is very likely to fall in 2003 for the third consecutive year. Rapid, sustained, and even economic growth is yet to be seen.

This experience raises serious doubts about the current industrial structure's ability to generate self-sustained growth. The counterpart of the processes of intra-firm and intra-industry trade specialization is that many, if not most, exporting sectors and firms, while dynamic, lack domestic linkages and a number of other industries have witnessed a "disintegration of linkages."[29] The consequences have been negative for the trade balance and learning processes. Moreover, the fragility of Mexico's pattern of industrial production and trade specialization goes beyond the lack of domestic linkages in export-oriented activities and the dependence of export demand on US economic activity. The increasing dominance of the maquiladora industry in export activities is a motive for concern. The maquiladora industry is characterized by a low potential for productivity growth, the counterpart of its high capacity of employment absorption. As the real exchange rate has appreciated again in the recent past and dollar wages have increased, profit margins have declined in the face of low and stagnant labor productivity. This, together with the US recession, has put a brake on the expansion of productive capacity and output in the maquiladora sector and has led to a sharp decline in employment starting in the third quarter of 2000. With no productivity growth, the maquiladoras constitute a sector that can only expand on the basis of low wages. Given the tendency of wages to increase in other sectors along with productivity gains, the maintenance of the "internal competitiveness" of the maquiladoras, i.e. their capacity to attract resources from the rest of the economy, would require a continuously undervalued currency.[30]

Financial liberalization, the capital surge and the financial crisis

If the efficiency and productivity effects of market reforms have been unable to make up for the loss of growth potential during the 1980s, what about their effects on external capital inflows and the prospects for increasing the rate of accumulation by these means? Would the shift in the market/state balance bring about a permanently higher flow of external savings, significantly greater than historical rates that would allow an increase in the rate of accumulation, despite the sharp decline of the domestic savings rate? Such was the optimistic outlook of many observers in the early 1990s, for whom Mexico, a model reformer and successful emerging market, would turn into a Latin American economic miracle. These optimistic expectations became rampant when NAFTA was approved in 1993.

Market reforms and positive external shocks, such as the fall in foreign interest rates in the early 1990s, together with the beginning of NAFTA negotiations, contributed in three main ways to a capital surge from 1990 to 1993. The first was the liberalization of domestic financial markets. (In a 1994 study on the determinants of capital inflows, Ros found that the opening of the bond market was the main determinant of the "change in asset preferences" during the period). The second was a drastic reduction in the country risk premium – an improved image of Mexico as a "good place to invest" – which resulted from the debt relief agreement, the fall in international interest rates and the repayment of foreign debt, financed by the large privatization revenues of 1991–1992. The third, which interacted with the reduction of country risk, was the real appreciation of the peso and the very high interest rates that prevailed in the initial stages of the disinflation program of late 1987.

The size and composition of capital inflows, heavily biased towards short-term portfolio investments, had three consequences on the economy. First, the continuous appreciation of the real exchange rate that was taking place in the midst of a radical trade liberalization produced a profit squeeze in the tradable sectors of the economy with negative consequences on investment (Ros, 2001). Second, as a result of the difficulties in intermediating massive capital inflows, an allocation of resources biased towards consumption rather than investment (Trigueros, 1998), reinforced the decline in the private savings rate, while the bias towards the production of non-tradable goods resulted, together with the real appreciation, in a slow economic expansion. Third, an increasing financial fragility, which resulted from the concentration of the inflows in highly liquid assets, accompanied a progressive deterioration of the banking system balance sheets (Trigueros, 1998).

These trends should have been a legitimate concern for economic policy. They were not. By 1993, the current account deficit reached levels of the order of 6–7 percent of GDP and by early 1994 the capital surge was over. Throughout 1994 the authorities financed the massive current account deficit through the depletion of international reserves. Clearly the government incorrectly diagnosed the causes of the macroeconomic disequilibria, as the pressure on the reserves and dilemmas of policy makers were considered temporary and would be corrected without needing to depreciate the exchange rate. No significant exchange rate depreciation was implemented on the grounds that it would rekindle inflation, and would "give alarming signs to the market," augment capital flight and trigger a balance of payments crisis. In any case such policy was steady, but surely being perceived as non-sustainable by investors in Mexico's capital and money markets. In the course of the year, the Bank of Mexico not only had to allow for increases in the interest rates on CETES and Tesobonos (Mexican Treasury Bonds), but had to allow for greater guarantees on the rates of return on government paper denominated in foreign currency. In any case, the foreign exchange reserves kept being depleted, ultimately creating the perception that macroeconomic policy was unsustainable. At the end of 1994, scarcely a year after NAFTA came into effect, the Mexican economy was in the midst of a financial crisis and on the brink of the worst recession since the great depression of the 1930s. Moreover, the country had been experiencing instability and political violence throughout 1994, starting with the armed revolt of the Zapatistas in January (the same day that NAFTA came into effect).

The boom and bust cycle that culminated with the banking crisis of 1994–1995, was a consequence, at least in part, of an excessive reliance on financial deregulation and capital market liberalization (Clavijo and Boltvinik, 2000; Lustig 2002; OECD 2002). The result of that cycle was a bankrupt banking system whose bailout added some 20 percentage points of GDP to the public debt and left those households and firms, mostly small and medium enterprises with no access to foreign finance, virtually without access to bank credit. It is ironic that the banking sector returned to a situation of credit rationing characteristic of the era of financial repression that preceded the financial liberalization of the late 1980s. This situation has been an obstacle to faster growth and has also reinforced the dual structure of the productive sector.[31]

Recent growth and investment performance

After the decline of 6.2 percent in real GDP in 1995 – the sharpest drop in more than fifty years – economic growth resumed in 1996–2000. However, its expansion abruptly stopped in 2001–2002 and GDP per capita actually declined in real terms. On average, from 1985 to 2002, GDP expanded at an annual rate of 2.2 percent, or barely half a percentage point above the rate of population growth. By the end of 2003, in constant dollars GDP will be barely above 20 percent of the US figure, a gap almost 10 percentage points wider than in 1981 and similar to the level recorded 50 years earlier. Thus in these five decades, in terms of real

GDP per capita the Mexican economy has so far failed to "catch up" in any significant way with its northern neighbor.

Crucial to the slowdown in Mexico's rate of economic expansion has been a weak investment performance.[32] The failure of capital formation to grow at a fast pace – after the years of decline during the debt crisis – has deterred the expansion and modernization of productive capacity and simultaneously restricted the growth of aggregate demand. Indeed, gross fixed investment followed a path similar to that of GDP in real terms. It increased rapidly during the oil boom, then collapsed in 1982–1987, and began a slow recovery in 1988 (Figure 7.1). This rebound gained some strength in 1990–1992, responding to the favorable expectations associated with the beginning of NAFTA negotiations. The recovery was cut short in 1995, but vigorously continued in 1996–2000. However, in 2001–2002 investment again collapsed in real terms. In synthesis, during the last two decades, the investment process has been wanting.

This poor performance is even more evident in the evolution of the investment/GDP ratio. During most of the 1970s this ratio followed a downward trend that was drastically but only temporarily offset by the oil boom, reaching a historical peak (26.5 percent of GDP) in 1981. However, the recovery was very short lived. In 1982–1983 the ratio fell again, placing its value way below 20 percent for the first time in years. It hovered around 18 percent thereafter and only began rising at the end of the 1980s. Its rise was sharply curtailed in 1995 when it dropped 5 percentage points, to reach an all time low of 14.6 percent. And as

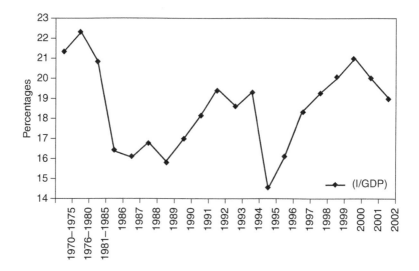

Figure 7.1 Investment to GDP Ratio, 1970–2002 (source: prepared by the authors from table 4 of Mattar, Moreno-Brid and Peres (2002), on the basis of ECLAC and INEGI data).

Note
The figures for 1970–1988 were calculated on the basis of data in 1980 constant pesos: figures for 1989–2001 were based on data in 1993 constant pesos.

mentioned above, in spite of its subsequent expansion, by 2001–2002 it stood at 19.5 percent, still below its 1980–1981 levels. These ratios are way below the 25 percent minimum that UNCTAD (2003) has identified as necessary to launch a process of high and sustained growth in less developed countries.

The disappointing performance of investment is a reason for concern over Mexico's future economic growth. What are the causes behind it? Were there any limitations or shortcomings in the macroeconomic reforms that failed to consider or misperceived the nature of key determinants of Mexico's investment process? Recent research on the topic has identified a set of factors that help explain Mexico's poor performance of investment.

First, the reforms were adopted in a stagnating economy under severe rationing in the access to foreign or domestic capital and finance. The adverse economic environment was aggravated by the fall in public investment, because "crowding in" between public and private investment has historically been more important than "crowding out" effects (UNCTAD, 2003).

In addition, the reforms had the explicit goal of eliminating all types of incentives, including measures to promote domestic investment both aggregate and in specific sectors. No attempt was made to orient domestic spending to investment as opposed to consumption expenditure. Such explicit refusal to promote investment was combined with the uncertainty inherent in any radical change in development strategy. Not surprisingly such uncertainty was far from favorable to investment, thus leading to the postponement or interruption of investment projects. The elimination of sector incentives had an especially strong adverse impact on manufacturing investment, given that manufacturing had traditionally been the most favored sector under the previous development model based on import substitution and state-led industrialization. The adverse incentives – exacerbated by the intense and sudden competition from imports – reduced manufacturing's relative rate of return, which in turn curbed investment. The appreciation of the real exchange rate in 1988–1994 vis-à-vis the US dollar, further conspired against investment in manufacturing and more generally in tradable goods sectors. While real exchange-rate appreciation can encourage fixed investment in developing countries by lowering the relative prices of imported machinery and equipment, it also shifts relative prices in favor of non-tradables, inducing a reallocation of labor and investment away from the production of tradable goods and services. This last effect appears to have dominated in the Mexican case.

State reform and the tasks of development policy

The other side of market reform is the retreat of the state and its restructuring. By shrinking in size, the chances improve that it will be able to do a better job in its priority tasks, or so the argument goes. However, while the state is smaller, it is not necessarily more effective. The tax burden continues to be extremely low by international standards (OECD, 2002). At 12 percent of GDP in the late 1990s, tax revenues are below those of Latin American countries with similar income per capita and well below those of OECD countries. As a result, the fiscal accounts continue to be highly vulnerable to changes in oil income, which still represent around a third of total government revenues. Together with the loss of policy instruments and the reorientation of monetary policy from growth to purely stabilization objectives as well as the volatility of external capital flows, this is the source of a major macroeconomic problem: the fact that it contributes to pro-cyclical macroeconomic policies that exacerbate the negative effects of shocks on economic activity.

Nor is the state necessarily more efficient. Mexico's fiscal adjustment did not encourage a greater internal efficiency of the public sector, despite, or perhaps because of, its massive character. Especially before 1985, fiscal adjustment was, by and large, achieved through deep cuts in public investment and the real salaries of public employees, hardly a useful means to improve the efficiency of the state and its bureaucracy. Moreover, the state's retreat has gone well beyond areas where the private sector has a comparative advantage. In fact, public infrastructure investment has been the main victim of fiscal adjustment in the context of falling oil prices. Giugale et al. (2001) strikingly illustrate with two figures the close correlation between oil price declines, fiscal deficit cuts and reductions in public investment (the correlation coefficient between the last two turns out to be 0.82 from 1980 to 1997). As a result, public investment was barely 3 percent of GDP in 2001–2002 down from 5 percent in 1994 and 10 percent in 1980–1981 (Table 7.6). It is also clear that, despite some positive recent trends in social spending, state disengagement has not served its main stated purpose: the expansion of social infrastructure. The main contribution of privatization revenues was to support (very effectively, no doubt) stabilization efforts. The revenues temporarily compensated for the inflation tax decrease and strengthened the capital account of the balance of payments through the financial assets that the private sector had to bring back home to purchase public enterprises on sale.

The implications of all this are more important than generally acknowledged because the priority tasks of the state, social policy in particular, are today far more formidable than in the past. This is so for several reasons. There is, first, the accumulated backlog of unmet social needs and the legacy of increased inequality from the 1980s. In the face of slow growth in agriculture and the expansion of the urban informal sector, the recovery of social spending in the 1990s has not prevented an increase in the number of poor and a persistently high inequality in income distribution. Lustig (2002) shows that income inequality measured by the Gini concentration coefficient increased quite sharply from 1984 to 1989 (around four percentage points) and then fell from 1989 to 1994 (although remaining slightly above its 1984 level). Then from 1994 to 2000, the OECD (2002) estimates show a slight increase in income inequality (the Gini rises from 0.477 to 0.481). Poverty rates (both extreme and moderate) show a similar behavior across time while the number of poor shows a continuous increase through 1994.

Second, there are at least two ways in which the present development pattern is exacerbating social disparities. The state retreat from agriculture and the reform of the land tenure system may have brought private capital and prosperity to some rural areas, but has also inadvertently tended to impoverish large masses of rural workers in a similar way that agricultural modernization under the Porfiriato did on purpose and on a much more massive scale. There has been a clearly differentiated behavior between the commercial sector producing exportable goods – which benefited from and responded positively to the reforms (exports have grown by 70 percent during the first five years of NAFTA) – and the ejido sector, which has not (imports grew by 60 percent affecting this sector which largely produces importable goods). Today, this sector barely survives on an increasing integration into non-farm activities (about 40 percent of its income comes from non-farm sources including remittances).[33] The overall stagnation of agricultural output and the persistence of rural poverty are related to the reforms themselves, as recognized by Giugale et al. (2001). The downward trend in real agricultural prices throughout the 1990s was strengthened by the removal of trade protection (and exchange rate overvaluation in the early part of the decade). The elimination of extension programs and technical assistance has affected a large proportion of small producers. The state's retreat from distribution was followed by the domination of marketing channels by oligopolistic intermediaries that depress the prices obtained by producers, affecting particularly the poorest areas. In the absence of competitive markets and without proper consideration to the large regional diversity and income heterogeneity of the Mexican countryside, liberalization did not yield the expected benefits.

On the other hand, the benefits of a greater integration with the international economy, and with the US in particular, are also being very unevenly distributed within the country. Greater integration has been accompanied by a substantial increase of the wage premium on skilled labor with a resulting relative decline in unskilled labor incomes, a major cause of persistent inequality. As documented by Godínez (2000) and Dussel Peters (2000), general regional trends from 1970 to 1985 pointed towards a de-concentration of economic activity (away from the main industrial centers in the metropolitan area of Mexico City, Nuevo León and Jalisco) and convergence of income levels. Since 1988, a process of divergence has been taking place, especially as the northern states – linked to export activities – have been rapidly increasing their share in national income. By contrast, the relatively poor south (with the exception of Quintana Roo, which benefited from the expansion of tourism) has been lagging behind. These regional trends are clearly linked to the economy's structural changes, such as the lagging grain agriculture, expanding export sectors of agro-industrial products, fruits and vegetables and the rapidly growing export-oriented manufacturing activities in the northern and central areas. Just as in the late eighteenth century the "opening of North Atlantic trade" exacerbated the "fragmentation of regional markets," there is today a tendency towards a deepening of regional disparities, especially between a prosperous north increasingly integrated with the US economy and a poor and backward south plunged into agricultural stagnation.

Finally, and no less fundamentally, by abandoning the trade and industrial policy instruments that have worked successfully in the past without any effective replacement, current development strategy encourages the exploitation of present rather than potential comparative advantages. The basic task of development policy – the task of changing and enhancing the present endowment of resources and, over time, shifting the pattern of comparative advantages towards higher value-added, technology-intensive activities – falls now fully, in the absence of industrial policy, upon social policies. A proportionate response to this challenge could actually make things better than otherwise (that is, than, under an active industrial policy with little social policy, for example), but our point is that the challenge itself is much bigger and the response remains to be seen. A less than proportionate response would lead to freezing the present stage of development – getting stuck in the relatively unskilled and low-pay tasks of the production processes of capital-intensive industries. This is a far from desirable prospect for a country that needs to grow rapidly to increase the living standards of its 100 million people.

Concluding comments

All this leads us to the final and most important aspect of the overall reform process, on which we can only raise the relevant questions. Is the shift in the market–state balance a sign that, after having reduced economic backwardness by state-sponsored industrialization, use of a different set of ideas becomes more suitable in the new stage, a shift that is the natural companion of the transition from Gerschenkronian to Schumpeterian entrepreneurship? Or is it still the case that "to break through the barriers of stagnation in a backward country, to ignite the imaginations of men, and to place their energies in the service of economic development, a stronger medicine is needed than the promise of better allocation of resources ..." (Gerschenkron, 1952)? Dealing with these questions falls outside the scope of this chapter, and of the wisdom of its authors. But on their answers rests Mexico's longer-term prospects for rapid economic development.

What we can say, however, is that the origin of the adjustment problems and the new problems created by the reform process are not being adequately perceived in current development policy. First, the notion that the crisis was brought about by the exhaustion of past development strategies should not be taken for granted, even though we would be very far from defending every single aspect of past development strategies. Secondly, the solution to the new obstacles may require more and better, rather than less, state participation in the economy. As we have tried to show, the source of these new problems has to be found in part in the retreat of the state, in such areas as public infrastructure investment. But as a result of the shift in ideological climate, very little attention is being given to these problems and to what government policy can do about them while, at the same time, too much is expected from the efficiency gains of market reforms. Is it the case that, just as a century and a half ago, the real obstacles to economic development are being misperceived?

Notes

1 This paper was presented at the LACEA meeting in Cholula, Puebla on October 10, 2003 and the EEA meeting in New York on March 4, 2005. The authors want to acknowledge the valuable research assistance of Mr Rubén Guerrero and comments on a previous version by Ted Beatty, Rolando Cordera, Amitava Dutt, Julie Lennox, Julio López, Martín Puchet, Ajit Singh, Carlos Tello and Samuel Valenzuela.

2 This chapter is intended to be an extended and much revised version of an essay published by the authors nearly ten years ago, at the time NAFTA was put in place (see Moreno-Brid and Ros, 1994).

3 Ethnic distinctions in the access to employment, justice and in fiscal treatment – which, among other things, had severely restricted capital and labor mobility – were formally abolished; many corporate privileges, including most of the guilds, were eliminated, while corporate property rights were limited to the Church and the Indian communities and town councils. The number of royal monopolies on the production and distribution of many commodities was reduced and their activities regulated; efforts were also made to modernize the judiciary and revise archaic judicial codes.

4 In the 55 years between independence and the Porfiriato, the presidency changed hands 75 times (Haber, 1989). The most disastrous consequence of the prolonged civil strife was the loss to the US of half of the national territory in the mid-nineteenth century. Fifty years after the 1848 Treaty which ended the US–Mexico war, and also after the beginning of the California "Gold Rush," the mineral output alone of the lost territories exceeded Mexico's total GNP (Coatsworth, 1978).

5 See, in particular, García Alba (1974) and Coatsworth (1978). The reason is that the effect of the tithe in pushing labor and capital out of private agriculture was probably very small because the Church itself, and the Indian villages, produced a major portion of the country's farm products and livestock. And the net effect on GNP was, in any case, probably positive since differences in productivity between private agriculture and the rest of the economy suggest that nonagricultural activities were already more productive than agriculture.

6 Another figure worth mentioning is Estevan de Antuñano, a creole industrialist, whose very many pamphlets best articulated the case for protectionism and industrialization.

7 For accounts of economic growth during the Porfiriato, see Beatty (2001), Rosenzweig (1965) and Solís (2000).

8 The importance of these obstacles to economic development was well recognized at the time. In the words of Matías Romero: "This nation ... has in its soil immense treasures of agricultural and mineral wealth, which now cannot be exploited due to the lack of capital and communications" (cited by Rosenzweig, 1965, translation by the authors).

9 The railway system expanded from 900 to 19,000 km in the 1880s. According to Coatsworth's estimates, this brought an 80 per cent reduction in freight costs per kilometer from 1878 to 1910.

10 The depreciation of silver was provoked by the adoption of the Gold standard towards 1870 in the advanced countries (Cardenas and Manns, 1989). It amounted to a continuous real devaluation of the Mexican peso of 26 percent throughout the 1890s. See Zabludovsky (1984) which assesses the view, held by Rosenzweig (1965) and Nugent (1973), that devaluation promoted export-led growth and the PPP view of Limantour, Porfirio Díaz's minister of finance, according to which the silver depreciation was ultimately reflected in the price level. Zabludovsky's evaluation of the evidence supports the first view.

11 Having defaulted on its external debt on six different occasions between 1824 and 1880, in 1889 the Mexican government finally reached an agreement with foreign bankers on rescheduling Mexico's foreign debt. By the early 1890s, the country's

access to international capital markets was restored and, from then until 1911, Mexico's external debt increased 300 per cent, mostly to finance public works in infrastructure.

12 Mining would most likely have remained abandoned without the railway expansion as neither the necessary capital inputs for its development nor the commercialization of mineral products would have been profitable.

13 As noted by Haber (1989), the extent of poverty was such that the increase in the price of corn due to any bad harvest would reduce workers' consumption of manufactures by enough to provoke a crisis in the cotton garment industry.

14 For accounts of finance, banking and industry during the Porfiriato, see Batiz and Canudas (1980), Haber (1989) and Bortz and Haber (2002).

15 For detailed accounts of the creation of the PNR and its role in long-term political stability, see Newell and Rubio (1984).

16 The Bank of Mexico was established in 1925, and started to operate as a central bank in the early 1930s as a response to the Depression. By then, the Public Agricultural Credit Bank had been established, and the creation of other banks followed. In 1933, the Budget Ministry created the National Finance Entity, which was soon to become Nacional Financiera, the first fully fledged development bank and the financial pivot for industrial and other long-term investment.

17 At the time of the War, in 1942, Mexico and the US signed a reciprocal free trade agreement committing both sides to freezing tariffs on various products. A year later, however, the agreement was cancelled and Mexico proceeded to raise trade tariffs and, for the first time, in 1944, imposed license requirements (King, 1970).

18 By 1972, the debt–GDP ratio and the debt-service–exports ratio had both reached 18 per cent (compared with 1 per cent in 1946). While these magnitudes did not yet imply a serious macroeconomic imbalance, they reflect the dynamic evolution of foreign indebtedness during the period.

19 The belief that development, especially social development, could be accelerated while sacrificing fiscal discipline was rightly criticized by orthodox economists at the time. See Solís (1977) for a forceful statement.

20 An adjustment for inflation was introduced in personal income taxation. A value-added tax and a new corporate income tax were established. The tax base broadened as loop-holes were closed, and the whole administrative and compliance process was simplified. The 1–5 minimum wage bracket went from contributing 58 percent of labor income tax collections in 1978, to 28 per cent in 1981; whereas the highest wage bracket – more than 15 minimum wages – went from 8 to 25 percent of the total. For a detailed description, see Gil Díaz (1987).

21 For a detailed analysis, see Ros (1993).

22 For a detailed review of the reform process, see Lustig (2002).

23 For an analysis of reforms in the domestic regulatory framework, see Lustig (2002) and Ros (1991). For an international comparison of policy reform in these areas, see Williamson (1990).

24 Under such conditions, a clear comparative advantage argument can be made for privatization, even if public enterprises had absolute efficiency advantages over private firms, for society as a whole would clearly gain from a reallocation of public investments from areas where social and private returns do not differ greatly from activities yielding a higher social/private returns differential.

25 See in the public capital literature, the studies by Aschauer (1989a, 1989b, 2000), Deno (1988), Munnell (1990, 1992) and Easterly and Rebelo (1993), among others.

26 For a detailed discussion of resource reallocation processes see Ros (1992) and, in particular, Moreno-Brid (1988) for an analysis of a most important aspect of these processes, the restructuring of the automobile industry and its role in the 1980s manufacturing export boom.

27 For a more detailed analysis, see Ros (1992, 1993).

28 For example, in the case of the auto industry, one of the star performers in the productivity growth recovery, the improvement appears to be associated with its special policy regime and the international developments in this sector since the late 1970s. In particular, the export-oriented investments of the late 1970s and early 1980s, following the 1977 reform of the automotive decree, must have made a significant contribution to the technical modernization of the industry, whose effects were only fully felt well into the 1980s as the new plants created by these investments came into operation and rapidly expanded their share in the industry's output (see Moreno-Brid, 1988). In the basic metals sector, the industry's rationalization has probably been determined by a government program with precisely that goal, and which included the shutdown and privatization of many public enterprises in a sector where the latter have traditionally shown a relatively high share of the industry's output.

29 Dussel Peters (2000) illustrates this with a case study of the pharmaceutical industry where the share of locally produced raw materials fell from around 80 percent in the late 1980s to around 20 percent in 1998.

30 See Frenkel and Ros (2003) for an analysis of the performance of the maquiladora industry in the 1990s.

31 Giugale *et al.* (2001) and Dussel Peters (2000) document how the credit decline affected differently large firms and small and medium enterprises, and the large and increasing gap between the export performances of these two types of enterprises.

32 For an extended analysis of the performance of investment in Mexico's manufacturing sector after the macroeconomic reforms see Moreno-Brid (1999).

33 See Giugale *et al.* (2001).

References

Aschauer, David A. (1989a) "Is Public Expenditure Productive?" *Journal of Monetary Economics* 23, pp. 177–200.

Aschauer, David A. (1989b) "Does Public Capital Crowd Out Private Capital?" *Journal of Monetary Economics* 24, pp. 171–88.

Aschauer, David A. (2000) "Public Capital and Economic Growth: Issues in Quantity, Finance and Efficiency," *Economic Development and Cultural Change* 48, pp. 391–406.

Batiz, José. A. and Enrique Canudas (1980) "Aspectos Financieros y Monetarios (1880–1910)." In *México en el Siglo XIX (1821–1910)*, edited by Ciro Cardoso, México, DF: Editorial Nueva Imagen.

Beatty, Edward (2001) *Institutions and Investment*, Stanford University Press.

Beatty, Edward (2002) "Commercial Policy in Porfirian Mexico: the Structure of Protection." In *The Mexican Economy 1870–1930. Essays on the Economic History of Institutions, Revolution and Growth*, edited by J. L. Bortz and S. Haber, Stanford: Stanford University Press.

Bortz, J. L. and S. Haber (2002) *The Mexican Economy 1870–1930: Essays on the Economic History of Institutions, Revolution and Growth*, Stanford: Stanford University Press.

Cárdenas, Eduardo (1985) "Algunas Cuestiones Sobre la Depresión Mexicana del Siglo XIX," *Revista Latinoamericana de Historia Económica y Social* 3.

Cárdenas, E. and C. Manns (1989) "Inflación y Estabilización Monetaria en México durante la Revolución," *El Trimestre Económico* 56(221), Mexico City: Fondo de Cultura Económica, January–March.

Clavijo, F. and J. Boltvinik (2000) "La Reforma Financiera, el Crédito y el Ahorro," in F. Clavijo (ed.), *Reformas Económicas en México 1982–1999, Lecturas El Trimestre Económico*, No. 92, Mexico City: Fondo de Cultura Económica.

Coatsworth, John (1978) "Obstacles to Economic Growth in Nineteenth-Century Mexico," *American Historical Review* 83(1), February, pp. 80–100.

Coatsworth, John (1989) "The Decline of the Mexican Economy, 1800–1860." In *América Latina en la Época de Simón Bolivar*, edited by Reinhard Liehr, Berlin: Colloquium Verlag.

Coatsworth, John (1990) *Los Orígenes del Atraso. Nueve Ensayos de Historia Económica de México en los Siglos XVIII y XIX*, México, D.F.: Alianza Editorial Mexicana.

Deno, Kevin T. (1988), "The Effect of Public Capital on U.S. Manufacturing Activity: 1970 to 1978," *Southern Economic Journal* 55, pp. 400–11.

Dussel Peters, Enrique (2000) *Polarizing Mexico: The Impact of Liberalization Strategy.* Boulder, Co.: Lynne Rienner Publishers.

Easterly, William and Sergio Rebelo (1993) "Fiscal Policy and Economic Growth," *Journal of Monetary Economics* 32, pp. 417–58.

Frenkel, Roberto and Jaime Ros (2003) "Macroeconomic policies, trade specialization, and labor market adjustment in Argentina and Mexico," Buenos Aires, CEDES, mimeo, unpublished.

García Alba, Pascual (1974) "Los Liberales y los Bienes del Clero," El Colegio de México.

Gerschenkron, Alexander (1952) "Economic Backwardness in Historical Perspective." In *The Progress of Underdeveloped Countries*, edited by Bert Hoselitz, Chicago: University of Chicago Press.

Gil Díaz, Francisco (1987) "Some Lessons from Mexico's Tax Reform." In *The Theory of Taxation for Developing Countries*, edited by David Newberry and Nicholas Stern, Oxford: Oxford University Press.

Giugale, Marcelo, Olivier Lafourcade and Vinh H. Nguyen (2001) *Mexico. A Comprehensive Development Agenda for the New Era*, Washington, DC: The World Bank.

Godínez, V. M. (2000) "La Economía de las Regiones y el Cambio Estructural," in F. Clavijo (ed.), *Reformas Económicas en México, 1982–1999, Lecturas El Trimestre Económico*, No. 92, Mexico City: Fondo de Cultura Económica.

Haber, Stephen (1989) *Industry and Underdevelopment: The Industrialization of Mexico, 1890–1940*, Stanford: Stanford University Press.

Hernández Laos, Enrique (1989) "Efectos del Crecimiento Económico y la Distribución del Ingreso Sobre la Pobreza y la Pobreza Extrema en México (1960–1988)," México, DF: Universidad Autónoma Metropolitana.

INEGI (1985) *Estadísticas Históricas de México*, México, DF: Instituto Nacional de Estadística, Geografía e Informática.

King, Timothy (1970) *Mexico: Industrialization and Trade Policies since 1940*, Oxford: Oxford University Press.

Kuntz Ficker, Sandra (2002) "Institutional Change and Foreign Trade in Mexico, 1870–1911." In *The Mexican Economy 1870–1930: Essays on the Economic History of Institutions, Revolution and Growth*, edited by Jeffrey L. Bortz and Stephen Haber, Stanford: Stanford University Press.

Lustig, Nora (2002) *México: Hacia la Reconstrucción de una Economía.* México, DF: El Colegio de México y Fondo de Cultura Económica.

Maddison, Angus (1989) *The World Economy in the 20th Century*, Paris: Development Centre of the Organization for Economic Co-operation and Development.

Maddison, Angus (2001) *The World Economy: a Millenial Perspective*, Paris: OECD.

Manzanilla Schaffer, Víctor (1963) "Reforma Agraria en México." In *Mexico: 50 Años de Revolución*, México, DF: Fondo de Cultura Económica.

Máttar, J., J. C. Moreno-Brid and W. Peres (2002) "Foreign Investment in Mexico after Economic Reforms," *CEPAL: Serie Estudios y Perspectivas*, No 10.

Moreno-Brid, Juan Carlos (1988) "The Motor-Vehicle Industry in Mexico in the Eighties," Geneva: ILO.

Moreno-Brid, J. C. (1999) "Mexico's Economic Growth and the Balance of Payments: a Cointegration Analysis," *International Review of Applied Economics* 13(2), pp. 149–59.

Moreno-Brid, Juan Carlos and Jaime Ros (1994) "Market Reform and the Changing Role of the State in Mexico: a Historical Perspective." In *The State, Markets and Development*, edited by Amitava Dutt, Kwan Kim and Ajit Singh, Cheltenham: Edward Elgar.

Mosk, Sanford (1950), *Industrial Revolution in Mexico*, Berkeley: University of California Press.

Munnell, Alicia H. (1990) "How Does Public Infrastructure Affect Regional Economic Performance?" In *Is there a Shortfall in Public Capital Investment?*, edited by Alicia Munnell, Boston: Federal Reserve Bank of Boston.

Munnell, Alicia H. (1992) "Policy Watch: Infrastructure Investment and Economic Growth, " *Journal of Economic Perspectives* 6(4), autumn, pp. 189–98.

Newell, Roberto and Luis Rubio (1984) *Mexico's Dilemma: the Political Origins of the Economic Crisis*, Boulder, Co.: Westview Press.

Nugent, J. B. (1973) "Exchange Rate Movements and Economic Development in the late XIX Century," *Journal of Political Economy* 84(5), September–October, pp. 1110–35.

OECD (2002) *OECD Economic Surveys: Mexico*. Paris: OECD

Ros, Jaime (1991) "The Effects of Government Policies on the Incentives to Invest, Enterprise Behavior and Employment: A Study of Mexico's Economic Reform in the Eighties," Working Paper No. 53, World Employment Programme Research, Geneva: ILO.

Ros, Jaime (1992) "Mexico's Trade and Industrialization Experience Since 1960: A Reconsideration of Past Policies and Assessment of Current Reforms," Helsinki: World Institute for Development Economics Research, WIDER.

Ros, Jaime (1993) "Trade Liberalization with Real Appreciation and Slow Growth: Sustainability Issues in Mexico's Trade Policy Reform," Helsinki: World Institute for Development Economics Research, WIDER.

Ros Jaime (1994) "Financial Markets and Capital Flows in Mexico." In *Foreign Capital in Latin America*, edited by José Antonio Ocampo and Roberto Steiner, Washington, DC: Inter American Development Bank.

Ros, Jaime (2001) "Del Auge de Capitales a la Crisis Financiera y Más Allá: México en los Noventa." In *Crisis Financieras en Países 'Exitosos'*, edited by Ricardo Ffrench-Davis, Santiago: CEPAL-McGraw Hill.

Rosenzweig, Fernando (1965) "El Desarrollo Económico de México de 1877 a 1911," *El Trimestre Económico*, 32(5), pp. 405–54.

Solís, Leopoldo (2000) *La Realidad Económica Mexicana: Retrovisión y Perspectivas*, México, DF: Fondo de Cultura Económica.

Solís, Leopoldo (1977) "A Monetary Will-O' the Wisp: Pursuit of Equity through Deficit Spending," Geneva: ILO.

Thomson, Guy (1986) "The Cotton Textile Industry in Puebla during the Eighteenth and Early Nineteenth Centuries." In *The Economies of Mexico and Peru during the Late Colonial Period, 1760–1810*, edited by Nils Jacobsen and Hans Jurgen Puhle, Berlin: Colloquium Verlag.

Trigueros, Ignácio (1998) "Flujos de Capital y Desempeño de la Inversión: México." In *Flujos de Capital e Inversión Productiva: Lecciones para América Latina*, edited by Ricardo Ffrench-Davis and Helmut Reisen, Santiago: CEPAL/OCDE, McGraw-Hill.

UNCTAD (2003) *Trade and Development Report 2003*, Geneva, UNCTAD.

Van Young, E. (1981), *Hacienda and Market in Eighteenth Century Mexico: The Rural Economy of the Guadalajara Region, 1675–1820*, Berkeley: University of California Press.

Van Young, Eric (1986) "The Age of Paradoxes: Mexican Agriculture at the End of the Colonial period, 1750–1810." In *The Economies of Mexico and Peru during the Late Colonial Period, 1760–1810*, edited by Nils Jacobsen and Hans Jurgen Puhle, Berlin: Colloquium Verlag.

Williamson, John (1990) "Latin American Adjustment: How Much Has Happened?" Washington, DC: Institute for International Economics.

Zabludovsky, J. (1994) "La Depreciación de la Plata y las Exportaciones," in E. Cárdenas (ed.), *Historia Económica de México, Lecturas El Trimestre Económico*, No. 64, Mexico City, Fondo de Cultura Económica.

8 The continuing relevance of the terms of trade and industrialization debates

José Antonio Ocampo and María Angela Parra

Introduction

Raúl Prebisch's conception of the world economy as a center–periphery system became perhaps the most distinctive feature of Latin American structuralist thinking in the early post-war years. Prebisch argued that the asymmetries between the center and the periphery of the world economy destroyed the basic premise of the international division of labor, making the transmission of technological change in the world economy "relatively slow and uneven." Thus, for developing countries, industrialization was not an end in itself, but the principal means at their disposal to obtain a share of the benefits of technological progress and gradually raise the standard of living of their population.[1] This was a very influential idea in practice, as it justified both industrialization in the developing world as the only way to overcome economic dependency, and the need to reform the international economic system, to break its asymmetric features and facilitate industrialization in the periphery.[2]

An element of this view of the world system was the hypothesis that the terms of trade of commodities – and thus of developing countries, which at the time were basically commodity-dependent in their export structure – tended to experience a long-term decline. This thesis, launched in the aftermath of World War II by both Raúl Prebisch and Hans Singer (then at the United Nations Department of Economic Affairs), has since generated a heated theoretical and empirical debate. According to Toye and Toye (2004), the Prebisch–Singer (P–S) hypothesis has continuing significance because it implies that, barring major changes in the structure of the world economy, the gains from trade will continue to be unevenly (and some would add, unfairly) distributed between nations exporting mainly primary products and those exporting manufactures. This could be, and has been, taken as an indicator of the need for both industrialization and protection.

The case for industrialization was, however, broader, and was indeed at the heart of most schools of development economics since their birth in the mid-twentieth century. For Singer, industrialization was necessary to take advantage of the externalities that it generates on other economic activities and the associated increases in productivity. In Prebisch's thinking, the case for industrialization was also based on the transformation of the production structures that characterize growing economies, which tend to reduce the relative weight of primary production and increase that of industry, a point made in more general terms by Simon Kuznets, among others, at the time.

In this chapter, we present a critical review of the terms of trade controversy and its relation to the industrialization debate. We argue that, notwithstanding the empirical validity of the Prebisch–Singer (P–S) hypothesis, it was not needed to justify industrialization in developing countries. In fact, the excessive focus on the terms of trade side-tracked the discussion from the broader consensus in place for some decades on the necessity of industrialization in order to take advantage of its externalities and dynamic economies of scale. This largely remains the case today, even without an accompanying consensus on how to achieve industrialization.

The chapter is divided into three parts. The first part reviews the terms of trade debate on theoretical and empirical grounds. The second explores the relationship between patterns of specialization and growth over the past four decades. As East Asian success has shown, industrialization, and especially the promotion of high technology production and exports, has been key to the rise of "the rest."[3] In contrast, specialization in primary commodities has not brought the benefits that believers in classical international division of labor would have expected. The third part of the paper presents some conclusions.

The terms of trade debate

Two theoretical variants

The history of the terms of trade debate can best be understood by referring to two different theoretical variants of the P–S hypothesis.[4] The first drew on the negative impact that the low income-elasticity of demand for primary commodities had on the terms of trade of developing countries. The second was based on the asymmetric functioning of factor and goods markets in the center and at the periphery of the world economy.[5]

The fundamental difference between the two variants is that, in the first case, the downward pressure on real commodity prices was generated through goods markets (i.e. via the *barter* terms of trade),[6] whereas, in the second, it was generated through factor markets (i.e. via *factorial* terms of trade)[7] and only indirectly, through the effects that production costs have in price formation, on the barter terms of trade. Another important difference is that the first variant applies only to primary commodities (or, more generally, to goods for which the income-elasticity of demand is inelastic), whereas the second affects all goods and services produced in developing countries, regardless of the characteristics of those goods and services or of their final demand.

The first variant of the hypothesis was based on the observation that, as noted, economic growth tends to trigger changes in the production structure over time and, in particular, generates a tendency towards a relative reduction in the size of the primary sector. This structural transformation is associated not only with the characteristics of final demand (especially the low income-elasticity of the demand for food products, i.e. Engel's law) but also with the fact that, in many cases, technological change in the production of manufactures entails reductions in raw materials costs or production of synthetic materials.

These variations in the production structure have important implications at the world level if the international division of labor is such that developing countries tend to specialize in the production of raw materials, while industrialized nations specialize in manufactures. This was certainly the case in the 1950s and continues to be true, to a certain extent, even today.[8] Under these circumstances, either countries specializing in primary goods will grow more slowly or the surplus of primary commodities will push down their relative prices. The pressure towards unequal rates of growth will be greater if the externalities generated by the production of manufactures (demand multipliers and the externalities associated with technological progress) are greater than those that characterize primary production.

The Keynesian and neoclassical literature of the 1950s and 1960s on the terms of trade largely focused on the characteristics of the demand and supply of different goods and services. According to Johnson (1954), the lower income-elasticity of the demand for raw materials ought to be reflected in slower economic growth in the countries specializing in those products or in a tendency for raw material prices to decline. This effect depends entirely on *income*-elasticity, but the lower the *price*-elasticity of the demand for raw materials is, the larger the decrease will be.

In a neoclassical (Heckscher–Ohlin) trade model, there are three types of factors that can affect terms of trade. First, relative prices depend on the income-elasticities of the demand for different goods and services. Thus, the terms of trade will move against countries specializing in income-inelastic goods. Second, terms of trade will improve if technological change in import-substitution industries is faster than in the rest of the world, and will decrease if faster productivity improvements take place in the export industries. Third, as countries tend to specialize in producing goods that require an intensive use of their more abundant factors, an increase in the supply of those factors will decrease a country's terms of trade. An increase in the scarce factors will have the opposite effect. The net effect of these three types of factors on the terms of trade of developing countries is indeterminate.

The second theoretical variant of the P–S hypothesis was structured in terms of the unequal distribution of the fruits of technological progress in primary versus manufacturing production. According to this variant, in the case of manufactures (especially high-tech nowadays) these benefits are distributed to producers in the form of higher incomes, but in the case of commodities (and possibly today simple manufactures) they are reflected in lower prices. This asymmetry results from the functioning of both goods markets (greater market power in manufacturing in relation to the primary sector, where production is highly atomized) and labor markets (greater organization of industrial workers).

At the international level, however, the asymmetry is also a reflection of the international division of labor. Because of the weaker long-term demand for raw materials, the relative surplus of labor displaced from primary activities tends to concentrate in developing countries, which, in turn, have more difficulty putting that surplus labor to work in new production sectors. The problems they face include political restrictions on migration to industrialized nations and the obstacles hindering late industrialization, which, in their view, are associated with the striking disparities between the countries of the "centre" and the "periphery" in terms of technological capabilities and the availability of capital. This situation tends to generate a larger surplus of labor in the developing countries which leads to a relative decline in the wages of developing-country workers and, hence, in those countries' terms of trade.

The "unequal exchange" theories developed in the 1970s argued that the asymmetric features in the economic structures of developed and developing countries that affect the costs of production were the main determinants of international prices.[9] In Emmanuel (1972), the "unequal exchange" concept is associated with the difference between value and price of production in Marxist theory. The observation that there is a trend towards equalization in profit rates at the international level, but not in wages, implies that there may be an interchange, at the same price, of higher direct and indirect labor contents (value) of goods and services coming from developing countries for lower labor contents of goods and services coming from the industrialized countries. Independent from the validity of this theory, the concept of "unequal exchange" can be linked to the idea that terms of trade evolution reflect more than anything the disparities in labor incomes between developed and developing countries.

This fits extremely well with Lewis' terms-of-trade theory (1977), according to which the international terms of trade are determined by relative wages in developing versus developed countries, which are determined, in turn, by the levels of productivity attained in the production of food (or of subsistence goods in general) in the two groups of countries. An increase in labor productivity that boosts real wages will have a positive effect on the terms of trade for the region where it takes place. In contrast, in the export sectors of the periphery, the entire impact of technological change in export sectors is transmitted ("exported") to the rest of the world via a decline in the terms of trade.

Hence, the trend in the terms of trade is not associated with the types of goods produced by one region or another but, rather, with that region which produces them. The North–South models developed in the 1980s can be viewed as a formalization of this type of analysis. The central characteristic of this literature was the use of the growth models developed in the 1950s and 1960s to analyze the international terms of trade. The models developed by Findlay (1980 and 1981) and Taylor (1983, chapter 10) in the early 1980s provided the more powerful formulation.[10] The essential element of these models is the central role played by asymmetries in the economic structures of the two regions. In the long run, the North appropriates the full benefits of its own technological change, while the South's productivity gains lead to a commensurate deterioration in its barter terms of trade (its technological changes are "exported"). This is a reflection of the asymmetrical effects that technological change has on real wages. While in the North wage increases are proportional to increases in productivity, in the South real wages are not affected by technological change, due to the existence of an unlimited surplus of labor in subsistence sectors. The corresponding effect is transmitted through production costs and is therefore unrelated to the type of good being produced or the demand for it.[11]

According to this type of analysis, the deterioration of the terms of trade may be better explained by differences among *countries* (developed versus developing countries, different levels of technological capacity, different organization of labor markets, presence or absence of surplus labor, different positions in international debt and trade markets, etc), rather than by the characteristics of the *goods* they export. This has generated another debate in which the point of contention is whether there are "commodity-like" characteristics of manufactures exported by developing countries that place these countries in double jeopardy in their attempts to escape from unequal exchange in world trade. This debate has generated what Athukorala (2000) calls the "new terms of trade pessimism," in the sense that it could be self-defeating for developing countries to industrialize. As we argue below, there is reason to believe that industrialization is by no means a self-defeating exercise, as reflected in the success of countries that, through proactive industrial policies, have been able to accelerate technological improvements and the diversification of their production and export structures.

The literature on the "fallacy of composition" has, however, given some cause for the "new terms of trade pessimism." In recent decades, the simultaneous entry of several countries into some markets evidently has led in some cases to an oversupply of exports, reflected in falling terms of trade for developing countries as a group and/or in high-cost producers being displaced from the market.[12] This fallacy of composition phenomenon can be identified not only in primary commodities and natural resource-based manufactures, most of which face low income-elasticities of demand in world markets, but also in low-tech manufactures and, more generally, manufactures that can be transferred easily from one country to another.

Indeed, the downward structural shift of non-oil commodity prices in the 1980s may be viewed as the result of the massive export supply generated by developing countries trying to adjust to the debt crises, and thus of the presence of a "fallacy of composition" effect.[13] As Singer stated

> A further element has been added to support the PST [P-S hypothesis], i.e. the debt pressure under which the poorer countries are compelled to export and earn foreign exchange at any price. The "fallacy of composition" ensures that the efforts of each country individually to improve its income terms of trade by increasing its own market shares must be at the expense of other countries under similar pressure which simultaneously try to increase their own individual market share.[14]

A similar phenomenon has thus affected both primary goods and manufactures exported by developing countries to the industrial world (see Figure 8.1 below).

As Singer's quote suggests, the downward shift of commodity prices in the 1980s reflects yet another phenomenon: the critical role that cyclical downswings have in the evolution of commodity prices, an issue that was at the center of Prebisch's and subsequently ECLAC's thinking on the subject.[15] Although the strong effects of low price-elasticity of demand for primary goods play a central role in the fall of commodity prices during cyclical downswings, the transformation of this cyclical fall in the terms of trade into a more permanent trend was seen by Prebisch and ECLAC as the result of the fall of relative *wages* between the center and the periphery that takes place simultaneously, and that reflects the relatively larger labor surpluses and weaker bargaining power of the labor force in the developing world. This mechanism thus fits better with the second variant of the P–S hypothesis.

Opposing views

Viner was the first major North American economist to call into question the P–S hypothesis.[16] His main arguments were directed against industrialization policies in general, but he also denied that there was a persistent or "secular" decline in the terms of trade of primary goods. He was the first of a long list of critics that included Ellsworth (1956), Morgan (1957), Meier (1958) and Harberler (1959). The quality-change argument was underscored by these North American critics. Ellsworth focused on the decline in railway and shipping costs that occurred in the particular period for which the original P–S empirical hypothesis was proposed. Nevertheless, he conceded that the decline between 1913 and 1933 was real enough, while contending that it was explained by a series of discrete causes.

Meier (1958) engaged in a broader critique of protection and deliberate industrialization. He argued that "even if there has been a deterioration [in the terms of trade] in the past, it does not follow that poor countries should now impose import restrictions to forestall an anticipated deterioration in their terms of trade." He went on to conclude that "although traditional theory envisaged foreign trade as an important activator of economic change, this has failed to occur in many poor countries. But the lack of 'carry-over' is to be attributed to domestic obstacles rather than to any international mechanism of inequality".

In Meier's view, the remedy did not lie, therefore, in policies of protection and deliberate industrialization at the expense of agriculture and foreign trade; it depended instead on the promotion of those domestic conditions – particularly in the political, social and institutional framework of the economy – that would permit the expansion of the export sector to induce secondary changes in the domestic sector. If this were accomplished, foreign trade might then also serve the poor countries as an "engine of growth." This discourse has been used over the years in various formulations, with the most recent being the emphasis on the links between institutions and development in the 1990s and 2000s.

While these scholars focused on criticizing industrialization policies, the substratum of the newly born Latin American "heresy," the empirical debate focused directly on trying to invalidate the P–S hypothesis. To this debate we turn next.

The empirical debate

In his seminal article, Prebisch (1950) studied the Board of Trade's mean price indices for British imports and exports, which he took to be representative of world prices for primary goods and manufactures, respectively. Based on those data, he argued that from the 1860s to the years leading up to World War II, the terms of trade had continually moved against commodity producers. Along the same lines, Singer (1950) claimed it was a historical fact that, since 1870, price trends had moved sharply against vendors of foodstuffs and raw materials and in favor of enterprises selling manufactures.

This and later evidence provided on the terms of trade of primary commodities was subsequently put to closer scrutiny. Spraos (1980) summarized the criticisms against the empirical evidence on which the P–S hypothesis was based around four major issues: (i) the relevance of the series analyzed; (ii) the inclusion of primary commodity exports of developed countries; (iii) the bias introduced by the use of f.o.b. values for exports and c.i.f. values for imports and the associated influence of transport costs; and (iv) the increasing quality and variety of manufactured products. Scandizzo and Diakosawas (1987) added three more issues: (i) the difference in the periods analyzed and the arbitrariness of their selection; (ii) the omission of productivity in the analysis; and (iii) the statistical procedures used.

While the findings of the empirical literature written up to the end of the 1970s were ambivalent, most of the studies of the 1980s tended to corroborate the P–S hypothesis.[17] Although the trend could not be confirmed for certain subperiods and commodities, the evidence indicated that, on average, real raw material prices trended downward throughout the twentieth century. This trend was also found to exist for raw materials (other than petroleum) as a group and for most products in the years after World War II.[18]

Ironically, the World Bank, by then the major advocate of trade liberalization, bolstered the empirical debate on the terms of trade in the late 1980s by giving support to the P–S hypothesis. Grilli and Yang (1988) constructed price series for 24 commodities and for seven indices using those series and concluded that there was indeed evidence of a long-term deterioration in real non-oil commodity prices. This was a milestone in the debate. Furthermore, the development of modern time-series econometrics provided new techniques to analyze the specific dynamics of the series.

Table 8.1 summarizes the findings of 25 studies on the subject published over the past 20 years. In terms of their conclusions, these studies can be divided into two broad groups. One group concludes that, while the secular trend in the terms of trade of non-oil commodity prices is not statistically significant, there is a

Table 8.1 Real commodity prices, historical inventory of results, (1985–2003)

Authors	Source of data	Method	Period	Trend[a]	Structural break(s)	Stepwise decrease
Sapsford (1985)	UN and WB	DT	1900–1982	–1.3	1950 (+)	
Sarkar (1986)	UN	DT	1953–1980	–0.9		
Scandizzo and Diakosawas (1987)	WB Food	DT	1900–1982	–0.3		
	WB Non-food	DT	1900–1982	–1.7		
Grilli and Yang (1988)	G-Y (GYCPI)	DT	1900–1986	–0.6		Yes
Cuddington and Urzúa (1988)	G-Y	ST	1900–1983		1921 (–)	
von Hagen (1989)	G-Y	CO	1900–1986			
Powell (1991)	G-Y	DT	1900–1986		1921, 1938, 1975 (–)	Yes
Helg (1991)	G-Y	DT	1920–1988	–0.3	1921 (–)	
Ocampo (1993)	G-Y	DT	1948–1987	–1.3		
Sapsford, Sarkar and Singer (1992)	G-Y	DT	1900–1983	–0.5	1921 (–), 1950 (+)	
	G-Y	DT	1922–1983	–0.5		
Ardeni and Wright (1992)	G-Y	DE	1900–1988	–0.6		
Cuddington (1992)	G-Y	DT and ST	1900–1983	–0.7	1921	
Cuddington and Wei (1992)	G-Y Arithmetic	DT	1900–1988	–0.3	1921 (–)	
	Geometric[b]	DT and ST[c]	1900–1988	–1.0		
Barros and Amazonas (1993)	B.M	DT	1948–1989	–0.1		Yes
Bleaney and Greenaway (1993)	G-Y	CE	1921–1986	–0.5	1921 (–)	
Reinhart and Wickham (1994)	IMF	DE	1900–1991	Negative	1980 (–)	
		DT	1925–1991			
León and Soto (1995)	G-Y Aggregated	DT and ST	1957–1993	–1.5	1973 (–)	Yes
	G-Y Weighted			–0.2		
Lutz (1996)	G-Y	CO	1900–1995	–0.4	1921 (–)	
Newbold and Vougas (1996)	G-Y	DT	1900–1995	–0.8	1921 (–)	
		ST				
Maizels, Palaskas and Crowe (1998)	EU	ST	1979–1994	–4.2	1980 (–)	
			–3.6			
Sapsford and Balasubramanyam (1999)	G-Y	DT	1900–1992	–0.7	1973 (–)	
				–0.9		
Lutz (1999)	G-Y Total	CO	1900–1995	–0.9	1920–21 (–) 1974 (–)	No
	Food			–0.4		
	Non-food			–0.4		
	Metals			–0.9		
Cashin and McDermott (2001)	TE	NP	1862–1999		1921 (–) 1985 (–)	Yes
Cuddington, Ludema and Jayasuriya (2002)	G-Y	DT	1900–1998	–1.3	1921 (–)	Yes

Source: Ocampo and Parra (2006a). WB: World Bank; UN: United Nations; G-Y: Grilli and Yang (1988); IMF: International Financial Statistics, International Monetary Fund; EU: EUROSTAT; TE: The Economist; CO: Cointegration; DE: Decomposition in cycle and trend; DT: Deterministic trend; ST: Stochastic trend; NP: Non-parametric test.

Notes
a Only statistically significant trend values are included.
b A geometric index is recalculated using the prices for the 24 products used by G-Y.
c The results are not conclusive and thus provide no basis for choosing between one and the other.
d If only one break in 1921 is included, then the trend ceases to be significant and the results would no longer be conclusive.

long-term deterioration attributable to one or more adverse structural downturns – and, equally important, no structural upturn. The other group finds that a negative long-term trend does exist, independently of structural breaks in the series. This fits in with the views of Bloch and Sapsford (2000), who contend that "a key element in reaching different conclusions (on the P–S hypothesis) is the inclusion of breaks or jumps in the data when estimating the trend relationship."[19]

Based on time-series analysis, however, the evidence of structural breaks is stronger than that for a secular decline. As we have argued in a previous publication,[20] rather than following a steady downward trend during the twentieth century, the terms of trade for commodities exhibit two major downward shifts: one after World War I and the other in the 1980s (see Figure 8.1). In both cases, these adverse shifts represent the delayed effects of the sharp slowdowns in the world economy that took place first after World War I and at the end of the "golden age" of the post-World War II period.[21] This accords with the conclusion reached by Bloch and Sapsford (2000) regarding the contemporaneity of structural breaks in the terms of trade and major changes in the rate of growth of industrial production at the world level. It also fits very well with North–South models, and with the results of most structural models, which show that industrial production is one of the main determinants of the terms of trade.[22]

Whatever the specific nature of the price dynamics involved, the recent empirical literature can thus be regarded as providing proof of the P–S hypothesis, although not necessarily for its original version or for its original period. It is

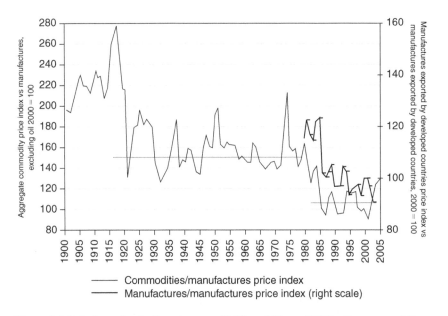

Commodities/manufactures price index
Manufactures/manufactures price index (right scale)

Figure 8.1 Relative price indices (source: Grilli and Yang (1988), Ocampo and Parra (2003) and United Nations (2004)).

worth noting, in particular, that a major conclusion of the empirical analysis is that the downward trend is a hallmark of the twentieth century, not the nineteenth. In fact, in keeping with the recent observations of Hadass and Williamson (2001), and contrary to the empirical evidence used by both Prebisch and Singer, existing series actually point to an improvement in real raw material prices in the late nineteenth and early twentieth centuries, as well as to a long-term improvement throughout the nineteenth century. These authors have also pointed out that the sharp reduction in shipping costs that occurred during those years benefited all countries. This is reflected in the improvement observed in the terms of trade for this period when prices are measured in a given location (i.e. f.o.b. export prices versus c.i.f. import prices).

Finally, it should be mentioned that, in recent years, demand from Asia, particularly from China, and emerging supply constraints in some commodity markets have strengthened commodity markets. But it is still too early to know if this improvement of commodity prices will be sustained. In the course of 2005, the pace of price increases decelerated, and non-fuel commodity prices are now expected to stabilize, if not decline somewhat, as new productive capacity is brought in stream.[23] In any case, even if Chinese-led world economic growth happens to keep prices in high levels for a longer period, other important reasons would still justify structural change and industrialization at the periphery.

The industrialization debate

The periphery's quest to industrialize

Based on the laws of diminishing returns in primary production and constant or increasing returns in manufactures, classical economists, going back to Adam Smith, postulated that the terms of trade of primary goods would show long-term improvement vis-à-vis manufactures. The policy implication of this hypothesis was that agricultural countries did not need to industrialize to enjoy the gains from technological progress taking place in manufactures. The free play of international market forces would distribute the gains from the industrial countries to the agricultural countries, through favorable terms of trade.[24]

By the time of World War II, however, it was increasingly believed that natural resource-based economies had reason to be pessimistic about their economic prospects. Kindleberger bolstered this conviction by suggesting, as early as 1943, that the only hope for a slackening in the long-run decline in basic material prices was industrialization of primary goods-producing countries.

> Inexorably ... the terms of trade move against agricultural and raw material countries, as the world's standard of living increases, and as Engel's law of consumption operates ... If the agricultural and raw material countries of the world want to share the increase in the world's productivity ... they must join in the transfer of resources from agriculture, pastoral pursuits and mining, to industry.[25]

Most schools of development economics captured this basic insight. Classical development economics thus dealt largely with the pre-conditions and the factors that would help to accelerate industrialization in developing countries.

Protectionism was already the rule since the late nineteenth century in the United States and most of Continental Europe, as well as in most Latin American countries and politically independent developing countries that had kept their autonomy to manage tariff policy. The Great Depression of the 1930s brought with it not only the collapse of international trade but the multiplication of bilateral trade agreements, and the increasing use of direct import controls and multiple exchange rates by many countries. To these processes we must add, as we saw in the previous section, the collapse of the commodity terms of trade in the 1920s, which the Great Depression reinforced, and the disturbances generated by war controls, in both World War I and II, that hit all export-dependent economies.

In the face of the collapse of international trade and the disintegration of multilateralism, the virtues of free trade thus seemed at best remote in the early post-World War II period. It would take some time to generate what, *ex-post*, turned out to be the period of most rapid growth of world trade in history, a prospect which was, at best, a dim hope in the immediate post-war years. Furthermore, most of the recovery of world trade in the early post-war period took place among industrial economies and thus provided limited opportunities for developing countries. Thus, looking at the opportunities that domestic markets provided to encourage industrialization was not only natural but, in a strong sense, forced by the circumstances.

This makes clear why the immediate post-World War II period was characterized in the developing world by a strong will to industrialize. Many countries, including particularly major Latin American nations, had already started to do so, largely as a response to the world economic disturbances in the inter-war period. In fact, the intellectual contributions of the Economic Commission for Latin America came to provide theoretical rationale for a process that was already in full swing.[26] The rising anti-colonialist movements in Asia and Africa gave industrialization an additional political push in those parts of the world, as an expression of national self-determination.

This was the context in which classical development economics was born and in which Prebisch and Singer generated their hypothesis. As Toye and Toye (2004) have stated,

> in the broader context of growing imbalance in the power of nations that characterized that period, it was possible to discern in this controversy [around the P–S hypothesis], not only a lively academic debate, but also the emergence of a contest around the ideology of economic nationalism in poorer countries in response to these changing political realities.[27]

We could add that it was also a response to evident *economic* realities of the previous decades: the collapse of the terms of trade for commodities, of multilateralism and of world trade.

Structural change and patterns of specialization

The idea that rising incomes are linked to a reduction in the relative weight of primary production and an increase of that of industry is associated with the work of Simon Kuznets, as well as the early work on the patterns of structural transformation by Hollis Chenery, Lance Taylor and others.[28] In fact, the link of industrial development to long-term economic growth is one of the strongest observed "regularities" in development. This is why classical development economics put industrialization at the center of the process of economic development. It is also why Prebisch placed the absorption of surplus labor generated by the shrinkage of primary goods sectors at the center of his theory of the terms of trade.

Old Engel's law is part of the story, as already pointed out, but equally important is the fact that industry revolutionizes primary production itself – through the provision of machinery and inputs for agriculture and mining – and has historically been the major mechanism for generating and transferring technological change. More broadly, the transformation of economies and societies that industrialization entailed opened the door to urbanization and to scientific achievements without precedents.

The strong technological externalities generated by manufacturing were the central argument behind Singer's call for industrialization. This is certainly more important than the terms for trade argument in his seminal article on the subject. Expressed in his own terms:

> In the economic life of a country and in its economic history, a most important element is the mechanism by which "one thing leads to another," and the most important contribution of an industry is not its immediate product ... and not even its effects on other industries and immediate social benefits ... but perhaps even further its effects on the general level of education, skill, way of life, inventiveness, habits, store of technology, creation of new demand, etc. And this is perhaps precisely the reason why manufacturing industries are so universally desired by underdeveloped countries; namely, that they provide the growing points for increased technical knowledge, urban education, the dynamism and resilience that goes with urban civilization, as well as the direct Marshallian external economies.[29]

The ongoing shift away from industry into services is now transforming the global economy. The rise of modern services (transport and communications, finance and services to enterprises, as well as modern state services) is, of course, as essential to industrialization as manufacturing itself, and has been at the center of all successful development experiences. In fact, the relative backwardness of some modern services was one of the major sources of problems that centrally planned economies eventually faced, and one of the causes of their eventual stagnation.

We also know that at high levels of income the dynamics of services eventually overtake that of industrialization, and that the revolution in information and communications technologies (ICT) has induced major changes in manufacturing itself. This has generated paths that may allow countries to go straight from primary production to services that some high-income primary producers (e.g. some oil economies) or small economies (e.g. high-income Caribbean economies) may follow. Services associated with the ICT revolution have become an essential ingredient of the success of others (e.g. India). Yet this still seems to be secondary to what appears as the almost inevitable path through industrialization in the process of economic development.

Structural transformation is not, in any case, a "once and for all" event, but an ongoing task and a continuous process that may encounter obstacles at any stage. In this context, steady growth can be seen as the result of a successful sequence of "innovations" in production structures (i.e. of micro- and, particularly, mesoeconomic processes), their intensity and the domestic linkages they generate. The ability to constantly generate new dynamic activities is, in this sense, the essential determinant of rapid economic growth.[30]

In developed countries, innovations are associated with technological waves – or, using Schumpeter's (1961) terminology, "new combinations" which may involve also innovations in the managerial processes, in industrial organization, in marketing and in the sources of raw materials, among others. In developing countries, innovations are more closely linked to the attraction of sectors, activities and technologies previously developed in the industrial world. Historically, this has involved processes of import substitution, export promotion or a mix of both strategies. In this context, although macroeconomic policy can certainly block or promote it, steady growth can be essentially seen as the result of a successful sequence of innovations in production structures. The sectoral (mesoeconomic) dynamics that this process involves are ignored or assumed to play a passive role in growth analyses that concentrate on institutional or macroeconomic features and policies. In contrast, sectoral dynamics play a central role in the "structuralist" tradition of economic thinking, broadly defined, where growth is viewed as the result of success in managing the dynamic transformation of production structures.

Industrialization policies in developing countries have been criticized on different grounds. As we saw in the previous part of this chapter, the most recurrent critique has been the one of protectionist policies, focusing particularly on misallocations of resources, corruption and inefficiency generated by import substitution policies. Although those are, undoubtedly, serious issues, it is important to recall that protectionism and industrial policies are almost universal features of the historical experience of today's industrial countries.[31] It is also interesting to note that the period in which those policies were common in developing countries, namely the 1950s to the 1970s, was also a time of widespread growth in the developing world and, as we will see below, includes the only period so far in history when there has been some convergence of incomes between developed and developing countries.

Although the rise of industrialization policies in the developing world took place when the world economy was still in shambles, the recovery of the world economy in the post-war years started to provide new opportunities for export development, particularly from the 1960s. Following his own brand of structuralist thinking, Chenery argued that the use of those opportunities was an important source of success in the developing world. More broadly, he argued that sustained economic growth required a transformation of the structure of production compatible with both the evolution of domestic demand and the use of the opportunities provided by international trade.[32]

This point was made in a more radical way by more orthodox thinkers, who argued that the "anti-export" bias generated by protection reduced the growth opportunities that export orientation provided.[33] Nonetheless, contrary to the simplistic view of the virtues of a structure of "neutral incentives," and more in line with the nuanced analysis of Chenery, the countries that outperformed the rest in the 1980s and 1990s were those that were able to deepen their industrialization through success in the world markets for high-technology manufactures: a strategy that, as we know, also involved strong state encouragement of industrialization.[34]

The opportunities for export development therefore did not eliminate the classical case for active industrialization strategies, though they certainly changed the type of industrialization needed. Lall (2001) argued, for example, that export structures, being path-dependent, have important implications for growth and development, with the highest technology products having the greatest benefits, in terms of spillover effects and dynamic scale economies (learning), as well as greater dynamism in world trade. Palma (2004) expressed a similar view based on the different capacity that low- vs. high-technology products have in inducing medium- and long-term productivity growth in the economy as a whole, as well as their relative dynamism in world trade. Hausmann, Hwang and Rodrik (2005) have also argued that the quality of exports, as indicated in the "income level" of a country's exports (i.e. an estimate of the weighted average income of countries exporting specific products, seen to reflect their technological content), is an independent determinant of economic growth. Diversification towards "dynamic products or sectors" in a particular period is especially important, as it limits the risk that the export market will get rapidly saturated and that prices will decrease (fallacy of composition), while increasing the possibility to exploit the potential of long-term productivity growth associated with export-oriented industrialization strategies.[35]

The capacity for adaptation and change is fundamental, as international market conditions change drastically over time and new developments create new export opportunities, while destroying old ones. Successful countries and regions in the last decades have thus shown a sustained effort to transform their specialization patterns over time and, particularly, to penetrate the market for technology-intensive manufactures.

Divergence and patterns of specialization in the developing world

Over the past two centuries the income gap between different regions and countries has increased notoriously.[36] The only exception to this trend is the period 1965–1973, in which the international per capita GDP gap decreased slightly. The story of the developing countries is thus one of "divergence, big time" vis-à-vis the industrial world,[37] with the late phase of the "golden age" being the only exception so far in history.

History has also shown considerable divergence among developing countries, particularly since the mid-1960s. Part of this divergence has been the result of several success stories ("miracles") at different times in various parts of the developing world (China and India being the most recent ones). Very few "peripheral" countries have joined the industrial "center" (Japan being the notable exception in this regard, perhaps with some of the "first-tier" Asian newly industrialized countries).

These miracles have been associated with success in the transformation of production structures. Thus, during 1970–2003, fast growth in China, South-East Asia and South Asia was associated with a rapid decline in the importance of agriculture and strong expansions of industry and services. According to Lall (2001) and Palma (2004), among others, East Asia's extraordinary performance is closely associated with the continuous effort, both by the State and the corporate sector, to promote a persistent industrialization drive and upgrade export production capacities.[38] In contrast, sluggish long-term growth after the 1970s in the semi-industrialized countries and in Central America and the Caribbean, as well as in countries in the Middle East and the Commonwealth of Independent States (CIS), was associated with a process of de-industrialization (of variable intensity).[39]

Over the past decades, the export structure of all developing country regions diversified away from primary goods and natural-resource intensive manufactures into low-, mid- and high-technology manufactures. The velocity of this diversification has been clearly associated with economic growth (Figure 8.2). China, the East Asian newly industrialized countries and South-east Asian countries diversified much faster (including into low-technology manufactures), followed by Latin America. The latter region, however, has been less capable of transforming success in export markets into growth dynamism.

The impact of integration into the world economy has depended on the circumstances under which it has taken place and on the policies pursued during the integration phase. Integration of Latin America and Africa (as well as Central and Eastern Europe) marked a sharp shift in development strategy, occurring in a "big-bang" manner and following the debt crisis (i.e. a period of weakness). This contrasts with the integration process in East Asia, which occurred from a position of strength and was characterized by a continuous and purposeful strategy of gradually opening up.[40] In the Schumpeterian terminology used by Ocampo (2005), in East Asia, the "creative" elements prevailed ("creative destruction"), while in other regions of the world, the "destructive" components of the restructuring process were stronger ("destructive creation").

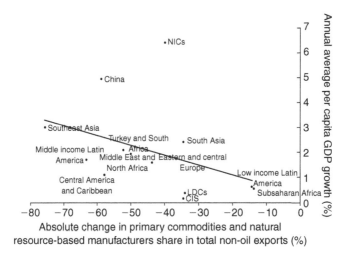

A. Primary commodities and natural resource-based manufactures dynamism and growth

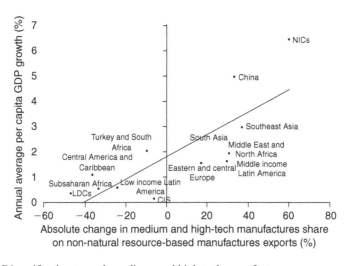

B. Diversification towards medium- and high-tech manufactures

Figure 8.2 Structural change in exports and growth, 1962–2000 (source: Authors'
calculations based on Maddison (2003) and Feenstra and others (2005)).

In the latter case, this reflected the destruction of many import-substitution
activities and the weak domestic linkages generated by new export sectors. The
capacity to capture a share of the value added in the production chain has in fact
differed widely between countries and regions. Those countries that have relied
on activities with limited value added and limited linkages with the rest of the
economy (e.g. maquila) benefited less from their structural change. In the terms

used by Palma (2004), unless the industries are firmly "anchored" in the domestic economy, their growth-enhancing capacity evaporates. Ocampo (2005) refers to these specialization patterns as "shallow."

Figure 8.3 provides a synthetic view of the relations between economic growth and specialization patterns, by showing the average performance in terms of per capita GDP growth rates across groups of countries according to their dominant export specialization pattern.[41] Growth divergence among developing countries, albeit present, was much less marked in the period 1962–1980 than during the final two decades of the century. Average rates of growth of countries specializing in primary products (PP) and natural resource-based (NRB) manufactures were relatively lower, at half of the rate of growth observed for other exporters. In short, industrialization beyond the processing of primary goods clearly paid off. Moreover, only a few exporters of PP and NRB manufactures were able to exceed the average annual rate of growth of per capita GDP of developed countries during the period (3.1 percent).

Divergence in performance among developing countries increased significantly in the period 1980–2000. There was a marked deceleration in the rate of growth of per capita income in all groups of exporters, except for those exporting high-technology manufactures. Producers of low-technology exports came next, reflecting the dynamic markets that have characterized some of these sectors. In contrast, none of the countries belonging to the groups of PP and medium-technology manufacture exporters had a growth rate that exceeded the average rate of growth of per capita GDP of the developed countries (2.2 percent), which was already lower than what had been observed in the previous period. For PP exporters, increasing participation in slow-growing markets was

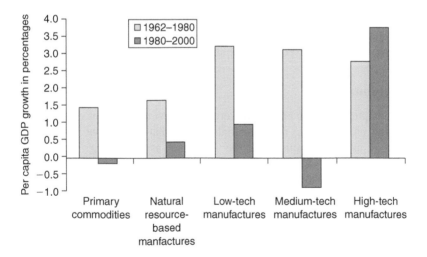

Figure 8.3 Per capita GDP growth average of countries specializing in each sector (source: Authors' calculations based on Maddison (2003) and Feenstra and others (2005)).

not enough to offset the adverse trends, such as lower average commodity prices, that prevailed during the period. This evidence clearly shows that the effects of trade on economic growth depend crucially on the type of products a country exports in a particular period, which are linked in turn to broader trends in world trade.

As Prebisch and Singer expected, reliance on natural resources has been associated with sluggish economic growth. This is confirmed above for both historical periods and is supported by a parallel body of research that shows that specialization in primary commodities has been associated in recent decades with poor growth performance, including growth collapses (long-term reductions in per capita income). Thus, Ros (2005) found that dependence on raw material exports – particularly mineral exports – is associated with growth collapses. Reddy and Minoui (2005) found that countries that suffered spells of real-income stagnation[42] were more likely to be dependent on primary commodity exports.

As we have shown in a previous study,[43] most countries that failed to increase shares in world markets were exporters of primary goods or natural resource-intensive manufactures, and all of them experienced either low growth or per-capita GDP contraction. Even, on average, success in increasing market shares in these sectors was associated with weak economic growth. Indeed, Chile, the Seychelles, Oman, Uganda and Egypt were the only countries in the sample of 96 analyzed that extracted GDP per capita growth above 2 percent during 1980–2002 from a strategy based on natural resources. In any case, many of those successful countries were increasingly processing their commodities and decreasing the reliance on pure primary commodities.

There is, finally, a strong association between a high dependence on a few commodities and poor growth performance. The group of least developed countries, comprising the poorest countries, showed the least export diversification, and the regions with the lowest growth records in Latin America and Africa continued to show higher export concentration ratios than those of other regions.[44]

Conclusions

In this chapter, we have presented a critical review of the terms of trade controversy and its relation to the industrialization debate. We have shown that the recent empirical literature can be regarded as providing proof for the Prebisch–Singer (P–S) hypothesis, although not necessarily for its original version or for the historical period to which it was originally applied.

This led us to underscore the importance for developing countries of industrialization, including the diversification of exports into manufactures. In this respect, the P–S hypothesis fit right into the mainstream of development thinking at the time of its publication. Development and industrialization were treated virtually as synonymous.[45]

The case for industrialization was, however, both broader and independent from the terms of trade debate. In fact, the excessive focus on the terms of trade side-tracked the discussion from what remained for some decades a broader consensus on industrialization as necessary to take advantage of its externalities and dynamic economies of scale; indeed, consensus on this rationale largely remains today, despite the lack of agreement on the means. Industrialization was thus seen as essential to increase productivity and to retain the fruits of this productivity in the developing world. And the emphasis fell on the links between industrialization and the building up of technological capacity, entrepreneurial skills and of human capital in general.

Other justifications for industrialization included the low income-elasticity of demand for commodities and the associated need to absorb surplus labor generated by the modernization of agriculture, and even (at the time, and in many areas, still today) by the absence of free trade arrangements in the world. Each of these arguments would have been sufficient to justify an active promotion of industrialization. In this light, it is peculiar that the "secular" decline of the terms of trade came to occupy such a central role in Latin American structuralism, providing for some time an easy target for criticism, as it failed to materialize during the period of booming world trade from the 1950s to the 1970s.[46]

As the share of manufactures in the exports of developing countries increased, it became necessary to break the identification of the terms of trade of developing countries with the terms of trade for commodities. This made increasingly relevant what we called the second variant of the P–S hypothesis, which links the terms of trade to the country where goods and services are produced, not to the nature of these goods. As we showed, there is some evidence that the terms of trade for the technologically simpler manufactures exported by developing countries have followed a trend similar to that of primary commodities. Moreover, both trends could be reflecting "fallacy of composition" effects in those countries' terms of trade.

Successful industrialization requires a persistent process of structural transformation. In the context in which the P–S hypothesis was formulated, the natural recommendation was industrial policy in the form of import substitution. Today, active participation in international markets matters, but the key to success seems to be the capacity to participate actively in dynamic markets (including those for several low-technology manufactures) and high-technology markets (which tend to be generally dynamic). The historical experiences of countries that have been more successful in benefiting from global markets suggest that industrial policy, albeit of other kinds, is still necessary. After all, this seems to have been the policy followed by all success cases through history.[47]

As Sapsford and Balasubramanyam have categorically stated, in relation to the P–S hypothesis, "There can be few hypotheses in economics that have stood the test of both time and new statistical techniques so well."[48] Based on the arguments and empirical evidence presented in the second part of our chapter, we can say something similar about the basic insight of classical development economics: that industrialization is an essential ingredient of development. This also seems to have stood very well the test of time.

Notes

1 Prebisch (1950), reproduced in Prebisch (1962), p. 1.
2 The United Nations, through the Economic Commission for Latin America (ECLA) (later ECLAC, when the Caribbean joined the Commission) and the Department of Economic Affairs, were at the center of this and parallel conceptual developments, with the United Nations Conference on Trade and Development (UNCTAD) becoming from its creation in 1962 the center of the debates on reform of the international economic system.
3 Amsden (2001).
4 See Ocampo (1993) for an extensive analysis of these two variants.
5 See also the typology developed by Rodriguez (1986) to summarize the debate that took place within ECLAC. He differentiates between what he calls the accounting version, the business cycle version and the industrialization version of the terms of trade debate. The first estimated the effects of this trend on income divergence between the center and the periphery. The second focused on the determinants of this deterioration and focused on the growing inequality in real wages between the center and the periphery, and the particular role of cyclical downturns in this dynamics. The third tied the decline in terms of trade and income divergence in the world economy to the industrialization process.
6 Ratio between export prices and the prices paid for imported goods and services.
7 Ratio between the relative incomes of the factors of production embodied in exports versus imports. One way of estimating this variable is to adjust the barter terms of trade to take into account the productivities of the factors used to produce tradable goods. A more straightforward option is to analyze relative trends in the prices of factors of production (especially labor) in developing vs. developed countries.
8 Singer (1991) stated that, although developing countries could not be identified with commodity exports in the same way as they could be in 1950, developing countries as a whole clearly remained net exporters of primary commodities and net importers of manufactures. This has changed in the past decades due to the surge of the newly industrialized countries of East Asia and, more recently, of China and India, but not for all developing regions. While the share of primary commodities and natural resource-based manufactures in Latin America and the Caribbean, Middle East and North Africa, and South Asia decreased substantially since 1960, to around 40 percent in 1996–2000, sub-Saharan Africa and the least developed countries specialization in this type of products is still overwhelming (United Nations, 2006a, Figure III.2).
9 See Ocampo (1986 and 1993) for an extensive analysis of these models.
10 For a comparison of these and other models, see Ocampo (1986). There is, of course, a large body of literature along these lines. See, for example, Darity (1990) and Molana and Vines (1989).
11 Consequently, contrary to the argument made by Hadass and Williamson (2001), this effect should be modeled under the assumption of equivalent (unitary) income elasticity for goods produced by the two regions.
12 Mayer (2003).
13 See Singer (1989, 1991 and 1999), Sarkar and Singer (1992) and Ocampo and Parra (2006b).
14 Singer (1999), p. 915.
15 See Rodriguez (1986).
16 Toye and Toye (2004), p. 131.
17 See, for example, among the earlier studies, Spraos (1980 and 1983), Sapsford (1985), Sarkar (1986), Evans (1987) and Scandizzo and Diakosawas (1987). See also the broader set of studies summarized in Table 8.1.
18 Ocampo (1993).

19 Bloch and Sapsford (2000), p. 478.
20 Ocampo and Parra (2003).
21 Maddison (1995).
22 In this chapter we only focus on the time-series debate. Another line of empirical research has focused on identifying the underlying causes of the behavior of relative commodity prices by developing "structural" models. See Ocampo and Parra (2006a) for a review of this literature.
23 United Nations (2006b).
24 Sarkar (2001).
25 Kindleberger (1943), p. 349.
26 Ocampo (2006).
27 Toye and Toye (2004), p. 110.
28 Kuznets (1966), Chenery and Taylor (1968) and Chenery (1979).
29 Singer (1950), p. 476.
30 Ocampo (2005).
31 Chang (2002).
32 Chenery (1980), p. 281.
33 Krueger (1980).
34 See Amsden (2001) and Wade (2004).
35 Mayer, Butkevicius and Kadri (2002).
36 Maddison (1995 and 2003); Bourguignon and Morrison (2002); Ocampo and Parra (2006b).
37 Pritchett (1997).
38 United Nations (2006a).
39 In fact, some countries began to de-industrialize rapidly, despite the fact that their level of income per capita was far lower than the levels found in other countries that had either de-industrialized, or that were beginning to de-industrialize at the same time (Palma, 2005). Palma argues that this resulted from several factors, including changes in economic policy in middle-income countries and the discovery of natural resources.
40 UNCTAD (2003).
41 See United Nations (2006a). Products are grouped into five categories according to natural resource and technological content on the basis of a methodological classification developed by Lall (2001). Products classified as SITC divisions 3 (fuel and energy) and 9 (non-classified products) are excluded from the analysis. While some degree of discretion is unavoidable, Lall's classification is based on indicators of technological activity in manufacturing.
42 Real-income stagnation is defined as negligible or negative per capita real-income growth for a significant uninterrupted sequence of years.
43 Ocampo and Parra (2006b).
44 United Nations (2006a).
45 Singer (1999), p. 912.
46 Furthermore, given the central role that the secular decline played, it is even more peculiar that it received little rigorous theoretical and empirical scrutiny by Latin American structuralists, which rarely went in their analyses much beyond the initial contributions of Prebisch. As we saw, the subsequent debate took place largely outside Latin America.
47 Chang (2002) and Wade (2004).
48 Sapsford and Balasubramanyam (1994), p. 1743.

References

Amsden, Alice (2001) *The Rise of the Rest: Non-Western Economies' Ascent in World Markets*, Oxford: Oxford University Press.

Ardeni, Giorgio Pier and Brian D. Wright (1992) The Prebisch–Singer Hypotheses: A Reappraisal Independent of Stationary Hypothesis, *Economic Journal* 102(413): 803–12.

Athukorala, Prema-Chandra (2000) Manufactured Exports and Terms of Trade of Developing Countries: Evidence from Sri Lanka. *Journal of Development Studies* 36(5): 89–104.

Barros, Alexandre Rands and Analice Amazonas, (1993) On the Deterioration of the Net Barter Terms of Trade for Primary Commodities, *UNCTAD Review* 4, Geneva: 99–119.

Bleaney, Michael and David Greenaway (1993) Long-Run Trends in the Relative Price of Primary Commodities and in the Terms of Trade of Developing Countries, *Oxford Economic Papers* 45(3): 349–63.

Bloch, Harry and David Sapsford (2000) Whither the Terms of Trade? An Elaboration of the Prebisch-Singer Hypothesis, *Cambridge Journal of Economics* 24: 461–81.

Bourguignon, François and Christian Morrison (2002) Inequality among world citizens: 1820–1992, *The American Economic Review* 92(4), September: 727–44.

Cashin, Paul and C. John McDermott (2001) The Long-Run Behavior of Commodity Prices: Small Trends and Big Variability, *IMF Working Paper* WP/01/68, Washington, DC, May.

Chang, Ha-Joon (2002) *Kicking away the Ladder, Development Strategy in Historical Perspective*, London: Anthem Press, Wimbledon Publishing Company.

Chenery, Hollis B. (1980) Interactions between Industrialization and Exports, *The American Economic Review* 70 (2), Papers and Proceedings of the Ninety-Second Annual Meeting of the American Economic Association, May: 281–7.

—— (1979) *Structural Change and Development Policy*, New York: Oxford University Press.

—— and Lance Taylor (1968) Development Patterns: Among Countries and Over Time, *The Review of Economics and Statistics* 50 (4), November: 391–416.

Cuddington, John T. (1992) Long-Run Trends in 26 Primary Commodity Prices, *Journal of Development Economics* 39: 207–27.

—— and Hong Wei (1992) An Empirical Analysis of Real Commodity Price Trends: Aggregation, Model Selection, and Implications, *Estudios Económicos* 7(2), July–December: 159–80.

—— and Carlos M. Urzúa (1988) Ciclos y Tendencias en los Términos netos de Intercambio: un Nuevo Enfoque, *Estudios Económicos* 3(2), El Colegio de México, Mexico, July–December: 169–204.

—— , Rodney Ludema and Shamila Jayasuriya (2002) Reassessing the Prebisch–Singer Hypothesis: Long-Run Trends with Possible Structural Breaks at Unknown Dates, *Georgetown University Working Paper*, October.

Darity, William (1990) The Fundamental Determinants of the Terms of Trade Reconsidered: Long-Run and Long-Period Equilibrium, *American Economic Review* 80(4), September: 816–27.

Ellsworth, Paul Theodore (1956) The Terms of Trade between Primary Producing and Industrial Countries, *Inter-American Economic Affairs* 10(1), Summer: 47–65.

Emmanuel, Arghiri (1972) *Unequal Exchange*, New York: Monthly Review Press.

Evans, David (1987) The Long-Run Determinants of North–South Terms of Trade and Some Recent Empirical Evidence, *World Development* 15: 657–71.

Feenstra, Robert C., Robert E. Lipsey, Haiyan Deng, Alyson C. Ma and Hengyong Mo (2005) World Trade Flows: 1962–2000, NBER Working Paper 11040, available at www.nber.org/papers/w11040.

Findlay, Ronald (1981) The Fundamental Determinants of the Terms of Trade, in Sven Grassman and Erik Lündberg (eds), *The World Economic Order: Past and Prospects*, London: Macmillan.

—— (1980) The Terms of Trade and Equilibrium Growth in the World Economy, *American Economic Review* 70(3), June: 291–9.

Grilli, Enzo R. and Maw Cheng Yang (1988) Primary Commodity Prices, Manufactured Goods Prices, and the Terms of Trade of Developing Countries: What the Long Run Shows, *The World Bank Economic Review* 2(1), January: 1–47.

Hadass, Yael S. and Jeffrey G. Williamson (2001) Terms of Trade Shocks and Economic Performance 1870–1940: Prebisch and Singer Revisited, *NBER Working Paper Series* 8188, Cambridge, MA, March.

Harberler, Gottfried (1959) International Trade and Economic Development, in J. D. Theberge (ed.), *Economics of Trade and Development*, Cairo: National Bank of Egypt.

Hausmann, Ricardo, Jason Hwang and Dani Rodrik (2005) It is not How Much but What you Export that Matters, Working Paper, Harvard University, John F. Kennedy School of Government, December.

Helg, Rodolfo (1991) A Note on the Stationarity of the Primary Commodities Relative Price Index, *Economics Letters* 36: 55–60.

Johnson, Harry G. (1954) Increasing Productivity, Income-Price Trends and the Trade Balance, reprinted in *International Trade and Economic Growth*, Cambridge, MA, Harvard University Press (1967).

Kindleberger, Charles P. (1943) Planning for Foreign Investment, *The American Economic Review* 33(1), Part 2, Supplement, Papers and Proceedings of the Fifty-fifth Annual Meeting of the American Economic Association, March: 347–54.

Krueger, Anne O. (1980) Trade Policy as an Input to Development, *The American Economic Review* 70(2), Papers and Proceedings of the Ninety-second Annual Meeting of the American Economic Association, May: 288–92.

Kuznets, Simon (1966) *Modern Economic Growth: Rate, Structure and Spread*, New Haven: Yale University Press.

Lall, Sanjaya (2001) *Competitiveness, Technology and Skills*, Cheltenham: Edward Elgar.

León, Javier and Raimundo Soto (1995) Structural Breaks and Long-Run Trends in Commodity Prices, *Policy Research Working Paper* 1406, The World Bank, January.

Lewis, W. Arthur (1977) *The Evolution of the International Economic Order*, Princeton, NJ: Princeton University Press.

Lutz, Matthias G. (1999) A General Test of the Prebisch–Singer Hypothesis, *Review of Development Economics* 3: 44–57.

—— (1996) Primary Commodity and Manufactured Goods Prices in the Long Run: New Evidence on the Prebisch–Singer Hypothesis, *Discussion Papers in Economics*, Department of Economics, University of Sussex, March.

Maddison, Angus (2003) *The World Economy: Historical Statistics*, Paris: OECD.

—— (1995) *Monitoring the World Economy 1820–1992*, Paris: OECD.

Maizels, Theodosios, B. Palaskas and Trevor Crowe (1998) The Raúl Prebisch-Singer Hypothesis Revisited, in David Sapsford and John-ren Chen (eds), *Development Economics and Policy*, London: Macmillan/St. Martin's Press.

Mayer, Jorg (2003) The Fallacy of Composition: a Review of the Literature, *UNCTAD Discussion Papers*, No. 166, February.

_____, Arunas Butkevicius and Ali Kadri (2002) Dynamic Products in World Exports, *UNCTAD Discussion Papers*, No. 159, May.

Meier, Gerald M. (1958) International Trade and International Inequality, *Oxford Economic Papers*, New Series, 10(3), October: 277–89.

Molana, Hassan and David Vines (1989) North–South Growth and the Terms of Trade: A Model on Kaldorian Lines, *The Economic Journal* 99, June: 443–53.

Morgan, Theodore (1957) The Long-Run Terms of Trade between Agriculture and Manufacturing, Report of the Detroit Meeting, September 7–10, 1956, *Econometrica* 25(2): 360.

Newbold, Paul and Dimitros Vougas (1996) Drift in the Relative Price of Primary Commodities: A Case Where we Care About Unit Roots, *Applied Economics* 28: 653–61.

Ocampo, José Antonio (2006) Latin America and the World Economy in the Long Twentieth Century, in K. S. Jomo (ed.), *The Great Divergence: Hegemony, Uneven Development and Global Inequality*, New Deli: Oxford University Press, pp. 44–93.

—— (2005) The Quest for Dynamic Efficiency: Structural Dynamics and Economic Growth in Developing Countries, in José Antonio Ocampo (ed.), *Beyond Reforms, Structural Dynamics and Macroeconomic Vulnerability*, Palo Alto: Stanford University Press, pp. 3–43.

—— (1993) Terms of Trade and Center–Periphery Relations, in Osvaldo Sunkel (ed.), *Development from Within: Toward a Neostructuralist Approach for Latin America*, Boulder, Co: Lynne Rienner Publishers.

—— (1986) New Developments in Trade Theory and LDCs, *Journal of Development Economics*, 22: 129–70.

—— and Maria Angela Parra (2006a) The Commodity Terms of Trade and their Strategic Implications for Development, in K. S. Jomo (ed.), *Globalization under Hegemony – The Changing World Economy in the Long Twentieth Century*, New Delhi: Oxford University Press, Chapter 6.

—— (2006b) The Dual Divergence: Growth Successes and Collapses in the Developing World since 1980, in Ricardo Ffrench-Davis and José Luis Machinea (eds), *Economic Growth with Equity; Challenges for Latin America*, London: Palgrave.

—— (2003) The Terms of Trade for Commodities in the Twentieth Century, *CEPAL Review*, No. 79, April: 7–35.

Palma, Gabriel (2005) Four Sources of "De-industrialization" and a New Concept of the "Dutch Disease," in José Antonio Ocampo (ed.), *Beyond Reforms, Structural Dynamics and Macroeconomic Vulnerability*, Palo Alto: Stanford University Press, pp. 71–116.

—— (2004) Flying-geese and Lame Ducks: Regional Powers and the Different Capabilities of Latin America and East Asia to 'Demand-adapt' and 'Supply-upgrade' their Export Productive Capacity. Unpublished manuscript, University of Cambridge, August.

Powell, Andrew (1991) Commodity and Developing Country Terms of Trade: What Does the Long Run Show?, *The Economic Journal* 101, November: 485–96.

Prebisch, Raúl (1950) *The Economic Development of Latin America and its Principal Problems*, New York: United Nations. Reprinted in *Economic Bulletin for Latin America* 7 (1962).

Pritchett, Lant (1997) "Divergence, Big Time," *Journal of Economic Perspectives* 11(3), Summer: 3–17.

Reddy, Sanjay G. and Camelia Minoiu (2005) Real Income Stagnation of Countries, 1960–2001. Unpublished manuscript, Columbia University, New York, March.

Reinhart, Carmen and Peter Wickham (1994) Commodity Prices: Cyclical Weakness or Secular Decline?, *IMF Staff Papers* 41(2): 175–213.

Rodriguez, Octavio (1986) *La Teoria del Subdesarrollo de la CEPAL*, Mexico, DF: Siglo XXI editors.

Ros, Jaime (2005) Divergence and Growth Collapses: Theory and Empirical Evidence, In José Antonio Ocampo (ed.). *Beyond Reforms, Structural Dynamics and Macroeconomic Vulnerability*, Palo Alto: Stanford University Press, pp. 211–32.

Sapsford, David (1985) The Statistical Debate on the Net Barter Terms of Trade Between Primary Commodities and Manufactures: A Comment and Some Additional Evidence, *The Economic Journal*, 95, September: 781–8.

—— and V. N. Balasubramanyam (1999) Trend and Volatility in the Net Barter Terms of Trade: New Results From the Application of a (Not So) New Method, *Journal of International Development* 11(6): 851–7.

—— (1994) The Long-Run Behavior of the Relative Price of Primary Commodities: Statistical Evidence and Policy Implications, *World Development* 22(11): 1737–45.

Sapsford, David, Prabirjit Sarkar and Hans W. Singer (1992) The Prebisch-Singer Terms of Trade Controversy Revisited, *Journal of International Development* 4(3): 314–32.

Sarkar, Prabirjit (2001) The North–South terms of Trade Debate: a Reexamination, *Progress in Development Studies* 1(4): 309–27.

—— (1986) The Singer–Prebisch Hypothesis: A Statistical Evaluation, *Cambridge Journal of Economics* 10(4): 355–71.

Sarkar, P. and H. W. Singer (1992) Debt Crisis, Commodity Prices, Transfer Burden, and Debt Relief, Institute of Development Studies, Sussex.

Scandizzo, Pasquale L. and Dimitris Diakosawas (1987) Instability in the Terms of Trade of Primary Commodities, 1900–1982, *FAO Economic and Social Development Paper* 64.

Schumpeter, Joseph (1961), *The Theory of Economic Development*, New York: Oxford University Press.

Singer, Hans W. (1999), Beyond Terms of Trade – Convergence and Divergence, *Journal of International Development* 11(6), September–October: 911–16.

—— (1991) Terms of Trade: New Wine and New Bottles? *Development Policy Review* 9: 339–51.

—— (1989) The Relationship between Debt Pressures, Adjustment Policies and Deterioration of Terms of Trade for Developing Countries (with Special Reference to Latin America), IDS Discussion Paper No. 260, University of Sussex.

—— (1950) The Distribution of Gains between Investing and Borrowing Countries, *American Economic Review* 40. Also published in David Greenaway and C. W. Morgan (eds), *The Economics of Commodity Markets*, Cheltenham: Edward Elgar, 1999.

Spraos, John (1983) El Deterioro de la Relación de Intercambio: Algunas Perspectivas, *Estudios Internacionales* 16(62), Santiago, April–June.

—— (1980) The Statistical Debate on the Net Barter Terms of Trade between Primary Commodities and Manufactures, *The Economic Journal* 90: 107–28.

Taylor, Lance (1983) *Structuralist Macroeconomics*, New York, Basic Books.

Toye, John and Richard Toye (2004) *The UN and the Global Political Economy: Trade, Finance and Development*, United Nations Intellectual History Project Series, Indiana University Press.

UNCTAD (2003) *Trade and Development Report 2003: Capital Accumulation, Growth and Structural Change*. United Nations Conference on Trade and Development, New York.

United Nations (2006a) *World Economic and Social Survey, Diverging Growth and Development*, New York.

—— (2006b) *World Economic Situation and Prospects 2006*, New York.

—— (2004) *International Trade Statistics Yearbook, 2003*, vol. II, *Trade by Commodity*, New York.

Von Hagen, Juergen (1989), Relative Commodity Prices and Cointegration, *Journal of Business and Economic Statistics* 7(4), October: 497–503.

Wade, Robert Hunter (2004) *Governing the Market: Economic Theory and the Role of Government in East Asian Industrialization*, second paperback edition, Princeton, NJ: Princeton University Press.

9 Strategies of "industrialization by invitation" in the Caribbean

Esteban Pérez Caldentey[1]

Introduction

This chapter describes the main elements of the development strategy known as "industrialization by invitation" and also analyses its effects and implications using two source cases: the English-speaking Caribbean countries and Puerto Rico. The strategy was first formulated by the Saint Lucian economist and Nobel Laureate, Arthur Lewis (1915–1991). Lewis envisaged industrialization as a process requiring the simultaneous development of agriculture and industry. Industry would absorb the surplus labor emanating from agriculture allowing the sector to increase its productivity and standard of living. The improvement in agricultural conditions would allow it to generate a demand for manufacturing products.

In the case of the English-speaking Caribbean countries (the West Indies), the low levels of income prevailing at the time meant that income would be spent mostly on food and shelter rather than on manufacturing. Lewis envisaged that the West Indies would be characterized by a coexistence of an excess demand for food and an excess supply of manufacturing. The solution lay in exporting manufacturing products and using the proceeds to purchase agricultural products.

However, the small volume of islands' trade prevented these economies from exporting on a competitive basis and Lewis recommended that instead of exporting, the West Indies should, through a series of policy measures, court foreign entrepreneurs to install and open their businesses and factories in the islands. Hence, the term, "industrialization by invitation."

Foreign capital would contribute to the acquisition and development of fundamental managerial, entrepreneurial and administrative skills that were absent in newly developing economies, such as those of the Caribbean. Over time, after a learning period, local entrepreneurs would possess the capacity to start their own ventures and the creation of their respective national industrial bases.

From the time of their independence, the industrialization by invitation strategy shaped the development path adopted by Caribbean economies and remains to this day a fundamental pillar of their economic policy.

This chapter is divided into four sections. The first describes the strategy of industrialization by invitation as conceived in Lewis' seminal paper, "The Industrialization of the West Indies" (1950). The second and third sections focus on the economic policies that were followed by English-speaking Caribbean countries and Puerto Rico and that were inspired by the strategy of 'industrialization by invitation'.[2] The last section centers on their effects and more precisely on whether they managed to spur the development of domestic industry and entrepreneurship.

The industrialization of the West Indies

Arthur Lewis (1950) first formulated the rationale and main elements of the development model of industrialization by invitation. Lewis' argument for industrialization rested on over-population in agriculture and even more so on the need to improve the productivity of agriculture by shifting labor to the manufacturing sector. Thus "the creation of new industries is an essential part of a program for agricultural improvement" (p. 831). Lewis did not view industrialization as an alternative to agricultural development but as a complement to it. As he put it (p. 832):

> There is no choice to be made between industry and agriculture. The islands need as large an agriculture sector as possible, and, if they could even get more people into agriculture, without reducing output per head, then so much the better. But, even, when they are employing in agriculture the maximum number that agriculture will absorb at a reasonable standard of living, there still will be a large surplus of labour, and even the greatest expansion of industry which is conceivable within the next twenty years will not create a labour shortage in agriculture. It is not the case that agriculture cannot continue to develop if industry is developed. Exactly the opposite is true: agriculture cannot be put on to a basis where it will yield a reasonable standard of living unless new jobs are created off the land.

In much the same way that the development of manufacturing was a precondition for the improvement in agricultural conditions, the latter was needed to provide a demand for the increase in manufactures.

However, the small size of the market and the shortage of cultivable land in the West Indies were two main constraints that prevented the complementarity between agriculture and manufacturing. The small size of the market for manufactures implied that the demand for manufacturing output would fall short of its supply. At the same time, the shortage of cultivable land meant that the supply of food would fall short of demand. The solution proposed by Lewis was to export the excess supply of manufactured products, which would finance the required imports of food products. The equality between manufacturing exports and agricultural imports would then provide the necessary balance for the simultaneous development of agriculture and manufacturing.

Nonetheless, Lewis doubted that Caribbean manufacturers would be poised to compete with existing suppliers in international markets. The limited amount of island trade precluded them from incurring into the cost of breaking into established export supplier markets. Based on the experience of Puerto Rico, he proposed "to persuade existing suppliers to open factories in the islands to supply their trade."

The strategy of industrialization by invitation consisted of three elements: the creation of a customs union; the creation of a special agency, the Industrial Development Corporation, to drive the industrialization process; and the provision of special incentives. The Industrial Development Corporation would put in place the necessary infrastructure and would offer the required incentives (protection, subsidies or tax holidays) to attract foreign investment.

According to McIntyre (1995, p. 60), the attraction of foreign investment was a means to acquire two of the main resources that were crucial to any development process, capital and entrepreneurial skills, which were lacking in the islands. In addition, foreign investment would generate processes of "learning by doing" and Caribbean entrepreneurs would eventually be able to start their own domestic firms and national industrial base.

The strategy of industrialization by invitation was applied in two different variants in the English-speaking Caribbean and in the Hispanic Caribbean, namely, in Puerto Rico. The following sections examine the main instruments used in each and the respective results.

Industrialization by invitation in the English-speaking Caribbean: the evolution of the tax incentives schemes

Following World War II and up to the middle of the 1970s most Caribbean economies passed and gradually perfected a series of fiscal incentive to attract foreign and local investment. The fiscal incentive schemes applied to direct and indirect taxes alike. More specifically, they included income tax holidays, tax exemptions and concessions, and export subsidies. Corporations were exempted from paying taxes on profits for a tax holiday period ranging from six to 15 years subject to their value added in the process of production. Firms were also allowed to carry forward their losses during the tax holiday period, and apply a declining capital depreciation schedule balance. Individuals were exempted from paying taxes on their interest earned income. On the indirect tax side, the provisions granted duty free imports of raw materials, equipment, machinery and spare parts, and exemptions for other taxes on international trade and transactions. Finally, subsidies were established for the provision of rental factory space and utilities; and tax concessions were granted for exporting companies.[3]

Caribbean economies sought to prevent competition among member countries for investment flows and an incentives race to the bottom by harmonizing the fiscal incentives legislation. The Caribbean Free Trade Association (1968) established that possibility by stating that the council "may on its own initiative recommend to Member Territories proposals for the approximation of incentive provisions within the Area."[4] The Agreement on the Harmonization of Fiscal

Incentives to Industry (June, 1973), signed one month before the Treaty Establishing the Caribbean Community and Common Market (July, 1973), pursued this initiative.[5]

The Agreement on the Harmonization of Fiscal Incentives noted in its preamble that the process of harmonization was a requirement for the formation of the Common Market. It viewed fiscal policy as a microeconomic tool providing incentives to develop the manufacturing, mining and tourism sectors. Incentives were granted to "approved enterprises," which referred to firms receiving benefits contemplated within the framework of the agreement. These could be conferred with established ceilings at the discretion of Member States. Approved enterprises were divided into three categories according to the "local value added content" considerations and enclave enterprises.[6]

More specifically the agreement sought to promote investment from domestic and foreign sources; reduce competition among members by placing a ceiling on benefits; target incentives at enterprises with high value added; and seek regional convergence by giving greater fiscal incentives to the less developed countries (LDCs).[7]

The instruments included, as with the preceding domestic legislation, profit tax holidays, tariff exemptions, export allowances for extra-regional exports following the expiration of the tax holidays, dividend payments, loss-carry forward and depreciation allowances. Table 9.1 below summarizes the fiscal incentives under the harmonization scheme. The scheme of fiscal incentives had a number of characteristics in terms of exemptions, its implementation procedure and its sectoral distribution.

First, the scheme was targeted mainly to promote industrialization in the LDCs of CARICOM. A World Bank report (1990) found that relative to their size the LDCs had a greater number of firms receiving fiscal incentives that the more developed countries (MDCs). As an example in 1989, the number of firms that benefited from fiscal incentives in St. Vincent and the Grenadines, and Saint Lucia was 85 and 82, respectively while Barbados and Belize had 48 and 39 firms each receiving fiscal incentives.

Second, the government's provisions included in the scheme, such as, rental subsidies, the facilitation of infrastructure, and human capital enhancement through the provision of training jointly with the perception that the incentives scheme was of a temporary nature, encouraged the establishment of labor intensive and footloose firms.

Third, at the sectoral level, the incentives schemes promoted the diversification of the productive base and stimulated the establishment of firms that specialized in non-traditional products. Firms in LDCs specialized in textiles, food processing and electronics. In the MDCs, firms under the incentives scheme specialized in electronics and plastics.

Fourth, The Treaty Establishing the Caribbean Community and Single Market was more timid and cautious in its approach to the harmonization of incentives that the Agreement on The Harmonization of Fiscal Incentives to Industry. The Treaty contains one article dealing with the Harmonization of

Table 9.1 Fiscal incentives of CARICOM economies, harmonization of Fiscal Incentives Act, 1973

Profit Holiday	Duration (number of years)		
	MDCs	Barbados	LDCs
When 100% of sales are exported extra-regionally	10	10	15
When the local value added exceeds 50% of total sales	9	10	15
When the local value added is comprised within a range of 25–49%	7	8	12
When the local value added is comprised within a range of 10–24%	5	6	10
When the industry is highly capital intensive: LDCs when the initial investment >EC$25 million MDC when the initial investment >EC$50 million	10	10	15
Tariff exemptions	For the duration of the above tax holidays, inputs, machinery and spare parts can be imported duty free; all materials and equipment for new factories can be imported duty-free		
Export allowance for extra regional exports after expiration of tax holiday When exports profits >61% of the total When export profits are comprised between 41 and 61% of the total When export profits are comprised between 21 and 41% of the total When export profits are comprised between 10 and 21% of the total	Tax relief of 50% up to 5 years Tax relief of 45% up to 5 years Tax relief of 35% up to 5 years		
Dividend payments	During the validity of the above tax holiday dividends paid to shareholders are tax exempt		
Loss carry-forward	Can carry forward losses for up to five years after the tax holiday expires		
Depreciation allowance	After the tax holiday expires, a deduction of up to 20% on any capital expenditure incurred		

Source: McIntyre (1995) and World Bank (1990)

Fiscal Incentives (Art. 40) which does not require member states signatory to the Treaty to harmonize incentives.[8] The Treaty undermined the need to harmonize tax incentives and to a certain extent the Agreement on the Harmonization of Incentives which, in fact, never entered into force.[9]

As a result, while the legal framework of the Agreement was conceived at a regional level, its implementation was carried out at the national level. Thus the regional interests in targeting did not necessarily coincide with that of the individual countries. CARICOM countries exhibited a different distribution of fiscal incentives by firms and sector.

Thus, at the same time that countries implemented the Harmonization Fiscal Incentives Act, they applied a comprehensive package of domestic tax incentives policy as part of their national development policies that were suited to the specificities of each of these economies and overhauled the regional incentives scheme. The national schemes remain to this day the main vehicle for the provision of tax incentives and the main tool for developing sectoral policies.[10]

The main legal texts establishing the tax concessions are found in Fiscal Incentives Acts, Hotel Aids or Ordinance Acts, and a range of exemptions applicable to international trade and transactions taxes. The duty exemptions are specified in the Common External Tariff Legislation and/or the Common External Tariff Schedules.[11] Some of these incentives are complemented by other measures such as the granting of residential rights and even the granting of the local nationality to foreign investors.

The Revised Treaty of Chaguaramas (2001) contemplates both a regional and unified investment policy and the harmonization of investment incentives among CARICOM member states (Art 68 and 69). The texts for the harmonization of investment, incentives and fiscal policies are expected to be approved in December 2005, June 2006 and December 2006 and respectively. Some of the recommendations on the provision of fiscal incentives of a report on an Action Plan for the Harmonization of the Investment Policy Framework (2004) include the removal of incentives granted on the basis of domestic value added or the development of exports, the simplification and streamlining of the current incentives regimes and the provision of incentives in accordance with WTO rules.

The current incentives scheme has not witnessed significant changes from its predecessors. The incentive provisions consist in personal income and corporate income tax holidays, allowing losses incurred during the holiday period to be written off against future profits, accelerated depreciation allowances on capital, investment allowances, corporate income tax reductions based on the local content of outputs, income tax reductions for productive activities highly intensive in foreign-exchange-earning, exemptions from international trade and transactions for selected productive activities, and tax holidays for offshore or export-oriented industries. The tax incentives are listed in Table 9.2 by Caribbean country.

Table 9.2 Tax incentives in CARICOM (2004)

	Import tariffs[a]	Taxation of consumption[b]	PIT Rate	CIT Rate	Tax holidays	Range in number of years of tax holidays	Reduced tax rate[e]	Investment allowance	Duty/VAT reduction	Accelerated depreciation	Enhanced depreciation
Antigua	14.2	15	55	35	Yes	5–15	Yes	No	Yes	No	No
Bahamas	50.2	–	–	0	Yes	5–20	No	No	Yes	No	No
Barbados	10.2	7.5–15.0	37.5	36	Yes	10–15	Yes	Yes	Yes	No	Yes
Belize	25.5	8,12	25.0	25	Yes	5–25	Yes	No	Yes	No	No
Dominica[c]	12.2	7.5 20	40.0	30	Yes	10–20	No	Yes	Yes	Yes	No
Grenada	11.6	5–8–10–15	30.0	30	Yes	10–15	No	No	Yes	Yes	No
Guyana	8.0	0–120	33.3	45	Yes	5–10	Yes	Yes	Yes	Yes	No
Jamaica	9.4	15,12.5,6.3	25.0	33.3	Yes		Yes	Yes	Yes	Yes	Yes
St. Kitts and Nevis	14.6	4–17	–	35	Yes	10–15	No	Yes	Yes	No	No
St. Lucia	13.9	5–35	25.0	33.3	Yes	10–15	Yes	Yes	Yes	Yes	No
St. Vincent and the Grenadines	9.4	5–40	40.0	40	Yes	20	No	No	Yes	No	No
Suriname[d]	16.1	5,7 5–25	38.0	36	Yes	10	No	Yes	Yes	Yes	No
Trinidad and Tobago	6.4	15	35.0	35	Yes	10	No	Yes	Yes	Yes	Yes

Source: Rider M. (2004) and Dos Santos and Bain (2004).

Note: Accelerated depreciation refers to deductions that can be made in a reduced time span. Enhanced depreciation refers to deductions for more than the value of the capital input.

a Refers to the effective import tariff rate.

b Barbados, Jamaica and Trinidad and Tobago have a value added tax. Belize has a sales tax. Dominica and Suriname have both a sales and consumption (excise tax). Antigua and Barbuda, Grenada, St. Kitts and Nevis, St. Lucia, and St. Vincent have a consumption (excise) tax.
– indicates non-existent.

c The sales tax and the Consumption and excise tax rates are 7.5 and 20%.

d Suriname sales tax rates are 5 and 7% and the consumption tax rates range between 5 and 25%.

e Antigua and Barbuda, can apply reduced tax rates and investment allowances or tax credit only through a special permit of the government. Grenada can apply investment allowances or tax credit only through a special permit of the government.

Industrialization by invitation in the Hispanic Caribbean: the case of Puerto Rico

From 1950 until 1986, "Operation Bootstrap" guided the orientation of economic policy. As stated by Bonilla and Campos (1982, pp. 133–4):

> Bootstrap strategists argued that the intolerable population pressures on resources constituted the root obstacle to economic advance and the necessary modernization of Puerto Rico. Their prescription was to find a low-cost approach to channel the movement of redundant Puerto Rican workers abroad while drawing energetic entrepreneurs to the Island from the United States. The necessary economic and social operations envisioned in Bootstrap were to be carried out through the agency of a newly designed political structure the commonwealth.[12]

It was conceived as a two-stage strategy. In the first stage, Puerto Rico would provide the social capital and the required infrastructure (Holbik and Swan, 1975; Cabán, 2002). These would be financed through the sale of bonds in the United States capital market and local taxes. Government expenditures and policies would provide, in turn, an important stimulus to the expansion of private investment, which took, in fact, a leading role during this phase. In the second stage, American firms would "be induced to locate through industrial sites through an elaborate incentives program. The incentives included: tax concessions, grants, subsidized rentals and utility rates and low wage rates" (Holbik and Swan, 1975, p. 16).

The first stage of the strategy was accompanied by significant government capital expenditures (education, transportation, housing, communications and irrigation) to provide a basis for the development of private enterprise.[13] This policy continued well into the 1960s as the focus of expenditure centered on roads and education (Holbik and Swan, 1975). Besides government intervention, the development of private enterprise was further enhanced by a policy of tax incentives deliberately aimed at encouraging domestic investment. One such example is the 1948 law granting tax incentives.

The 1948 law exempted from income, property and excise taxes in Puerto Rico, new industries established in 1947. The level of exemption granted was established at 100 percent until 1959 and 75, 50 and 25 percent in the following three years (Lewis, 1949). As Lewis saw it the law benefited only:

> (a) Puerto Rican capitalists who establish new industries; (b) U.S. capitalists who move from the U.S. to Puerto Rico; (c) by a special provision of the U.S. Tax Law a capitalist who resides in the U.S. but who derives 80 percent of his income from Puerto Rico, including 50 percent from active conduct of a business in Puerto Rico (probably a rare species) …. Tax exemption thus benefits the small American capitalist who is willing to transfer to Puerto Rico, and the large American capitalist who is willing to

use his Puerto Rico profits to expand his assets in Puerto Rico. But it would not help a large American corporation which built a branch plant in Puerto Rico and wished to use the income to declare dividends to its American shareholders.

Thus the tax laws and incentives benefited domestic investment.

The attraction of foreign direct investment was directly tied to a policy of federal and local fiscal incentives.[14] At the local level during Phase II, the Industrial Incentives Act (1978) sought to homogenize the existing Puerto Rican tax legislation with that of the rest of the United States. This meant the elimination of the regime of local tax exemptions, which had been in place since the late 1940s and which had provided a stimulus to the expansion of domestic investment. More importantly the 1978 Act encouraged the development of the services sector by granting a tax break of 50 percent to export-oriented service firms engaged in "distribution, consulting, accounting, banking and computer systems." According to Dietz (2001) "this contributed to the shift in overall production toward services and the emergence of ... the 'high finance' stage of industrialization."

At the federal level, Section 931 of the United States internal revenue tax code in force until 1976 allowed United States corporations to "exclude their profits from any US tax liability on so-called possessions income, as long as these profits were not repatriated to the US during the 'life' of the corporation." As also noted by Dietz (2001), this law "led to 'ghost' closings of corporations at the end of their Puerto Rican exemption period so that profits could be repatriated. These firms would be then reconstituted with a new exemption period in Puerto Rico until a subsequent ghost liquidation took place so that profits could again be remitted tax free."

The tax reform act of 1975 replaced Section 931 with Section 936. It provided a tax credit "equal to the full amount of the United States corporate income tax liability on income generated by production, trade or investment activities of an active business in a United States possession." This incentive "sheltered a large proportion of corporate income taxes generated by profits of production facilities located in Puerto Rico. The intent was to promote development of the Puerto Rico economy and the reduced costs also encouraged production of materials for export."[15] Investment income was also exempted from the federal income tax provided that at least three-quarters of all profits came from trade or production activities and provided that the income was earned and invested in Puerto Rico.

Section 936 was, without doubt, a significant tax incentive act as it was estimated that more than 90 percent of those corporations that qualified for tax exemptions under Section 936 were located in Puerto Rico. However the law also led to a concentration of industry in manufacturing and pharmaceuticals. In fact the drug and pharmaceuticals industry received half of the tax benefits granted by section 936 of the tax reform act of 1975.

While Puerto Rico officially abandoned the policy guidelines of "operation bootstrap" in the late 1980s and early 1990s, the government still viewed tax incentives as a fundamental part of their development policy. In the 1990s the tax legislation underwent important changes whose effects are not yet visible for the last years of the sample but which could have an important effect on the convergence trajectory of Puerto Rico to the United States.

Since 1993 the United States has gradually sought to suppress the special and differential tax treatment received by Puerto Rico. In 1993 the Omnibus Budget Reconciliation Act imposed cutbacks in the program of tax incentives for new investments by retaining the investment tax credit while imposing limits on the income-based tax credit. The latter decreased by five percentage points a year in 1995 – from 60 percent of profits in 1994 to 40 percent of qualified labor costs in 1998.

In 1996, Section 936 was repealed through the Small Business Job Protection Act and granted a phase out of ten years for current beneficiaries. Section 936 was replaced by Section 30A which allowed only wages to be tax deductible for US firms already established in Puerto Rico. In turn, Section 30A was set to expire at the end of 2005.

The authorities have proposed an amendment to Section 956 of the federal tax code, which would allow controlled foreign corporations (CFC) to repatriate 90 percent of their profits to related or parent operations in the United States tax-free. The income-based option of the Omnibus Budget Reconciliation Act will remain at its 1998 level. The reduction of tax incentives is estimated to increase from US$111 million in 1996 to US$2,686 in 2006 (Dusenbury and Liner, 1997).

At the local level the authorities have sought to offset the negative effects of the 936 Section phase out. As a result they passed the Tax Incentives Act of 1998 providing an exemption from Puerto Rican taxes for approved firms.[16] As well there are tax incentives for employment. An important change in the structure of the tax incentive system is that it "has shifted from large tax exemptions to low tax rates."[17] In 2001, the authorities approved the Export Law (August 2001) in an effort to "promote the distribution of products through existing channels such as multinationals retailers and joint venture agreements."[18] This law raises the tax credit from 10 to 25 percent when buying products which are manufactured in Puerto Rico.[19]

Invitation by industrialization: economic effects and implications

This section analyses the effects of the policies followed in the English-speaking Caribbean and Puerto Rico that were inspired by the strategy of industrialization by invitation. The focus is on whether the policies that were followed were successful in attracting foreign capital and on whether foreign capital was able to spur the development of domestic industry.

In the case of the English-speaking Caribbean, official assistance aid constituted the main form of net long-term foreign financial flows at least until the end of the 1980s. Available data indicate that these represented on average 65 percent per year of the total between 1981 and 1990.

During the 1990s the trend was reversed and official aid flows diminished considerably. Net official flows of resources, including grants, declined from 59 to 6 percent of the total between 1990 and 2000 (see Table 9.5 below). In 2002 official development and assistance and official aid represented 12 percent of total foreign exchange receipts. This highlights the greater reliance on private capital flows to finance development projects. Private capital flows increased eightfold, from US$326.4 million in 1990 to US$2,929 million in 2000.

This trend responded partly to domestic policy changes of donor countries as well as the adoption of structural change and outward-oriented policies in receiving countries and the reduction of capital controls and development of international financial markets. It also reflected a modification in the perception of the usefulness of official capital flows as a major contributor to development. Official capital flows switched their role from a fundamental engine of development to a complement of private flows. Finally, successful developing countries such as some Caribbean countries were viewed as graduates of concessional aid ready to take on the challenges of commercial borrowing. This allowed donor countries to reorient official aid to regions with high levels of poverty or that were in the process of restructuring their economies towards market-based systems.

Foreign direct investment (FDI, hereafter) increasingly substituted official assistance flows. FDI represents the main component of private capital flows in the Caribbean. During the 1990s, net FDI in the sub-region grew significantly, representing an increase from 8 to 10 percent of GDP on average, remaining at 5 percent of GDP between 2000 and 2002. FDI represents more than 20 percent of gross fixed capital formation (World Bank, 2005). The bulk of FDI is sourced in the United States followed by Europe. In 2002, net FDI flows accounted for a quarter of total foreign exchange receipts (see Table 9.3).

At the sectoral level, FDI inflows were concentrated on resource based-sectors: mining (bauxite and precious metals) (Guyana, Jamaica and Suriname), energy (petroleum) (Trinidad), agriculture (Barbados, Belize, Organization of Eastern Caribbean States – OECS), forestry (Guyana), and tourism services (OECS, Bahamas, Barbados). According to the World Bank (World Bank, 2005) the most significant growth of FDI was registered in Jamaica and the OECS.

In the case of the OECS, FDI is destined mainly to the tourism industry. As shown in Table 9.4, between 1997 and 2004 tourism received 60 percent of total FDI in the OECS outstripping by far any other sector. Also tourism and manufacturing are the only two sectors that receive foreign direct investment on a yearly basis. However, the inflows to the manufacturing sector are negligible (less than 1 percent of the total).

In the case of Puerto Rico, FDI did not increase, at least during the first decade of the implementation of "Operation Bootstrap" (1950 to 1960). In this regard Padin (2003, pp. 285–6) states: "US firms attracted to Puerto Rico in the 1950's were relatively small, labor intensive operations in declining sectors with

Table 9.3 Foreign exchange receipts for the Caribbean, by category and in percentage of the total, 2002

Country	Foreign direct investment, net inflows	Net current transfers	Official development assistance and official aid	Net service receipts	Total
Antigua and Barbuda	0.0	2.6	5.9	91.5	100.0
Bahamas, The	12.7	0.0	0.4	86.9	100.0
Barbados	2.3	23.3	0.5	74.0	100.0
Belize	21.6	34.6	20.0	23.8	100.0
Dominica	13.6	17.5	36.9	32.0	100.0
Grenada	42.7	17.1	7.2	33.0	100.0
Guyana	35.1	31.9	51.7	–18.7	100.0
Jamaica	27.1	53.8	1.4	17.7	100.0
St. Kitts and Nevis	51.5	23.2	18.3	7.0	100.0
St. Lucia	21.0	5.9	14.7	58.5	100.0
St. Vincent and the Grenadines	25.5	9.7	3.8	61.0	100.0
Suriname	0.0	0.0	–10.0	110.0	100.0
Trinidad and Tobago	71.8	4.9	–0.7	24.0	100.0
Total	29.4	23.1	4.1	43.3	100.0
Average	25.0	17.3	11.5	46.2	100.0

Source: World Development Indicators (2005)

Table 9.4 OECS, share of foreign direct investment per economic sector, 1997–2004 (%)

Sector	1997	1998	1999	2000	2001	2002	2003	2004	Average
Tourism	60.12	74.83	81.56	63.86	47.04	56.67	35.43	60.99	60.06
Manufacturing	1.53	0.16	0.40	1.20	1.90	0.24	0.52	0.74	0.84
Transportation	0.00	0.00	0.00	0.00	0.00	0.00	0.00	0.00	0.00
Construction	2.89	0.92	0.00	0.00	0.00	0.00	5.56	11.48	2.61
Sporting	2.06	6.24	1.14	0.00	0.00	0.00	0.00	0.00	1.18
Medical	0.00	0.00	0.00	0.00	0.24	0.34	0.00	0.00	0.07
Financial	0.00	0.00	0.00	0.00	0.24	1.20	0.00	0.00	0.18
Banking and Insurance	1.42	0.00	0.74	0.30	0.00	0.00	0.00	0.00	0.31
Commercial	2.11	0.00	0.00	4.84	0.84	0.00	0.00	0.00	0.98
Petroleum	1.50	0.08	0.25	0.00	0.00	0.00	0.00	0.00	0.31
Education	0.00	0.72	1.88	0.00	0.00	0.00	1.47	0.00	0.81
Agriculture	0.00	3.12	2.04	0.62	0.25	0.67	0.28	0.01	0.48
Other	28.36	13.94	11.99	29.18	49.48	40.87	56.73	26.79	32.17
Total	100.00	100.00	100.00	100.00	100.00	100.00	100.00	100.00	100.00

a grim future in the United States ... The turn to private foreign direct investment was initially so uncertain that each new plant was celebrated with the
orchestrated fanfare of a development agency fearful of losing public support for
its efforts."

For the following decade (the 1970s) Morley (1980, p. 183) stresses that,
"The number of new factories in operation as a result of 'Operation Bootstrap'
grew from 548 in 1957–1958 to 1,003 in 1964–1965 and then jumped dramatically to 1,674 in 1967–1968 when heavy capital investments were beginning to
establish a foothold in the Puerto Rican economy."

Foreign direct investment, which represented 5 percent of GNP in the period
1947–1971 rose to 11 percent in the period 1971–1986.[20] The take off in foreign
investment at the beginning of the 1970s responded in part to the change in the
tax legislation, as the 1948 act was replaced with a new and more comprehensive tax exemption act in 1963 and later in 1969 by the increase in the flexibility
in the granting of tax incentives given to the government. The 1963 tax act
granted exemptions of up to 100 percent on earnings ranging for a period of ten
to 17 years. Also the tax exemption period could be expanded when a firm opted
for 50 percent exemption on earnings combined with full exemption on local
taxes. Table 9.5 shows the composition of net financial flows for CARICOM
economies.

The rise in FDI was reinforced by the adoption and implementation of sections 931 and later 936 of the United States tax code. Section 936 was without
doubt, a significant tax incentive act as it was estimated that more than 90
percent of those corporations that qualified for tax exemptions under Section
936 were located in Puerto Rico. However the law also led to a concentration of
industry in manufacturing and pharmaceuticals. In fact the drug and pharmaceuticals industry received half of the tax benefits granted by section 936 of the tax
reform act of 1975.

In both the English Caribbean and Puerto Rican cases the large increases in
FDI have generated few spill-over effects. As put by the World Bank in a recent
report on the English-speaking Caribbean: "FDI has contributed little to
dynamic specialization in higher valued added production due to limited knowledge transfers and weak research and development spillovers."[21]

In the case of the English-speaking Caribbean economies there is preliminary
empirical evidence that shows that FDI flows went into those economies that
had the highest levels of domestic investment. The correlation coefficient
between FDI for 1991–2000 and gross domestic investment as a percentage of
GDP for 1981–1990 was found to be 0.53. More recent empirical analysis shows
that there is a negative statistical relationship between the levels of FDI and
domestic investment (the correlation coefficient is –0.21 and –0.22 for
1990–1997 and 1998–2003).

However, the change in FDI is not in any way related to the change in gross
domestic investment (the change between both as a percentage of GDP was
found to be 0.003 for 1991–2000). The data show that domestic investment as a
percentage of GDP has remained unchanged at the regional level and in many

Table 9.5 Composition of net financial flows for CARICOM economies (% total 1990–2000)

	1990	1991	1992	1993	1994	1995	1996	1997	1998	1999	2000
Total net financial flows	100	100	100	100	100	100	100	100	100	100	100
Total net long term	85.73	107.64	90.94	102.54	103.70	72.10	128.90	72.68	105.29	73.27	100.00
Official flows	59.25	92.44	29.22	39.18	14.85	23.50	14.56	5.82	13.43	6.86	6.34
Grants	33.88	64.12	20.43	35.32	20.66	24.11	25.78	16.10	20.70	17.38	4.76
Loans	25.37	28.33	8.79	3.86	-5.82	-0.61	-11.22	-10.28	-7.26	-10.51	1.58
Private flows	26.49	15.19	61.71	63.36	88.85	48.60	114.34	66.86	91.86	66.40	93.65
Debt flows	-42.55	-27.52	-12.64	-14.16	-11.22	-19.88	-6.28	-4.77	7.32	-0.04	33.69
Commercial bank loans	-12.07	-1.12	-4.07	-1.86	-3.30	-6.26	-8.27	-2.46	-2.69	-4.65	4.99
Other	-24.56	-26.41	-8.57	-12.30	-7.92	-13.63	1.98	-2.31	10.01	4.62	28.70
Foreign direct investment	69.04	42.71	74.35	77.53	100.07	68.48	120.62	71.63	84.54	66.44	59.96
Short term debt flows	14.27	-7.64	9.06	-2.54	-3.70	27.90	-28.90	27.32	-5.29	26.73	0.00

Source: On the basis of World Bank and ECLAC data.

country cases this ratio has decreased. On average for CARICOM countries the ratio of investment to GDP was 28 percent during 1981–1990 and remained at that level between 1998 and 2003 (27 percent) (see Table 9.6).

In the case of Puerto Rico, gross formation of fixed capital as a percentage of GNP averaged 21 percent during the first two decades of Operation Bootstrap reaching a peak of 31 percent. During the last decade of Operation Bootstrap the said ratio declined to 17 percent reaching an overall low of 11 percent by the end of the 1960s (see Table 9.7).

In the case of the English-speaking Caribbean, the revealed preference for foreign over domestic investment has underpinned a pattern of productive specialization characterized by the predominance of the services sector and natural resource activities, the decline of agriculture and the stagnation of the manufacturing sector. The GDP agricultural and manufacturing shares have

Table 9.6 Gross domestic investment in the Caribbean, 1980–2003 (% GDP)

Country	1981–1990	1991–2000	1998–2003
Antigua and Barbuda	33.8	33.6	29.0
Barbados	18.6	15.2	15.0
Belize	23.6	25.9	19.0
Dominica	31.1	29.0	21.0
Grenada	34.0	37.0	37.0
Guyana	28.0	31.3	22.0
Jamaica	23.1	28.1	30.0
St. Kitts and Nevis	37.7	42.6	46.0
Saint Lucia	26.8	23.6	26.0
St. Vincent and the Grenadines	28.9	28.7	32.0
Trinidad and Tobago	20.3	20.7	22.0
Average	27.8	28.7	27.2

Source: World Bank (2002; 2005)

Table 9.7 Puerto Rico: selected indicators 1947–2002

	1947–1971	1971–1986	1986–2002
(GDP-GNP)/GNP (%)[a]	0	23	47
Gross fixed capital formation as % of GNP	21.0	17.0	21.9
Foreign direct investment as % of GNP	5.2	10.94	n.a.
Foreign direct investment as % of gross fixed domestic investment	10.9	41.32	n.a.

Source: On the basis of official information. United States Department of Commerce (1979).

Notes
GDP is the gross domestic product and GNP is the gross national product. n.a. = not available.
a Includes the first and last data points of the corresponding phases. In the case of Phase II the ratio of Foreign Direct Investment as % of GNP and that of foreign direct investment as % of gross fixed domestic investment covers the years 1971 to 1976.

Table 9.8 Sectoral growth rates, GDP shares and contribution to GDP, 1960–1990 (averages by decade)

	Agriculture	Manufacturing	Services
Sectoral growth			
1960s	1.4	4.9	5.3
1970s	0.5	7.0	5.8
1980s	0.3	4.6	4.9
1990s	1.2	3.9	3.3
GDP shares			
1960s	13.7	37.6	49.9
1970s	16.6	25.8	54.3
1980s	12.5	25.3	58.9
1990s	9.8	25.1	61.6
Contribution to GDP			
1960s	0.2	2.0	3.9
1970s	0.0	2.0	3.3
1980s	0.1	1.1	2.8
1990s	0.1	0.8	2.4

Source: World Bank (2005).

decreased from 14 to 10 percent and 38 to 25 percent between the 1960s and the 1990s, while that of services has risen from 50 to 62 percent in the same period (see Table 9.8 below).

The respective governments have actively promoted those activities which are foreign exchange intensive through a gamut of fiscal incentives which impaired the use of taxation as a tool to achieve a more equitable distribution of income or to equilibrate the budget. Fiscal policy is mainly a microeconomic tool providing incentives to develop activities in selected economic sectors. The instruments include profit tax holidays, tariff exemptions, export allowances for extra-regional exports following the expiration of the tax holidays, dividend payments, loss carry forward and depreciation allowances.

This, in turn, has encouraged the development of the duality of existing productive structures and sectors. But most important, in the English-speaking Caribbean, the productivity and performance of the "dynamic sectors" (natural resource and services sectors) have never been able to compensate or offset the decline and underperformance of the "stagnant and laggard sectors." Moreover, the efforts to develop foreign exchange earning sectors have not managed to improve their economic performance. Indeed, all economic sectors have witnessed declines in their rates of growth in the past 30 years (see Table 9.8).

This is also clearly reflected in the roughly steady deterioration of the export performance of goods and services. The deteriorating export performance can be measured by the export performance ratio. It is measured by the ratio of exports to the average propensity of imports (i.e. the ratio of imports to GDP). When exports are equal to imports, the export performance ratio is equal to GDP. The

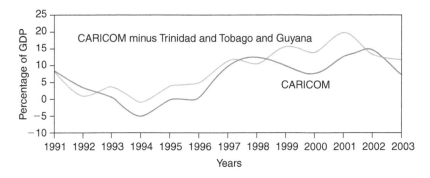

Figure 9.1 Export performance ratio, average for CARICOM 1991–2003.

export performance ratio can be computed in terms of percent deviation from GDP. A value of 0 would indicate a state of external equilibrium. A value greater than 0 in percentage shows the percent deviation of the external account from its equilibrium value.

This measure was obtained for each CARICOM economy and then an average was obtained. As can be seen from Figure 9.1 the export performance ratio expressed as a percentage deviation from GDP is characterized by three movements. The export performance was computed for CARICOM and for a subgrouping, excluding Trinidad and Tobago, and Guyana. The first movement is a decline lasting from 1991 until 1994. During this period the export performance of CARICOM economies on average improved. The year 1994 marks a point of inflection from the previous trend after which the export performance deteriorates steadily until 2002. In 1994, CARICOM economies on average had equilibrium in their balance of payments. Eight year later in 2002, their export performance had deteriorated to a value equivalent to 20 percent of their combined GDP. The third period shows some improvement in the export performance ratio.

The worsening of CARICOM's export performance is reflected in the loss of market share in its major export markets both in goods and tourist services including CARICOM, the European Union (EU) and the North American Free Trade Agreement (NAFTA) (see Tables 9.9 to 9.11). Between 1985 and 2002, the export market share of Caribbean countries in regional trading blocs such as NAFTA and Western Europe has decreased from 0.71 to 0.27 percent and from 0.15 to 0.10 percent, respectively (see Table 9.9).

In the same vein intraregional trade has also declined for the majority of CARICOM member States. The OECS, the LDCs and the MDCs (if Trinidad and Tobago is excluded) have lost intraregional market share. The OECS intraregional share dropped from 2.4 to 1.4 percent of the total between 1980 and 2003. For the same period, the LDCs share declined from 2.5 to 1.8 percent of the total. Finally, the MDCs share (excluding Trinidad and Tobago) decreased from 4 to 2 percent in the said period. Moreover, the share of intraregional trade has declined for most CARICOM countries (see Table 9.11 below).

Table 9.9 CARICOM's import market share in goods in regional trading blocs, 1985–2002 (%)

Regional bloc	1985	1990	1995	2000	2002
NAFTA	0.71	0.43	0.32	0.24	0.27
Western Europe	0.15	0.13	0.12	0.10	–
Andean Community	0.40	0.96	0.41	0.24	0.56
Marcos	0.30	0. 34	0.19	0.11	0.14
CACM	0.20	0.18	0.38	0.74	1.34

Sources: Competitive Analysis of Nations (2002) and WITS (2005).

Note
– denotes not available.

The stagnation/deterioration of export performance is not limited to goods but also affects services, which is important because services also play an important social role and have a major impact on the financial stability of a country, growth and the balance of payments. Moreover, the services sector has traditionally been identified as the sector that will provide the impetus for growth in the future and thus should be the main contributor to output, growth, employment and the provision for basic needs.

The deteriorating export performance has made these economies forever dependent on foreign capital. The pressing need for foreign exchange has shaped and geared most of their internal policies to the attraction and capture of foreign exchange rather than to goals linked to domestic economic development. The opportunity can be partly measured by the monetary value of the fiscal incentives referred to above.

The cost of fiscal incentives has been exceptionally high as illustrated by some of the smaller economies of the Caribbean. In the case of St. Kitts and Nevis, according to the International Monetary Fund (IMF) data, more than 58 percent of imports (equivalent to 31 percent of GDP) are exempt from import duties, 50 percent from the consumption tax and 39 percent from the service charge. Of this total the fiscal incentives act accounts for 14 percent of all the imports (representing 7.3 percent of GDP) that are exempted from the payment of duty, consumption tax and service charges.

In the case of Puerto Rico, Operation Bootstrap encouraged the development of "highly capital intensive" industries such as the pharmaceutical industry, which is highly capital intensive and did not favor the creation of employment. Indeed it was estimated in 1987 that the level of employment in pharmaceutical companies represented less than 3 percent of the total employment generated in Puerto Rico. Also they represent less than 18 percent of the total employment generated by companies benefiting from the tax exemptions granted in Section 936.

Operation Bootstrap ultimately also boosted profit repatriation flows. If the repatriation of profits is measured by the difference between the GDP (income

Table 9.10 Foreign direct investment (% GDP)

	1990	1991	1992	1993	1994	1995	1996	1997	1998	1999	2000	2001	2002
Anguilla	19.7	11.3	25.6	10.1	15.0	23.7	42.1	23.8	29.8	36.3	36.4	24.9	13.7
Antigua and Barbuda	15.5	13.3	4.6	3.3	5.0	6.4	3.6	4.0	4.4	5.6	5.0	7.8	5.5
Barbados	1.2	2.0	1.7	0.1	2.3	-0.3	1.2	1.4	0.7	2.2	6.0	3.6	6.8
Belize	3.3	3.1	1.8	1.3	7.5	7.2	2.5	5.0	2.7				
Dominica	7.7	8.4	10.7	6.6	10.5	24.7	7.6	10.3	3.0	8.0	4.7	6.4	4.3
Grenada	5.8	6.3	9.0	8.1	7.3	7.2	6.6	10.6	13.9	11.0	8.8	8.6	19.8
Guyana	4.1	8.0	36.9	13.6	8.8	8.6	8.4	7.0	6.7	6.7	9.5	7.9	–
Jamaica		1.4	9.8	7.3	10.2	5.5	8.1	-0.1	2.0	-0.1	6.0	12.1	5.4
Montserrat	14.3	14.4	7.9	7.8	11.3	5.0	-0.7	6.3	6.8	23.4	9.9	10.2	0.6
St. Kitts and Nevis	6.0	4.9	2.5	6.9	6.9	8.9	14.3	7.2	11.1	19.0	29.2	24.1	22.8
St. Lucia	10.8	1.8	0.9	6.9	6.3	5.9	3.2	8.3	13.3	12.4	7.1	7.7	7.2
St. Vincent and the Grenadines	3.9	4.2	6.4	13.2	19.4	11.6	15.3	31.5	28.0	16.9	8.4	10.2	9.2
Trinidad and Tobago	2.2	2.5	3.1	8.8	10.5	5.5	6.2	17.2	11.6	5.5	8.1	6.2	7.1
Average all	8.3	6.5	9.9	7.7	9.0	8.9	9.1	9.9	10.7	11.9	10.9	10.4	12.5
Standard deviation	6.0	4.6	10.7	3.7	4.7	7.4	11.0	9.2	9.1	9.9	10.0	6.7	13.1
Average OECS	10.5	8.1	8.5	7.9	10.2	11.7	11.5	12.7	13.8	16.6	13.7	12.5	16.0
Average Larger	1.9	3.5	3.6	7.4	8.0	4.8	6.0	6.4	5.2	3.6	7.4	7.5	14.5
Average RBE with Guyana	2.1	3.5	13.3	7.5	7.6	5.7	5.5	8.5	8.6	6.5	6.7	6.4	–
Average RBE without Guyana in 1992	2.1	5.4	1.0	7.5	7.6	5.7	5.5	8.5	8.6	6.5	6.7	6.4	–
Average SBE	8.4	6.0	5.4	4.4	5.8	6.2	8.0	6.4	8.3	12.4	11.7	9.8	15.0

Source: ECLAC on the basis of official data.

Note
SBE = service based economies, RBE= resource-based economies, – denotes not available.

Table 9.11 Intraregional trade shares of exports and imports, 1980–2003

	1980	1985	1990	1995	2000	2003
Intra-regional trade share (exports)						
Antigua and Barbuda	0.27	0.26	0.27	0.00	0.13	0.00
Barbados	0.92	2.30	1.66	1.79	1.59	1.70
Belize	0.10	0.10	0.21	0.11	0.12	0.30
Dominica	0.10	0.31	0.34	0.38	0.42	0.43
Grenada	0.04	0.23	0.17	0.12	0.16	0.18
Guyana	0.91	0.53	0.33	0.00	0.90	–
Jamaica	0.99	1.38	1.76	1.19	0.66	–
Montserrat	0.00	0.01	0.01	0.01	0.00	0.02
St. Kitts and Nevis	0.07	0.17	0.09	0.04	0.04	0.01
St. Lucia	0.25	0.29	0.53	0.34	0.17	0.46
St. Vincent and the Grenadines	0.11	1.09	0.69	0.54	0.31	0.34
Suriname	0.00	0.00	0.00	0.23	–	–
Trinidad and Tobago	5.88	6.88	6.60	11.94	13.19	17.22
CARICOM	9.66	13.36	12.39	16.70	17.17	20.65
OECS	0.85	2.35	2.11	1.45	1.24	1.44
LDC's	0.95	2.45	2.32	1.56	1.36	1.75
MDCs	8.70	11.09	10.34	15.15	16.35	18.91
MDCs without Trinidad[a]	2.82	4.21	3.75	3.21	3.98	1.68
MDCs without Trinidad[b]	9.06	10.56	7.52	6.39	7.59	–
Intra-regional trade share (imports)						
Antigua and Barbuda	0.73	0.77	0.68	–	–	–
Barbados	1.69	2.22	2.16	1.71	2.14	4.24
Belize	0.04	0.06	0.26	0.18	0.13	0.22
Dominica	0.22	0.34	0.50	0.44	0.37	0.57
Grenada	0.28	0.39	0.51	0.49	0.54	0.9
Guyana	1.54	1.98	0.49	0.00	0.91	–
Jamaica	1.45	1.07	1.74	3.52	3.72	–
Montserrat	0.07	0.10	0.16	0.00	0.04	0.04
St. Kitts and Nevis	0.16	0.25	0.32	0.32	0.34	0.56
St. Lucia	0.45	0.60	0.96	0.94	0.74	1.16
St. Vincent and the Grenadines	0.28	0.36	0.56	0.50	0.46	0.67
Suriname	0.00	0.00	0.00	0.70	–	–
Trinidad and Tobago	1.92	2.45	1.57	1.08	1.17	1.21
CARICOM	8.81	9.72	9.21	9.86	10.96	9.58
LDCs	1.62	2.03	2.65	1.60	1.54	2.40
MDCs	6.60	7.72	5.95	6.99	7.94	5.45
MDCs without Trinidad[a]	4.68	5.27	4.39	5.92	6.77	4.24
MDCs without Trinidad[b]	10.13	7.96	5.55	8.16	6.78	–

Sources: On the basis of data provided in 2003 and 2005 by the CARICOM Secretariat and CAN (2002).

Note
– denotes not available. a/ Adjusts for intraregional trade. b/ Accounts for intra and extra regional trade.

produced in Puerto Rico) and the GNP (income available in Puerto Rico) as a percentage of GNP, it is seen that throughout the 1940s and 1950s the ratio was negative, standing at 6 percent of GNP on average. It turned positive in 1960 and rose steadily throughout the period. During the 1960s the ratio equaled 4.4 percent on average. In the following three decades, the difference of GDP and GNP to GNP increased to 17, 37 and 48 percent, respectively. In 2002, it again risen to 57 percent.

The widening gap between the income produced and that available in Puerto Rico was accompanied by a marked shift in the distribution of wealth towards foreign-owned assets. Puerto Rican nationals saw the share of non-local direct investment increase from 26 to 44 percent between 1970 and 1980. At the same time Puerto Rican National Wealth, expressed as a percentage of total assets, steadily declined from 81 to 23 percent between 1950 and 1980.

Conclusion

The attraction of foreign direct investment is a key ingredient of developing country's long-run development policy and strategy. Inflows of FDI are viewed in a positive light as these narrow the financing gap of most developing economies. They help to reduce the shortage of domestic savings while at the same time increase the supply of foreign exchange.

More importantly the act of investment can generate a positive economic value to the recipient country if its social returns exceed the private returns (the increase in real income deriving from the investment is greater than the increase in income of the foreign investor). The positive expected effect of FDI has led governments to adopt a series of measures to attract long-term foreign capital.

Foreign direct investment can generate a positive value through spillover effects that improve productivity and export performance. Spillover channels include imitation, learning-by-doing, acquisition of skills, competition and higher value-added exports. However, the evidence regarding the benefits of spillover and more generally FDI is at best mixed. The empirical evidence presented in this chapter for Puerto Rico and the English-speaking Caribbean goes further and shoes that FDI can actually have detrimental effects on the recipient economies.

In the case of Puerto Rico the take off in foreign investment occurred at the beginning of the 1970s. It ultimately materialized into a growing divide between the income produced by Puerto Ricans and that available to Puerto Ricans. At the same time there was a marked shift in the distribution of wealth towards foreign-owned assets and a rise in the rate of unemployment. The take off was also one of economic decline and of absence of convergence between Puerto Rico and the rest of the United States economy.

In the case of the English-speaking Caribbean countries FDI exhibited weak linkages with the rest of the economy and did not manage to improve their perform-ance or competitiveness. The policies geared to attract FDI have in fact aggravated the key constraint of the Caribbean, the balance-of-payments constraint.

The existing literature on development economics and FDI has analyzed in depth the conditions that attract FDI. However, little attention has been paid to the conditions under which FDI can be beneficial to the recipient countries. This is due to the fact that traditional theory believes, in a dogmatic way, that FDI is "a driver of growth or development." The evidence in this chapter argues that this is not necessarily the case.

Notes

1 ECLAC Sub-regional headquarters for the Caribbean (Port of Spain, Trinidad and Tobago). The opinions here expressed are the author's own and may not coincide with those of ECLAC. Comments are welcome and can be sent to esteban.perez@eclacpos.org.
2 "Export-Led Industrialization by Invitation" is the more correct expression. It was coined by Best (1976).
3 See, Downes (2004).
4 Art. 23(3). The Caribbean Free Trade Association in The CARICOM System (2003).
5 See Agreement on the Harmonization of Fiscal Incentives to Industry in The CARICOM System (2003), p. 172.
6 The Agreement defined 'Approved Enterprise' as an enterprise which is approved by the relevant authority of a Member State for the purpose of conferring a benefit under the Harmonization of Fiscal Incentives to Industry Scheme.
7 In this sense the Agreement on Harmonization recognized the Principle of Special and Differential Treatment as being applicable within the Caribbean Common Market. This is also the case of the Treaty. In this respect see for example Art. 40(2) of the Treaty in the CARICOM System (2003), p. 215. The LDCs include the OECS (Antigua and Barbuda, Dominica, Grenada, Montserrat, St. Kitts and Nevis, St. Lucia, St. Vincent and the Grenadines) and Belize. The MDC's comprise The Bahamas, Barbados, Jamaica, Guyana, Suriname, Trinidad and Tobago.
8 The Treaty states that: "Member Status shall seek to harmonize such legislation as directly affect fiscal incentives to industry ... seek to establish regimes for the harmonization of fiscal incentives to agriculture and tourism ... study the possibility of approximating income tax systems and rates with respect to companies and individuals." See Treaty, Art. 40, in The CARICOM System (2003), p. 215.
9 CARICOM System (2003), p. 171.
10 Tax incentives are the main tool of industrial policy for CARICOM economies.
11 Some of these exemptions are granted under the Conditional Duty Exemptions of the Common External Tariff. The list includes among others, exemptions granted to industry, agriculture, fisheries, forestry, mining, tourism activities and shipping. See Common External Tariff of the Caribbean Common Market (Volume 3). Caribbean Community Secretariat, Georgetown, 1997.
12 The Commonwealth of Puerto Rico was established in 1952.
13 Holbik and Swan (1975, p. 25) write: "Heavy expenditures were made in subsequent years on education, transport, housing, telephones, irrigation, and power. A permanent improvement program was established outside the budgetary process to ensure steady progress. By 1967 the economy had developed to the point that it could support a $69 million program to finance expenditures of $14 million in industrial and tourist facilities, $11.4 million for new schools, $10.8 million for new housing, $9 million for land purchases, and $7.4 million for rural water supplies. In addition, a highway allocation of $7 million was to be lent by a New York bank in a project that would reach $40 million, the largest single credit transaction ever handled by Puerto Rico." The expenditure in infrastructure can also be seen as a component of social tranquility required for the success of Operation Bootstrap.

14 Arthur Lewis sought that the main incentive to attract foreign capital to the Caribbean was lower labor costs. Lewis sought to supplement this by a policy of fiscal incentives. The protectionist side to this development model came at a later stage. In fact, Lewis, rather than arguing in favor of protection from imports, stated the case for export subsidies. As he put it (p. 886): "Most of the industries will have to export, and if they are to do this, they must be able to compete on the world market; and if they can compete there, they will not need protection in the domestic market."

15 See, The Urban Institute. Targeting Export Markets for Puerto Rico. 1997.

16 The law establishes a maximum 7 percent flat corporate tax and some qualified companies are eligible to pay as little as 2 percent. In addition the law contemplates a special 0–2 percent tax rate, a 200 percent super-deduction for research and development and job training costs, accelerated depreciation for fixed investment, and a 100 percent deduction on real and personal property taxes during the initial first year construction.

17 See, Commerce in Puerto Rico. EIU. 2003.

18 Promoexport and the internationalization of Puerto Rico's Producers. Promoexport. Memo. 2003.

19 See, Ley Num 110. (2001) in *Nuevas Leyes para Promover el Desarrollo Económico de Puerto Rico*. San Juan, Puerto Rico (2002).

20 The scant empirical data available on FDI validates this hypothesis. Between 1960 and 1967 total United States investment in Puerto Rico increased from $1.4 to $5 billion and continued to expand to $10, $15 and $20 billion in 1973, 1976 and 1978, respectively (Bonilla and Campos, 1982, pp. 135 and 136)

21 World Bank (2005), p. 48. In general the evidence regarding the positive spillover effects of foreign direct investment is mixed. See, Gorg and Greenway (2004).

References

Best, Lloyd (1976) "The Choice of Technology Appropriate to Caribbean Countries," Working Paper, No 15, Center for Developing Areas Studies, McGill University.

Bonilla, Frank and Ricardo Campos (1982) "A Wealth of Poor: Puerto Ricans in the New Economic Order," *Journal of the American Academy of Arts and Science* 10(2), pp. 133–76.

Cabán, Pedro (2002) "Puerto Rico State Formation in a Colonial Context," *Caribbean Studies* 30(2), July–December, pp. 170–215.

CAN (2002) Competitive Analsys of Nations. Software. The World Bank and ECLAC, 2002.

CARICOM (2003) *The CARICOM System, Basic Instruments*, edited by Duke Pollard, The Caribbean Law Publishing Company Limited. Kingston.

CARICOM Secretariat (2002) "Final Report on Component III, Inventory of non-tariff, trade restricting measures applied by member states of the Caribbean Community."

CARICOM Secretariat (2002) "Review of Trade Policy Instruments and Administrative Practices Governing the Operation of the CARICOM CET and Rules of Origin." Final Report. Trevor Hamilton and Associates.

CARICOM (2001) *Revised Treaty of Chaguaramas Establishing The Caribbean Community Including the CARICOM Single Market and Economy*.

Dietz, James (2001) "Puerto Rico: The 'Three-Legged' Economy," *INTAL* 15, December, 5, pp. 247–73.

Dos Santos, Paulo and Laurel Bain (2004) "Survey of the Caribbean Tax Systems," CARICOM.

Downes, Andrew S. (2004) "Arthur Lewis and Industrial Development in the Caribbean:

An Assessment," Paper presented at the conference on 'The Lewis Model after 50 years: Assessing Sir Arthur Lewis:' Contribution to Development Economics and Policy,' University of Manchester, July 6–7, 2004.

Dusenbury, Pat and Blaine Liner (1997) "Targeting Export Markets for Puerto Rico," The Urban Institute. September.

EIU (2003) *Commerce in Puerto Rico*. February 2003.

Gorg, Holger and D. Greenway (2004) "Much Ado about Nothing? Do Domestic Firms Really Benefit from Foreign Direct Investment," *World Bank Research Observer*, 19(2), Fall, pp. 171–97.

Holbik, Karel and Philip L. Swan (1975), "Industrialization and Employment in Puerto Rico, 1950–1972," Studies in Latin American Business, No 16, Bureau of Business Research, The University of Texas at Austin.

Lewis, W. Arthur (1950) "The Industrialization of the West Indies." In *Sir William Arthur Lewis, Collected Papers, 1941–1998, Vol. II*, edited by Patrick A. M. Emmanuel, Institute of Social and Economic Research, University of the West Indies, Barbados, pp. 824–99.

Lewis, W. Arthur (1949) "Industrial Development in Puerto Rico. In *Sir William Arthur Lewis, Collected Papers 1941–1988, Vol. II*, edited by Patrick A. M. Emmanuel, Institute of Social and Economic Research (Eastern Caribbean), University of the West Indies, Barbados, pp. 793–823.

McIntyre, Arnold M. (1995) *Trade and Economic Development in Small Open Economies: The Case of the Caribbean Countries*, Westport: Praeger.

Morley, M. (1980) "Dependence and Development in Puerto Rico." In *The Puerto Ricans: Their History, Culture and Society*, edited by Adalberto López, Cambridge: Schenkman Publishing Company.

Padin, Jose A. (2003) "Puerto Rico in the Post War: Lliberalised Development Banking and the Fall of the Fifth Tiger." *World Development*, Vol 31.

Promoexport (2003) "Promoexport and the Internationalization of Puerto Rico's Pproducers." Mimeo. March.

Rider, Mark (2004) "Corporate Income Tax and Tax Incentives," Working Paper 04–28, Georgia State University, Andrew Young, School of Policy Studies.

United States Department of Commerce (1979), *Economic Study of Puerto Rico, Volumes I and II*, Washington, DC: United States Department of Commerce.

World Bank (2005) *Organization of Eastern Caribbean States. Towards a New Agenda for Growth*. World Bank, Washington, DC.

World Bank (2002a) *Caribbean Group for Cooperation in Economic Development. Development Assistance and Economic Development in the Caribbean Region: Is there a correlation?* Discussion Draft. World Bank, Washington, DC.

World Bank (2002b) *Caribbean Group for Cooperation in Economic Development. Macroeconomic Volatility, household vulnerability, and institutional and policy responses*, Discussion Draft. World Bank, Washington, DC.

World Bank (1990) *The Caribbean Common Market. Trade Policies and Regional Integration in the 1990's*, World Bank, Washington, DC.

World Integrated Trade System (2005) World Bank, Washington, DC: World Bank.

10 Anglo-Saxon versus Latin American structuralism in development economics

Diego Sanchez-Ancochea[1]

Introduction

The conviction that developing countries are structurally different to developed ones and that specific theories and policy recommendations are required to address their problems dominated the discipline since its birth in the 1940s to the 1970s. The neoclassical counterrevolution of the early 1980s dramatically changed this vision and completely reshaped the boundaries of the discipline. Neoclassical development economists concentrated on issues of macroeconomic adjustment and static allocation of resources, and recuperated the idea that a sole common theory could be used for both developed and developing countries.[2] In the last few years, however, the lack of success of standard neoclassical economics in explaining underdevelopment and promoting growth has shown the need to recuperate the work of the "pioneers of development" (e.g. Lewis, Hirschman, Rosenstein-Rodan, Nurkse and Myrdal) and readapt it to the current state of the world.[3]

Early development economists followed a structuralist approach, concentrating on the study of long-term structural change and on the identification of bottlenecks and rigidities that were characteristic of developing countries.[4] They all shared similar doubts about the efficiency of the price mechanism and a conviction that government intervention and planning was necessary to achieve development (Arndt, 1985). They also believed that an increase in productivity, a modernization of the agricultural sector and industrialization were all necessary conditions to achieve high and sustainable rates of growth in the long run.

Despite the numerous positive elements of their empirical and theoretical approach to economic development, the Anglo-Saxon (AS) structuralists deserve criticism for at least two reasons. First, although some authors recognized that the lack of foreign exchange constituted a constraint on economic growth, they did not pay enough attention to the relation between developed and developing countries. Second, they all had a limitless faith in the capacity of the state to intervene efficiently in the economic system (Taylor, 1996).

Overcoming the first problem was one of the key contributions of a different type of structuralism, the one developed in Latin America under the leadership of the Economic Commission for Latin America and the Caribbean (ECLAC) during the 1950s and 1960s.[5] For the Latin American (LA) structuralists, developed and developing countries (center and periphery in their terminology) are two different components of a common world economic system; the evolution of the center determines to a great extent the structural characteristics of the periphery. In particular, developed countries' control of the process of technological innovation, together with their responses to periodic financial crisis, has a major impact on developing countries' ability to secure long-term economic growth and export success; at the same time, country-specific institutional characteristics in Latin America determine their ultimate development paths.

This ability to analyze the interaction between global processes and the domestic particularities of Latin American countries from a historical perspective makes LA structuralism particularly relevant in the current global era. While mainstream economists have begun to recognize the contribution of AS structuralists to development economics (Krugman, 1997; Ray, 2000), they could probably learn even more from the work of Raúl Prebisch and his colleagues.

By comparing and contrasting the central claims of both AS and LA structuralism, this chapter shows the unquestionable contribution that both made to the understanding of economic development. By taking into account both internal and external forces, I also argue that the LA version is particularly useful to understand the evolution of the region and, more importantly, may be more relevant for development studies under globalization.

This chapter begins with a critical discussion of AS structuralism, and its key theoretical underpinnings. The next section introduces ECLAC's theory of development based on the notions of center and periphery. The last section compares and contrasts both approaches and briefly underlines their potential contribution for the future evolution of development economics.

Anglo-Saxon structuralism in development economics

Development economics emerged as a sub-discipline of economics in 1943 with the publication of Rosenstein-Rodan's "Problems of Industrialization of Eastern and South-Eastern Europe." While various historical, political and ideological factors contributed to its creation, the Keynesian criticism of neoclassical economics and its defense of government intervention were particularly important. Most early development economists were in England during the 1940s and participated both in the academic planning debate that took place at that time and also in the development of the Keynesian revolution (Little, 1982).[6] Many of them were also of Eastern European decent and were thus highly influenced by the relative backwardness of that region (Jameson and Warner, 2003).

While the term structuralism is not found in any of the early writings on development (Arndt, 1985), later economists like Chenery (1975) and Little (1982) used it to refer to the first development economists and to distinguish their work from neoclassical economics and neo-Marxism. In their account AS structuralism is based on the following assumptions about the economy:

1   The economy is inflexible and economic change is constrained by obstacles, bottlenecks and other rigidities (including foreign exchange shortages).
2   Aggregate demand is low and sectoral demands, especially demand for food, are price-inelastic. As a result, adjustment to equilibrium between supply and demand is slow and requires large changes in relative prices, which have a large influence on income distribution.
3   Development requires a radical transformation in the structure of production. Without industrialization, it is not possible to increase employment, productivity and income per capita and to reduce poverty.
4   The market alone cannot solve the problems of developing countries because the price mechanism has at least three major flaws: it is not always a good signaling mechanism, economic actors may not respond to price changes in the "right" way, and factors of production tend to be immobile (Arndt, 1985).
5   For them externalities and economies of scale are much more important than what neoclassical economists usually assume.

In their analytical models AS structuralists usually ignored the influences of prices, concentrated on real output changes, and assumed fixed relationships between quantities (which allowed them to use input–output matrixes and linear programming). Their theories, which varied greatly in their level of mathematical sophistication, were based on the following key concepts: complementarities and poverty traps, linkages and dualism (based on the existence of surplus labor).

Complementarities, poverty traps and balanced growth

A central claim of a significant number of the AS structuralists was that many investments are complementary, so that the expansion of production in one sector is only profitable if it is accompanied by the expansion of production in other sectors. Rosenstein-Rodan (1943) was the first one to develop this idea through his famous example of the shoe factory. In his 1943 paper he compared two different situations. In the first one, a large shoe factory is created in a developing area, which does not trade with the rest of the world. In this case, it is obvious that the firm will not be able to survive unless workers spend all their wages on shoes (something very improbable!). In the second situation, a whole series of industries, which produce all the goods that workers consume, are set up. This productive system will be viable because the expansion of one commodity, by generating new income and thus demand for other commodities, will provide the other industries with new markets (Basu, 1984). As a result, all firms will make profits, industrialization will succeed and output and income per capita will increase.

In this account, underdevelopment is caused by the inability of firms to benefit from the existence of complementarities in demand. Each capitalist, when making her/his investment decisions, does not take into consideration the positive effect that an expansion of his/her supply will have on other capitalists. As a result, the economy falls into a poverty trap, which can only be overcome with a coordinated effort by several firms.

Many other AS structuralists shared the idea that in each economy there are multiple possible equilibria and that developing countries are trapped in one with low income per capita.[7] Nurkse (1953), for example, developed the concept of vicious circles of poverty. For him a vicious circle of poverty is a "circular constellation of forces [that] tended to act and react upon one another in such a way as to keep a poor country in a state of poverty" (Nurkse, 1953 cited in Basu, 1984, p. 10). This set of forces is of two types (Bustelo, 1998): forces of supply (e.g. low production per capita, low propensity to save, lack of capital, low productivity) and forces of demand, including low purchasing power and the small size of the market.

For Leibenstein (1957), high demographic growth together with a high propensity to consume caused by the imitation of the consumption patterns of developed countries (the so-called "demonstration effect" or "Duesenberry effect") led to a "quasi-stable" equilibrium with low income per capita. Leibenstein also developed the "critical minimum effort hypothesis," which is based on the assumption that in every economy there is a minimum level of feasible investment; when such level is reached, the economy starts to grow (Basu, 1984).

Since the poverty trap is caused by a pervasive coordination failure, allocation of resources is not efficient and the market alone cannot succeed in achieving high rates of growth. As a result, for most AS structuralists government intervention was indispensable. The state should undertake public investment projects and promote and coordinate private investment through the elaboration of medium-term plans. This idea led to the design of investment programs which were based on estimations of shadow prices and input–output matrixes and which benefited from the advances in linear programming (Little, 1982).

For most of these authors, government planning should follow a strategy of balanced growth, that is, "investment would have to proceed simultaneously in the economy's various sectors and industries in the same proportions in which the buying public apportions the expenditure of its additional income among the outputs of those sectors and industries" (Scitovsky, 1987, p. 55). The balanced growth approach concentrated on matching domestic demand and domestic output without paying too much attention to international trade. It argued for a policy of import-substitution industrialization (ISI), and rejected the idea that countries should specialize according to their comparative advantage.

Linkages and unbalanced growth

Some AS structuralists, led by Albert Hirschman, while also concentrating on the role of bottlenecks, external economies and complementarities, did not see balanced growth as the best strategy for industrialization. In their opinion, this strategy required too many financial resources and a huge planning effort and it underestimated the efficiency gains that a dynamic comparative advantage could provide (Bustelo, 1998).

For Albert Hirschman (1958, p. 5), "development depends not so much on finding optimal combinations of resources and factors of production as on calling forth and enlisting for development purposes, resources and abilities that are hidden, scattered or badly utilized." In particular, an optimal strategy for development should increase the ability of economic agents to make investment decisions, which in Hirschman's account was a central problem in developing countries. He believed that a simultaneous investment effort in many sectors was not required and promoted instead the adoption of a policy of unbalanced growth. This strategy rested on the idea that a concentration of investment in a few sectors would induce increases in supply in related sectors through the creation of sectoral shortages and imbalances.

For the proponents of unbalanced growth the selection of the key sectors of the economy, which received different names such as "leading sector" (Rostow), the "propulsive industry" (Perroux), or the "development block" (Dahmen) (all cited in Hirschman, 1987), was a key task for the planning authorities. For Hirschman (1958), governments should favor industries with a strong interdependence or linkages with other sectors of the economy. He defined two different types of linkages: backward and forward linkages. An activity A has backward linkages when it stimulates an increase in investment and production of sectors that act as inputs in its production process, while it has forward linkages when it induces the creation of new activities that utilize the output of activity A.

At first it appeared that the development of input–output models would make the measurements of linkages easy. In fact, during the 1960s and 1970s different indicators of forward and backward linkages based on the Leontief inverse matrix were developed.[8] Nevertheless, Hirschman himself ended up recognizing that an exact measurement of backward and forward linkages during the process of development is impossible. This is so because "output tables cannot reveal which additional industrial branches are likely to be created in the wake of industrial investment in a given product line" (Hirschman, 1987, p. 211). They cannot show the impact of technological innovation and the usage of new inputs in the process of industrialization either. As a result the notion of linkage slowly became more an analytical concept used to deal with theoretical problems in development economics than a policy instrument for planning. The realization of this fact led Hirschman to extend the meaning of the concept and use it to study the "causal links between technology, ideology, institutions and development" (Hirschman, 1987, p. 220). In some of his later books, Hirschman introduced new concepts such as fiscal and social linkages and started to think of specific commodities as "acting as a multidimensional conspiracy in favor of or against development within a certain historical and sociopolitical setting" (cited in Syrquin, 1992).

The debate over balanced and unbalanced growth, which gave rise to a large body of theoretical and empirical literature in the 1950s and 1960s, was not completely satisfactory (Little, 1982). First of all, the difference between the two strategies with respect to the role of international trade was not as great as it is usually assumed. In fact, both Rosenstein-Rodan and Nurkse acknowledged that imports and exports are important and thought that balanced growth can enlarge the opportunities for trade. Second, both approaches coincided in the need for government planning but promoted two different ways of doing it. Those who favored balanced growth insisted on the convenience of planning at the macro-level while Hirschman and others believed that project and sectoral plans would be more efficient. Third, both approaches shed some light on different dimensions of the development process. Balanced growth theorists were correct in pointing out the need for some balance between different sectors of the economy.[9] They were, however, too optimistic about the technical and financial ability of the state to lead a big push in an efficient manner and without facing foreign exchange constraints. Meanwhile, the unbalanced growth theorists' belief that certain sectors could act as engines of growth and development was accurate, but their faith in the ability of private actors to respond to imbalances and shortages effectively was not warranted. Finally, the idea that the controversy between both approaches could be resolved through empirical research was overoptimistic. On the one hand, an unbalanced path (if such a thing can be effectively measured) does not imply that a strategy of planned imbalances has been followed. On the other hand, a successful unbalanced growth policy should give rise at the end to a balanced structure of production (Syrquin, 1992).

Dualism and surplus labor

A basic assumption shared by most AS structuralists was that developing economies were dualistic. An economy is dualistic when it is divided between two different sectors: a modern sector and a traditional one. There are two sets of asymmetries between the two: an asymmetry in the production methods employed and an asymmetry in organization (Ray, 1998). The modern sector, which is usually identified with manufacturing, is characterized by a relatively high level of income, high productivity, capital intensive methods of production and wage employment. Meanwhile, in the traditional sector, which includes not only agriculture but also informal urban activities, productivity is low, a vast majority of the population is very poor, capital is not intensively used and output is distributed following "conventional norms" (such as equal distribution among members of a family) rather than marginal products.

While the original idea of dualism was introduced by Boeke (1953) in a study of the Indonesian economy, it did not become a central concept in development economics until one year later when Arthur Lewis (1954) published his seminal paper "Economic Development with Unlimited Supply of Labor."

Lewis's main assumption was the existence of surplus labor in the agricultural sector, which implied that labor could be transferred to modern sectors without raising wages, and without loss of output in the traditional sector. He also assumed that all profits were saved and all wages consumed and that new investment was concentrated in the modern sectors. Under these assumptions Lewis developed a model of development in which labor was transferred from the traditional sector to the modern-industrial one until all the surplus labor was eliminated through a virtuous circle of investment and profits.

While Lewis's theory of development with surplus labor has received extensive criticisms, his conceptualization of the process of structural change has been very influential.[10] Moreover, his conclusion that the elimination of the structural differences between traditional and modern sectors is the main cause of growth in the first stages of development and is required to sustain growth in the long run seems to be accurate, as the experience of most industrialized and semi-industrialized countries clearly shows.

An initial evaluation of the contribution of AS structuralists to economic development

The structuralist approach developed by the early development economists is full of interesting insights and realistic explanations of the causes of underdevelopment. Their understanding of the development process was more sophisticated than that of most neoclassical economists. Focusing on the long-term determinants of economic expansion, AS structuralists highlighted the complex and dynamic character of the process of structural change. This perspective helped them move beyond the insistence on macroeconomic adjustment and static efficiency, instead emphasizing the importance of increasing productivity and reducing supply bottlenecks

Long-term development involves shifts in the structure of demand and production that move countries into higher productivity paths. As important as the expansion of the factors of production is, the promotion of high-productivity sectors with strong linkages with the rest of the economy has always been a more relevant feature of what Kuznets (1966) called modern economic growth.[11]

Looking at the overall structure of the economy and the interaction between different sectors also allowed AS structuralists to elaborate an alternative view of comparative advantages and of how markets worked. Comparative advantages are not given but can be created and change over time and industrialization is the only way to assure high rates of growth in the long run.

The abundance of supply bottlenecks, economies of scale and complementarities in developing countries also make planned industrialization indispensable. As such, government planning is important to secure a non-inflationary and sustainable development path. Investment decisions from both the public and the private sector need to take into account the possibility that production shortages in different sectors can limit the growth potential of the economy; investment decisions should also contribute to the promotion of linkages between the most dynamic sectors and the rest of the economy.

The existence of duality in developing countries was another major contribution of AS structuralists and, as will be discussed later, of LA structuralists as well. Differences between economic sectors in terms of productivity and factor income have a substantial influence on the economic, social and political evolution in Latin America and beyond. This was clearly the case when AS structuralists elaborated the first notions of duality, and is still the case within the current process of globalization

AS structuralists, however, were unable to move beyond their initial conception of duality – concentrated on differences between the rural and urban sectors – and understand the limitations of urbanization and modernization. In particular, their concentration on the promotion of the industrial sector resulted in an insufficient analysis of the informal sector and the development of agriculture (Bustelo, 1998).

Excessive accent on industrialization went hand in hand with too much faith in the success of state intervention (Taylor, 1996). This assumption was problematic for two reasons. First, it put too much weight on the limited administrative apparatus of developing countries (Chenery, 1975). Second, it did not take into consideration the possibility that the state could be allied with non-modernizing social actors (such as landowners) or that civil servants and politicians could have objectives other than improving the social welfare of the country as a whole.

Their faith in state intervention was partly a reflection of their times (Keynesian economics was dominant in developed countries), but also of their lack of attention to the class structure and to the possibility that growth may be constrained by conflicts of interests between different economic actors. Kalecki's work on economic development constitutes one of the exceptions to this absence. For him the central problem of developing countries (a supply bottleneck in the agricultural sector) was caused by the class structure of the rural areas.[12]

The main problem of AS structuralists, which is still shared by most mainstream development economists, was their excessive concentration on domestic forces. By studying developing countries in isolation and not paying sufficient attention to the structure of the global economy, AS structuralists failed to understand the specific difficulties of developing countries. Although many of the pioneers of development criticized the Ricardian theory of comparative advantages, they still believed that a close relation between developed and developing countries would always be positive for both sets of countries, something LA structuralists successfully criticized.

The Latin American structuralism of ECLAC

The theories just discussed are considered structuralist because they concentrate on the long-term technical relations between different sectors, in addition to explaining how the composition of output changes over time and how these changes influence the performance of the economy. In this view the term structure refers to "the relative importance of sectors in the economy in terms of production and factor use" (Syrquin, 1988, p. 206) and to "certain objective-quantitative relations among components of the system-say, between effective demand and aggregate employment" (Lowe, 1955, p. 581).

Structuralism has a very different meaning in other contexts. Structuralism as an approach to scientific knowledge is inspired in Piaget's studies on psychology, Chomsky's transformational grammar and Levi-Strauss's research in anthropology (Jameson, 1986). Its objective is to go behind the observable elements of reality and search for the interdependencies and relations that are hidden behind them (Sampedro and Martínez, 1969). Keat and Urry define various characteristics of this approach, five of which are very relevant for the following discussion (Jameson, 1986, p. 226):

1   Each system should be studied as "an organized set of interrelated elements and not broken down into individual elements and studied atomistically."
2   As already stated, the objective is to identify the deep structure, which lies behind the directly observable and knowable social reality.
3   The meanings of observed events and objects in the world are socially rather than naturally constructed.
4   Social systems can be analyzed by means of binary oppositions.
5   Structures change over time and as a result specific phenomena can have very different meanings in different historical periods.

Latin American structuralism should be placed within this methodological tradition (Jameson, 1986). LA structuralism, which has its origin in the Raul Prebisch's (1949) study *"El Desarrollo Económico de la América Latina y Algunos de sus Principales Problemas"* published by ECLAC, tried to explain the deep characteristics of the economic structure of Latin American countries through the analysis of the world economy as an integrated system with a center (developed countries) and a periphery (developing countries).[13]

The approach developed by Prebisch has four basic analytical components (Bielschowsky, 1998): a historical approach, based on the binary opposition center–periphery; an analysis of the international insertion of Latin America; the study of the domestic determinants of economic growth and technological progress; and an evaluation of the arguments in favor and against state intervention.[14]

ECLAC's theory of underdevelopment is based on a historical analysis of capitalist development. For this approach the initial process of capital accumulation and diffusion of technical progress took place asymmetrically in different countries. Some of them became *centers* (first the United Kingdom, later the United States, Europe and Japan) because they benefited first from the newly created capitalist techniques. Meanwhile, the rest of the world, the periphery, was left behind in the use of new technologies and in the implementation of new ways of organization.

Center and periphery are structurally different. In the centers technical progress (the basic variable to explain the evolution of capitalism) spread rapidly to all sectors of the economy giving rise to an equilibrated, homogeneous and diversified structure of production. On the other hand, the periphery was historically specialized in the production of primary goods for export, which was the only sector that benefited from technological innovations. As a result, economies in the periphery are characterized by two key features: heterogeneity and specialization. Heterogeneity is a similar concept to that of duality and was understood as the coexistence of a highly productive export sector and a vast majority of backward activities that use traditional technologies and have very low productivity. Specialization in very few sectors took place because new investments were concentrated on primary goods for export, while the growing demand for other goods and services was satisfied through imports.

These differences between center and periphery, generated by the asymmetric distribution of technological change, are also at the heart of the increasing inequality in per capita income between both sets of countries. This process was the result of higher labor productivity growth in the center than in the periphery but, especially, of a long-term deterioration in the terms of trade of primary goods.

The hypothesis of the deterioration in the terms of trade of developing countries was formulated independently by Singer and Prebisch in 1950 (Prebisch, 1950; Singer, 1950). It was originally based on the analysis of the British terms of trade during the period 1873–1938 under the assumption that they were a good representation of those between center and periphery and it was extended later for the post- World War II years.

The various documents published by ECLAC during the early 1950s gave two main theoretical explanations for the deterioration of the terms of trade (ECLAC, 1951; Prebisch, 1950). The first one stressed the existence of structural differences between the labor market of the centers and that of the periphery. In developed countries the rate of unemployment is lower and trade unions are very powerful. As a result, prices are relatively sticky and do not decrease in times of crisis. Meanwhile, wages in the periphery are very flexible because workers are poorly organized and the rate of unemployment and disguised unemployment is very high.

Capitalists in the centers are also in a better position to protect their profits during recessions than those in the periphery for two reasons. First, markets in developed countries are highly concentrated and competition is limited. Second, demand for primary goods from the periphery depends on the evolution of industrial output in the centers.

A second explanation for the deterioration of the terms of trade (which become more popular within the Anglo-Saxon literature) concentrated on the existence of lower income elasticity of demand for primary goods than for industrial products. This was due to Engel's Law and to the increasing use of synthetic inputs instead of raw materials in the manufacturing sector.

The relations between centers and periphery are not static but vary over time. For ECLAC from the 1800s to 1950 there were two main models or stages of development in Latin America. Until the interwar period there was an outward-oriented model characterized by trade openness, specialization in primary exports, which were the engine of growth, and high dependence on imports to match output and demand.

The changes that the world economy experienced during the economic crisis of the 1930s led to a shift in the model. In particular, the substitution of the United Kingdom for the United States as the leading economy in the world was very important. While the United Kingdom had always been an open economy with a high level of imports, a very low share of imports in GDP characterized American development after the Great Depression. As a result of this shift in the center of power, Latin American countries started to experience increasing trade deficits and were forced to reduce their own import coefficients. This was the main cause of the rise of a new inward-oriented model and of a spontaneous process of import-substitution industrialization.

According to ECLAC's analysis, the heterogeneous and specialized character of the Latin American economies, however, reduced the positive effect of this process of spontaneous industrialization. In particular, the process was constrained by the existence of external imbalances, structural unemployment and sectoral imbalances. Spontaneous import substitution did not result in a reduction of the trade deficit because imports of intermediate and capital goods were increasingly required to expand the productive capacity of the new industrial sector. At the same time, primary exports increased slowly and import substitution did not proceed at the required rate.

Dependence on the rest of the world in terms of technologies was also one of the main reasons behind the high levels of unemployment. The problem was made worse by the insufficient rate of capital accumulation, the concentration of investment in a few sectors and the incapacity of traditional sectors to absorb an increasing labor supply. Low and concentrated investment also resulted in structural imbalances; as a result, bottlenecks appeared in the supply of infrastructure, transport, energy and, especially, agricultural goods.[15]

The existence of trade deficits, sectoral imbalances, structural unemployment and inflation clearly showed that a spontaneous process of industrialization conducted by market forces was not sustainable in Latin America. This conclusion led Prebisch and other economists of ECLAC to insist on the need for a planned process of industrialization. For Prebisch industrial development was "an unavoidable prerequisite for development" (cited in Eatwell, Milgate and Newman, 1987, p. 319). It would increase the overall level of labor productivity and per capita income and it would solve all the problems derived from the deterioration of the terms of trade.

The failure of spontaneous industrialization had clearly shown the need for active state intervention in the process of industrialization. The state should be in charge of promoting particular sectors through the creation of public companies but, especially, should focus on planning. Plans should determine variables such as the sectoral composition of investment as well as the desired level of foreign capital and imports to avoid bottlenecks and imbalances. At the same time, the allocation of resources between sectors should follow the principle of equalization of marginal productivities. The state should promote those sectors in which the differences in productivity with respect to developed countries are lower.

Industrialization also required protection of the domestic market in those sectors in which higher productivity in the centers was not compensated by lower nominal wages in the periphery. While the LA structuralists were accused of promoting over-protection, Prebisch always insisted on the fact that protection should be kept to the minimum required to be effective.

The use of a historical methodology allowed Prebisch and other LA structuralists to slowly shift their focus and their policy recommendations as industrialization developed in the region. Prebisch, for example, was an early critic of the way in which industrialization had been promoted in Latin America in the 1950s (Love, 2005). Based on the analysis of the experience in different countries, he concluded that protection had been excessive and insisted on the importance of regional integration and a reduction of income inequality. The need to promote a better income distribution as a precondition to achieve sustainable economic growth was also a central theme of one of his last books, *Capitalism Periférico. Crisis y Transformación.*

A critical assessment of the approach

The LA structuralist theory of underdevelopment shares most of the strengths of the AS approach, including a concentration on the long run, an insistence on the need for structural change in the periphery and a rejection of the theory of comparative advantages and of the ability of markets to allocate resources efficiently in a dynamic sense. On the other hand, its methodology and some of its conclusions are useful to overcome some of the drawbacks of AS structuralism, as it will be shown in the final section of this chapter.

Despite its strengths, LA structuralism has been criticized by both neoclassical and radical economists for different reasons. In the 1950s neoclassical economists such as Haberler and Viner criticized the hypothesis of the deterioration of the terms of trade and claimed that the empirical evidence that supported it was very weak (Bustelo, 1998). In the following decades (especially during the 1970s and 1980s) neoclassical economists continued to attack the thesis of ECLAC on two different fronts.[16] On the one hand, they tried to show the negative effects that protection had produced on the allocation of resources, on the choice of technique and, more generally, on the overall efficiency of developing economies. On the other hand, neoclassical political economists developed various criticisms of interventionism, which were centered on the idea that politicians and bureaucrats are self-interested and do not pursue the welfare of the population as a whole.[17] In the last few years, however, they have come to realize the importance of effective state intervention and some type of industrial policy once again (World Bank, 1997, 2004).

Heterodox economists were sympathetic with the structuralists' insistence on external factors as determinants of underdevelopment in Latin America. Nevertheless, they criticized ECLAC for its lack of understanding of the severity of the external constraint and for their lack of analysis of Latin America's social structure. In particular, radical economists elaborated the following criticisms:

1   For some of them LA structuralism was basically a reformist school, which did not denounce sufficiently the exploitative character of international relations and which criticized the conventional theory of international trade only from within (Palma, 1987).

2   LA structuralist theory of underdevelopment completely ignored the social relations of production and its interrelation with the structure and the forces of production (Palma, 1987).

3   ECLAC should not only study the international insertion of Latin America in the world economy but also the domestic causes of underdevelopment. In particular, Arturo Bonilla maintained, the problem of Latin American countries "should be examined in terms of the capacity of Latin American economies to generate a social surplus and above all to understand the forms in which it is utilized" (cited in Cypher, 1990).

4   Lack of a theory of the state. In ECLAC's theories the state was assumed to be "an exogenous agent that could be brought in to correct economic imbalances, and, by assumption, it had no interests except those that led to the most efficient and rapid form of industrialization" (Cypher, 1990, p. 44). For many critics ECLAC's policy proposals had to be completed with a better understanding of the structure of the state and, especially, of its relation with different social classes.

Conclusion

The description of the main elements of LA structuralism has shown that there is an element of truth in Chenery's (1975) contention that Raul Prebisch was a member of what I have called AS structuralism. Both AS and LA structuralists shared many theoretical concepts, and offered similar policy recommendations. The concepts of duality and heterogeneity, for example, were similar. Both of them were used to illustrate the radical differences between various sectors in developing countries and to emphasize the negative impact that backwardness in the traditional sector has in the overall performance of the economy.

More generally, both approaches stressed the activity-specific nature of economic growth – something completely ignored by neoclassical economists. Structuralists from different schools emphasized that the best way to increase labor productivity and economic growth in developing countries is to expand those (industrial) sectors with higher productivity.

At the same time, complementarities and bottlenecks are extremely important in the process of economic growth in the periphery. AS and LA structuralists believed that sectoral imbalances were more important in developing countries that in developed ones; as a result, a process of industrialization could not succeed unless bottlenecks in the agricultural and export sectors were overcome and complementary investments simultaneously promoted.

These theoretical similarities also gave rise to a convergence in policy recommendations. Both approaches maintained that industrialization is a necessary condition for economic development and that market forces alone will never produce the required changes in economic structure. As a result, they argued that government intervention is indispensable and that protection of the domestic market, planning and the promotion of capital accumulation should be the basic tasks of the state.

The fact that both approaches shared many ideas on the problems of developing countries and on the solutions to them is not surprising. They both appeared more or less simultaneously and were influenced by the same historical circumstances and theoretical developments. Most economists from both schools were, for example, primary witnesses of the Keynesian revolution and their vision of the world changed because of it.[18] Also, Rosenstein-Rodan's pioneering paper on development in Eastern Europe exercised a great influence on both groups. In fact, Aníbal Pinto, a well-known Latin American structuralist from the first generation, argued that Rodan's arguments in favor of industrialization impressed Prebisch and other Latin Americans more than any other theory (Love, 1996).

Their relative convergence can also be explained by the numerous contacts that economists from both groups maintained. In particular, several Anglo-Saxon economists visited Latin America at least once invited by ECLAC. Kalecki was in Mexico in 1953 and gave several lectures on the problems of underdevelopment where he underlined the influence of bottlenecks in the agricultural sector on inflation and growth (Arndt, 1985).[19] In 1956 Raul Prebisch hired Kaldor for three months to work in Santiago. His main task was to advise ECLAC on their first studies on fiscal policies but he also gave more than twenty lectures on various topics. Although his final paper received many criticisms and was never published by ECLAC, his ideas on bottlenecks were very influential (Palma and Marcel, 1989). One year later Hollis Chenery was also invited to Santiago to lecture. During his time there, he tried to stimulate interest in input–output analysis and linear programming for investment planning and also discussed the theories of Rodan, Lewis and Nurkse with his Latin American colleagues (Arndt, 1985).

Despite these many contacts between economists from the two groups, the approaches are substantially different in the methodologies employed and also in some of their main conclusions. The approach of ECLAC is much broader and deeper than that of AS structuralism. For Jameson (1986, p. 227) ECLAC's originality and the secret of its success has rested "upon his [referring to Prebisch] ability to isolate a deep structure of the international economy, one which is convincing and provides a framework for a broad-reaching program of research on the surface structures and mechanisms and which suggests policies to deal with them." LA structuralists employ a historical-structural method to identify the basic interrelation between countries in the world economy, which are then used to explain the observable characteristics of Latin American countries. According to ECLAC's analysis, during the early stages of capitalist development, technical progress was distributed asymmetrically among countries and a binary opposition between centers and periphery was created. It was this initial insertion in the world economy and not domestic factors that determined the structure of production and the potential for growth of each country.

The superiority of LA structuralism over many of the theories developed by AS structuralists is not only rooted in its ability to describe the world economy as an integrated system. It is also connected with the fact that the institutional characteristics of markets (e.g. degree of monopolization, trade union power) are taken into consideration when discussing underdevelopment.[20] LA structuralists's own mistake, however, is that they studied these socio-economic elements only superficially and did not complete them with an analysis of social classes.

These methodological and analytical differences between the two approaches explain their divergence in some central conclusions:

1   Latin American economists put more emphasis on the historical differences between developed and developing countries, which makes economic growth in the periphery harder. In Bielschowsky words (1998), Prebisch's objective "was not to compare peripheral underdevelopment with the history of the central economies like Rostow (1956) wanted, but to identify their particular historical experiences, in which different sequences and results than those of central development should be expected."[21] As it has already been argued several times, the main characteristic of ECLAC's theory was precisely the distinction it drew between developed and developing countries.

2   Rejection of the hypothesis, shared by both AS structuralists and neoclassical economists, that developed and developing countries are linked in a mutually beneficial set of relations.

3   Insistence on the historical particularities of different periods. LA structuralists use an inductive methodology that emphasizes the constraints and opportunities of different stages of capitalism. This helps them to elaborate time-specific policy recommendations.

At a time when mainstream economists are paying more attention to the contribution of the A-S structuralists and are modeling their ideas on complementarities, indivisibilities and other market failures (for a discussion of this approach see, for example, Mookherjee and Ray, 2000), it is important to emphasize the superior analytical power of LA original structuralism. The sharp divergence between different developing countries since the 1950s has undermined the assumption of a unique and inevitable path to capitalist modernization. At the same time, the radical changes that the global economy has experienced since the 1980s with the consolidation of neoliberal globalization have clearly demonstrated the usefulness of a historically bound analysis of economic development.

In fact, economic globalization makes LA structuralism – particularly, complemented with a better appreciation of the state and its relation with various social forces – more relevant than ever before. Only if we incorporate changes in the global economy and in the behavior of transnational corporations into the analysis of the domestic economic structures, will we succeed in devising new alternatives for equitable economic growth in Latin America.

Notes

1 I thank Matías Vernengo and other participants at the Conference on Latin American and Caribbean Economic Thought at the Eastern Economic Association Annual Conference, New York, March 2005 for their valuable comments to an earlier draft.

2 It is true that in the 1980s there was also a revival of interest in growth theory, partly caused by the lack of convergence in per capita income between developed and developing countries (Romer, 1994). New growth theory, however, concentrates primarily on developed countries and does not study structural change.

3 This need is even recognized by mainstream economists working in the neoclassical tradition. For a textbook example see Ray (1998).

4 For an excellent overview of the pioneers as well as autobiographical accounts of their views and work on economic development, see Meier and Seers (1984).

5 The Latin American structuralists shared with their Anglo-Saxon counterparts their excessive faith in the state and lack a valid theory of state intervention. In fact, both structuralist approaches to economic development require a much better understanding of the internal structure of the state and of its relations with society. In recent times the applied work of different political economists (such as Amsden, Evans and Chang) has contributed to solve this limitation. For a review of their ideas, see Sanchez-Ancochea (1999).

6 Many of the "pioneers of development" have a similar biography. They were born in developing countries (most in Eastern Europe, some in India, Latin America and the Caribbean), studied in the United Kingdom and finished working in the United States. For a brief biography of Rosenstein-Rodan, Hirschman, Lewis and Nurkse, see Eatwell, Milgate and Newman (1987).

7 Mainstream development economists have recuperated this idea since the early 1990s. Different models emphasize the existence of complementarities through demand (Murphy, Shleifer and Vishny, 1989), through "roundaboutness" in the production process (Ciccone and Matsuyama, 1996) or through the financial system (Acemoglu and Zilibotti, 1997) as an explanation of multiple equilibria and poverty traps.

8 See Syrquin (1992) for a discussion of different measurements of linkages and for a summary of different empirical studies that tried to measure the value of linkages in different sectors of the economy.

9 This was, for example, stressed by Kalecki (1976). Although he did not explicitly promote balanced growth in the industrial sector or a big push, he claimed that in order to have a non-inflationary expansion of the economy the rates of growth of industry and agriculture would have to be balanced.

10 For textbook presentations of Lewis's model and a review of its main criticisms, see Basu (1984) and Ray (1998).

11 Some mainstream economists have recognized the importance of changes in the structure of production, and have developed growth models where these elements play a central role. See, for example, Kongsamut, Rebelo and Xie (1997).

12 For a review of Kalecki's comparative ideas on developed and developing countries and his theory of the state, see Sanchez-Ancochea (2000).

13 For the presentation of the ideas of the LA structuralists I mainly rely on Rodriguez (1980) and Prebisch's seminal paper published in Spanish in 1949 and in English in 1950.

14 Bielschowsky (1998), Di Filippo (1998) and others argue that these elements are shared by all the theories developed by ECLAC in the five decades since its creation. It is not clear, however, whether the neostructuralist proposals of the last few years (see, for example, ECLAC, 1990), which have been published under the heading of "Productive Transformation with Equity," really follow the same approach as the original structuralism or not.

15 For the LA structuralists these problems were not only a constraint on economic development but also the main cause of the inflationary pressures that Latin American witnessed during those years. The structuralist theory of inflation has its origin in a paper published by Juan Noyola in 1956 and was further developed during the 1960s by economists such as Osvaldo Sunkel (Arndt, 1985).

16 These criticisms were not only directed to LA structuralism but also to most early development economists, who defended the need for protection of the domestic market and believed that the state should play an active role in structural change in developing countries.

17 For a brief but accurate presentation of both sets of arguments, see Shapiro and Taylor (1990).

18 Raul Prebisch, for example, wrote several articles on *The General Theory* and a text-book on Keynesian economics called *Introducción a Keynes* during the 1940s.

19 One of the lectures was published in both Spanish and English and can be found in Kalecki (1976).

20 These characteristics were also analyzed by Kalecki in his studies of developing countries but not by other A-S structuralists who worked on underdevelopment all their lives.

21 The translation to English is mine.

References

Acemoglu, Daron and Fabrizio Zilibotti (1997) "Was Prometheus Unbound by Chance? Risk, Diversification and Growth," *Journal of Political Economy* 105.

Arndt, Heinz W. (1985) "The Origins of Structuralism," *World Development* 13(2).

Basu, Kaushik (1984) *The Less Developed Economy. A Critique of Contemporary Theory*, New York: Basil Blackwell.

Bielschowsky, Ricardo (1998) "Evolución de las Ideas de la CEPAL," *Revista de la CEPAL*, Special Edition, October.

Boeke, Julius H. (1953) *Economics and Economic Policy of Dual Societies as Exemplified by Indonesia*, New York: Institute of Pacific Relations.

Bustelo, Pablo (1998) *Teorías Contemporáneas del Desarrollo Económico*, Madrid: Editorial Síntesis.

Chenery, Hollis (1975) "The Structuralist Approach to Development Policy," *American Economic Review*, 65(2).

Ciccone, Antonio and Kiminori Matsuyama (1996) "Start-up Costs and Pecuniary Externalities as Barriers to Development," *Journal of Development Economics* 49.

Cypher, James (1990) "Latin American Structuralist Economics: An Evaluation, Critique, and Reformulation." In *Progress Toward Development in Latin America. From Prebisch to Technological Autonomy*, J. Dietz, and D. James, (eds), London: Lynne Rienner Publishers.

Di Filippo, Armando (1998) "La Visión Centro-Periferia Hoy," *Revista de la CEPAL*, special edition, October.

Eatwell, John, Murray Milgate and Peter Newman (eds) (1987) *The New Palgrave. Economic Development*, New York: W.W. Norton & Co, American edition 1989.

ECLAC (1951) *Theoretical and Practical Problems of Economic Growth*, Mexico City.

ECLAC (1990) *Transformación Productiva con Equidad. La Tarea Prioritaria del Desarrollo de América Latina y el Caribe en los Años 90*, Santiago, Chile: United Nations.

Hirschman, Albert (1958) *The Strategy of Economic Development*, New Haven: Yale University Press.

Hirschman, Albert (1987) "Linkages." In *The New Palgrave. Economic Development*, edited by John Eatwell, Murray Milgate and Peter Newman, New York: W.W. Norton & Company, American edition 1989.

Jameson, Kenneth P. (1986) "Latin American Structuralism: A Methodological Perspective," *World Development*, 14(2).

Jameson, Kenneth P. and James Warner (2003) "The Role of Eastern Europe in Development Economic's History," University of Utah.

Kalecki, Michal (1976) *Essays on Developing Economies*, Atlantic Highlands, NJ: Humanities Press.

Kongsamut, Piyabha, Sergio Rebelo and Danyang Xie (1997) "Beyond Balanced Growth," *NBER Working Papers*, No 6159.

Krugman, Paul (1997) *Development, Geography and Economic Theory*, Cambridge, MA: The MIT Press.

Kuznets, Simon (1966) *Modern Economic Growth: Rate, Structure and Spread*, New Heaven, CT: Yale University Press.

Leibenstein, Harvey (1957) *Economic Backwardness and Economic Growth*, New York: Wiley.

Lewis, W. Arthur (1954) "Economic Development with Unlimited Supply of Labor," *The Manchester School of Economic and Social Studies* 22.

Little, Ian M. D. (1982) *Economic Development. Theory, Policy, and International Relations*, New York: Twentieth Century Fund.

Love, Joseph (1996) "Las Fuentes del Estructuralismo Latinoamericano," *Desarrollo Económico*, 36(141).

Love, Joseph (2005) "The Rise and Decline of Economic Structuralism in Latin America: New Dimensions," *Latin American Research Review* 40 (3).

Lowe, Adolph (1951) "On the Mechanistic Approach in Economics," *Social Research*, 18.

Meier, Gerard and Dudley Seers (1984) *Pioneers in Development*, Washington, DC: World Bank.

Mookherjee, Dilip and Debraj Ray (2000) *Readings in the Theory of Economic Development*, Oxford: Blackwell Publishers.

Murphy, Kevin, Andrei Shleifer and Robert Vishny (1989), "Industrialization and the Big Push," *Journal of Political Economy* 97.

Nurkse, Ragnar (1953) *Problems of Capital Formation in Developing Countries*, Oxford: Basil Blackwell.

Palma, Gabriel (1987) "Structuralism." In *The New Palgrave. Economic Development*, edited by John Eatwell, Murray Milgate and Peter Newman, New York: W.W. Norton & Company, American edition 1989.

Palma, Gabriel and Mario Marcel (1989) "Kaldor on the 'Discreet Charm' of the Chilean Bourgeoisie," *Cambridge Journal of Economics* 13.

Prebisch, Raúl (1950) *The Economic Development of Latin America and its Principal Problems*, New York: UN Economic Commission for Latin America and the Caribbean.

Ray, Debraj (1998) *Development Economics*, Princeton, NJ: Princeton University Press.

Ray, Debraj (2000) "What's New In Development Economics?" *The American Economist*, 44.

Rodríguez, Octavio (1980) *La Teoría del Subdesarrollo de la CEPAL*, México, DF: Siglo Veintiuno Editores, second edition, 1981.

Romer, Paul (1994) "The Origins of Endogenous Growth," *Journal of Economic Perspectives*, 8(1).

Rosenstein-Rodan, Paul (1943) "Problems of Industrialization of Eastern and South-Eastern Europe," *Economic Journal* June–September.

Sampedro, José Luis and Rafael Martínez Cortiña (1969) *Estructura Económica. Teoría Básica y Estructura Mundial*, Madrid: Ariel, second edition, 1970.

Sanchez-Ancochea, Diego (1999) "The Role of the State in Structural Change: an Institutional Approach," *Transregional Center for Democratic Studies Working Papers*, New York: New School for Social Research.

Sanchez-Ancochea, Diego (2000) "Are Developed and Developing Countries Structurally Different? An Analysis of Kalecki's Economics," mimeo.

Scitovsky, Tibor (1987) "Balanced Growth." In *The New Palgrave. Economic Development*, edited by John Eatwell, Murray Milgate and Peter Newman, New York: W.W. Norton & Company, American edition 1989.

Shapiro, Helen and Lance Taylor (1990) "The State and Industrial Strategy," *World Development* 18(6).

Singer, Hans W. (1950) "The Distribution of Gains between Investing and Borrowing Countries," *American Economic Review* 40.

Syrquin, Moshe (1988) "Patterns of Structural Change," in H. Chenery and T.N. Srinivasan (eds), *Handbook of Development Economics*, Vol. I, The Netherlands: Elsevier Science Publisher.

Syrquin, Moshe (1992) "Linkages and the Strategy of Development." In *Towards a New Development Strategy for Latin America: Pathways from Hirschman's Thought*, edited by Simón Teitel, Washington, DC: Inter-American Development Bank and The John Hopkins University.

Taylor, Lance (1996) "Growth and Development Theories," New York: New School for Social Research.

World Bank (1997) *World Development Report, 1997*, New York: Oxford University Press.

World Bank (2004) *Inequality in Latin American and the Caribbean: Breaking with History?* Washington, DC: World Bank Annual Research Study on Latin America and the Caribbean.

11 Economic ideas and policies in historical perspective

Cairú and Hamilton on trade and finance

Matías Vernengo[1]

Introduction

Keynes famously argued that the world was ruled by ideas and little else. For him the power of vested interests was greatly overstated. Even if one believes that Keynes' faith in the power of ideas is exaggerated it seems reasonable to suppose that ideas influence policies to some extent. Yet, the history of ideas, including economic ideas, in Latin America has been traditionally neglected. In his classic book on Brazilian economic development, Celso Furtado suggested that, in part, the relative backwardness of Brazil with respect to the United States was the result of the economic ideas of their respective founding fathers. Furtado contrasted Alexander Hamilton's early defense of industrialization with the economic liberalism of José da Silva Lisboa, the Viscount of Cairú. Liberal economic policies halted the industrial beginnings in Brazil, according to this view.[2]

Two important limitations of Furtado's thesis must be noted. First, while it is correct to note that Brazilian liberals imported their principles from abroad, it is clear that these were modified for domestic consumption. In that sense, Cairú was considerably less naive than presumed by Furtado. In other words, the defense of an open economy, integrated to the world economy, in which agricultural production would prevail over the incipient industrial interests, should be seen as a discourse for landowners and the mercantile class connected to the slave trade.

Second, the emphasis on liberalism presupposes that international trade and the international division of labor are at the center of the divergent development paths of Brazil and the United States and other successful industrializers of the nineteenth century. However, modern readings of Hamilton's contributions suggest that his defense of tariffs was related fundamentally to public credit considerations and only to a lesser degree to a belief in the benefits of protectionism. In that respect the limited understanding of public financial issues seems more relevant to understand the limitations of the early nineteenth-century Brazilian intelligentsia.

The eighteenth century saw the rise of Britain to economic hegemony, and that was evident for both Cairú and Hamilton. It is now accepted that part of the explanation for the British take off is related to the development of a market for its national debt. The rise of banks, joint-stock companies and the increasing national debt threatened the traditional values of society. Alexander Hamilton was, contrary to conventional wisdom at the time, aware of the positive effects of a national debt. Hamilton famously argued that a national debt, if not excessive, would be a blessing. Nothing similar can be seen in Cairú's writings.

In the United States a thriving market for public debt surged after Hamilton's plan to fund the national debt, and around a third of the domestic debt was held by foreigners in 1795. The United States creditworthiness rose in the world, and the existence of a relatively safe asset that paid a moderately positive rate of return meant that financial markets could develop. The degree of development of Brazilian financial markets was by comparison tepid, to say the least. No significant public debt in domestic currency was developed, and the financial and banking sector remained underdeveloped. Since Gerschenkron economists have emphasized the role of banks and financial institutions in the process of development of late comers.[3] In this respect, it is Cairú's conservative political views and his relatively naive view of public finances, rather than his liberalism, that acted as a constraint on economic growth.

Economic liberalism and patrimonialism

In the wake of Napoleon's invasion of the Iberian Peninsula, the Portuguese royal family escaped to Brazil, and transferred its capital to Rio de Janeiro. Among the first measures of the regent D. João was to open the ports to the friendly nations, on 28 January 1808. This was a momentous measure, since it eliminated single-handedly the Portuguese trade monopoly with the colonies, the so-called Colonial Pact. Given that Portugal was occupied by French forces there was little else to be done. Average tariffs on manufactured goods were halved to 24 percent *ad valorem* for all countries, and later the tariffs on Portuguese goods were reduced to 16 percent.

It is generally accepted that the decision to open the ports and to reduce the tariffs was heavily influenced by the ideas of José da Silva Lisboa.[4] At the time of the arrival of the Portuguese royal family in Brazil, José da Silva Lisboa was a government bureaucrat and retired professor of moral philosophy in Salvador, Bahia. That changed almost immediately. In February 1808 a new chair of political economy was created by the regent and José da Silva Lisboa was appointed to it. In a couple of months the future Viscount of Cairú went from minor bureaucrat in a colonial province to major player in the capital of the Kingdom.

More importantly, in February 1810 Portugal and England signed the Trade and Navigation Treaty, which reaffirmed previous treaties – including the infamous Treaty of Methuen of 1703 – that reduced the average tariff on British products to 15 percent, that is, below that charged on Portuguese goods. Average tariffs in Britain were around 45 to 55 percent and in the United States between 35 and 45 percent (Bairoch, 1993, p. 40). Clearly, in comparison with Britain and the United States, Brazil was an ocean of liberalism. The treaty with

Portugal was not significantly different from the so-called unequal Treaties that were imposed under British pressure on China in the aftermath of the Opium Wars (1839–1842).

The origins of the Portuguese dependence on England went back to the end of Iberian Union (1580–1640). Portuguese dependency achieved its maximum through the Methuen Treaty. The Treaty stipulated that Portuguese restrictions on English cloth and woollen manufactures be lifted. In return, Britain guaranteed a lower tax on Portuguese wine than on French wine. The result was that Portuguese cloth manufacture was strangled in its infancy, and a switch towards wine production led to a reduction of foodstuff production. This, in turn, led to an increase in foodstuff imports and inflation. More importantly, free trade ruined Portuguese industry.[5] Instead of developing a dynamic garment and textile industry, Portuguese capital flowed massively into winemaking. On the other hand, England expanded its garment and textile industry and the achievement of a larger-scale production meant a reduction in costs. Indeed, English competitiveness in the sector increased. The discovery of gold in Brazil also played its role in these arrangements by financing Portugal's unfavorable balance of payments. This had another effect in helping London become the world's bullion market, and eventually to take over the role of main financial market from Amsterdam. In other words, dominance in trade was closely related to dominance in financial markets.

Table 11.1 shows that higher average tariffs do not seem to have constrained the rate of growth in Britain and the United States. It is, in fact, the relatively open Brazil that stagnated. It should be noted that initial conditions where quite different in the three countries. While manufacturing production had thrived in Britain and to a lesser extent in the United States, the Alvará of 1785 had closed all cloth production in Brazilian territory. Initial conditions and policy measures (protectionism) may have played a role in the divergent growth paths. Bairoch (1993, p. 53) argues that "there is no doubt that the Third World's compulsory economic liberalism in the nineteenth century is a major element in explaining the delay in its industrialization."[6]

However, it should be noted that neither Cairú's ideas nor the economic policies of D. João were intrinsically designed to curtail industrial development in Brazil. In fact, the Alvará of 1785 was cancelled on 1 April 1808 with the intent of promoting local manufacturing.[7] In addition, tariffs on raw materials imported

Table 11.1 Protectionism and growth

	Average tariffs c.1820	GDP per capita growth 1820–1870
Brazil	15–24	0.20
United Kingdom	45–55	1.26
United States	35–45	1.34

Sources: Bairoch (1993) and Maddison (2001).

by local manufacturers were eliminated, as well as export taxes. Cairú, although well acquainted with the works of the physiocrats, believed that the manufacturing sector contributed to the generation of surplus and, hence, to capital accumulation.[8] Novais and Arruda (1999, p. 17) correctly point out that Cairú should be seen as an eclectic author who brings together elements of mercantilist, physiocratic and classical economic political economy (i.e. Adam Smith's) thinking.

Cairú defended the notion of free trade with the background of the restrictive Colonial Pact in the back of his mind. In that respect, Cairú's works should be seen less as a defense of free trade and more as an attack on the privileges and monopolies enforced by the Brazilian position as a colony. Novais and Arruda (1999, p. 24) argue that pragmatism rather than ideology played a role in Cairú's free trade recommendations. In fact, in his *Observações sobre a Franqueza da Indústria e Estabelecimento de Fábricas no Brasil*, Cairú noted that England used protectionism to stimulate local production and increase domestic employment (Lisboa, 1810, pp. 101–2). He noted, however, that Brazil was a relatively unpopulated country and that the employment of the scarce labor force on agriculture would be more productive.[9] Only industries related to national security (e.g. gun powder production) should be stimulated artificially (ibid., p. 125). He also suggested that lack of effective demand implied that there were intrinsic limits to domestic production, and that prohibitions against importing manufactures would lead to retaliation from foreign nations and would ultimately have a negative effect on domestic production (ibid., pp. 104–5).[10]

In that respect, Cairú's pragmatic reasons, related mainly to the abundance of land and the scarcity of labor, meant that Brazil should specialize in the production of agricultural goods, while manufactures should be imported from Portugal and other nations. The idea that pragmatism rather than ideology was behind Cairú's defense of free trade is an important one, since it contradicts traditional economic historiography, as noted by Novais and Arruda (1999, p. 25). In that respect, the role of Cairú in the resistance to the re-colonization of Brazil[11] and his role in the modernization of the country should be seen as part of his contribution to the construction of the Brazilian Nation State (Novais and Arruda, 1999, p. 26; Rocha, 2001, p. 32).

This new view of Cairú's role while relevant in pointing out the pragmatism of his economic recommendations, and his role in Nation building, relegates to a secondary role Cairú's position as a defender of the status quo in the colony. In fact, there is no contradiction in noting that Cairú's views on free trade were in part related to the pragmatic limitations that a country still in formation would face, and the fact that he represented the economic interests of the dominant landed class.[12] Emília Viotti da Costa (2000, p. 53) notes that Brazilian liberals, "whatever their social origin or professional affiliation ... were linked by family or clientele to the export-import groups ... represented an elite closely tied to agriculture and trade [, and] it was according to the interests of these groups that they organized the nation."

Freedom, equality and self-government were aspirations of Brazilian liberals, as much as their counterparts in Europe. However, as noted by Viotti da Costa

(2000, p. 56), these ideals took a special meaning in Brazil. Freedom and equality meant freedom from the monopolies and privileges of the Colonial Pact, and free speech was related to the right to criticize the Portuguese privileges. Self-government was related to political independence from Portugal, and the control of the State by landed interests, which meant the maintenance of slavery and no significant social change. Patrimonialism rather than liberalism is a better characterization of the political institutions that were developed in the transition to independence. The institutions that emerged consolidated oligarchic power and a system of patronage that dated from colonial times.[13]

In sum, while the revisionist view of Cairú is correct in pointing out that he was more eclectic in his economic views, and not just a defender of *laissez faire*, it goes too far in disconnecting him from landed interests.[14] However, by emphasizing the eclecticism of Cairú's contribution the revisionist view indicates that the reasons for Brazilian underdevelopment in the first half of the nineteenth century are not limited to its liberal trade policies.[15] The underdevelopment of financial markets in the first half of the nineteenth century, and the contrast with the United States, suggests that it is in this respect that the ideas of Cairú and Hamilton should be compared.

Public debt and development

The eighteenth and nineteenth centuries were dominated by the principles of sound finance, and balanced budgets, but government debt, albeit in moderation, was seen as a blessing by some. For example, Alexander Hamilton the first Treasury Secretary and main strategist of the economic system in the post-independent United States did in fact argue for the development of a national public debt as a form of providing a strong central government. For Hamilton an excess of public debt was if possible to be avoided. However, once debt was incurred he believed it could be used for public good, and eventually become a blessing. This view, we argue, had an important influence on American fiscal policies. Hamilton saw government debt and a national public bank as the pillars of the British economic success that he wanted to emulate in America.[16]

The British public finance revolution dated back to the foundation of the National Debt in 1693, and the Bank of England in 1694. As a general rule, conservatives saw the debt as an inappropriate increase in the power of the crown and a threat to individual liberties. On the other hand, Whigs saw public debt as the basis for the development of the financial sector, and the expansion of trade. The Glorious Revolution then represents a victory for the Whigs, and of the financial and commercial interests of the City.[17] It appears that while other factors were essential for the Industrial Revolution, the national debt and its relation to the developing financial sector of the eighteenth century were also a crucial component.

It is important to note that conventional wisdom about the British experiment was highly negative. Among the founding fathers of political economy, David Hume and Adam Smith clearly expressed negative ideas about government debt.

The usual identification of Hume as a Tory – in particular because of his historical writings – means that his views on public debt are usually associated with the conservative party. Hence, Rotwein (1955, p. lxxxvi) in his introduction to Hume's writings on economics argues, "what he [Hume] seeks to show is that the inevitable continued rise in debt will not only have the gravest consequences for society but will ultimately terminate in total bankruptcy."

While it is clear that Hume was concerned, and was critical of the increasing size of public debt, he was not a dogmatic critic of the fiscal policies of the crown. He clearly refers to the ill resulting from public debt, but he also claims that some good results from a national debt (Hume, 1955, pp. 90–107). Adam Smith was more concerned about the dangers of bankruptcy than the possibilities for expanded trade that government debt facilitated (Smith, 1776, Book 5, pp. 689–947). However, one must note that Smith thought that taxes hindered capital accumulation in a way that government debt did not. As noted by Winch (1998, p. 13) McCulloch criticized both, Hume and Smith, for not perceiving that output growth made the burden of debt easier to carry.

David Ricardo's contributions to the question of public finances have cast a long shadow. Ricardo was even more concerned than his predecessors about the negative effects of taxes and public debt on capital accumulation, and considered the British debt, together with the Corn Laws, one of the two great evils plaguing the nation (Winch, 1998, p. 18). For Ricardo (1817, pp. 150–2) taxes either reduce capital accumulation or force tax payers to reduce consumption. Debt, as deferred taxes had the same effect, and, hence, Ricardo, a Radical connected to Jeremy Bentham and James Mill, was for paying down government debt, and maintaining a relatively low level of taxes – measures that at that time were opposed by both Whigs and Tories. Thomas Malthus – personal friend and main intellectual foe of Ricardo – not surprisingly held different views regarding government debt. As a moderate Whig, Malthus was against paying down public debt, on the grounds that it allowed debt holders to expand consumption and effectual demand, a result that was prevented by Say's Law in the Ricardian system (Ferguson, 2001, pp. 129–30).

The influence of Adam Smith on Alexander Hamilton has been established long ago (Bourne, 1894). However, it is clear that Hamilton was quite heterodox in his views on debt, and owed more to financial market practitioners and policy makers than to political economists regarding his views on debt. This is particularly important, since Hamilton's views on public credit are among the most important legacies of the Washington administration. Hamilton admired the Swiss banker Jacques Necker,[18] and was influenced by the ideas of the merchant Robert Morris (Ferguson, 1961, p. 109).

In addition, in the United States the acceptance of non-convertible currencies and debts was more widespread than in Europe or any Latin American colony. As early as 1712 the North American colonies had set up land banks, which lent money against mortgages on land. Land bank emissions eased the fiscal constraint of colonial governments. Money was created on demand, and it did not lead to inflation.[19] Beyond the land banks, unconvertible currency finance was relatively common. According to Ferguson (1961, p. 10) the system worked as follows: "the governments met expenses by issuing a paper medium, whether currencies or certificates, directly to individuals; they redeemed this paper, not by giving specie to those who held it, but by accepting it for taxes or other payments."[20] The North American experience with land banks, and paper currency, in addition to the British development of public debt markets, following on the steps of Dutch finance, were all important influences on Hamilton.

As the first Treasury Secretary in Washington's administration Hamilton sent three Reports to Congress that are of interest to us. The first report sent on 9 January, 1790 was on public credit and dealt with the accumulated debts of the states during the war of independence. Hamilton argued that all debts should be consolidated and assumed by the Federal government since the debts had been incurred in a common cause, and that the debt should be funded in order to improve the public credit of the nation. By funding Hamilton meant guarantee the revenues to pay for the interest, but not necessarily the principal, on the debt. The plan involved the transformation of devalued notes into perpetual annuities with relatively low rates of interest, following the example of British consols. Resistance to his plan led to the famous bargain with Jefferson and Maddison, by which the plan was approved in exchange for the transfer of the capital from New York to Philadelphia and then to somewhere in Virginia on the margins of the Potomac River.

Hamilton emphasized that the Federal government should have the power to tax to support national credit. The new government should have the power to tax imports, which would be the fundamental source of revenue followed by excise taxes. He also proposed that specific taxes were earmarked for the payment of interest, while the payment of the principal could be delayed indefinitely. In that respect tariffs play a more important role in raising revenues than as a protectionist measure per se. Hamilton also argued for bounties (i.e. subsidies) to render American products more competitive abroad, and guarantee an influx of bullion. These measures are outlined in his *Report on Manufactures*, requested by Congress in January of 1790 and sent in December of the following year.[21]

The final task in Hamilton's financial plan was the creation of a national bank, outlined in the *Report on a National Bank* sent to Congress on 13 December, 1790. The Bank was an important, if subsidiary, part of his plan to establish the public credit of the United States. Three-quarters of the price of a share of the bank had to be paid with public bonds rather than cash. Further, the bank served as the fiscal agent of the administration, where revenues were deposited, supplying bank notes by which taxes were paid and providing loans in emergencies.

The effects of the Hamiltonian program were impressive. Revolutionary bonds that were traded at less than 25 percent of their face value were selling around the end of Washington's first term at 120 percent of par. Around the end of Washington's second term almost a third of the national debt was held by foreign investors, and by the beginning of the nineteenth century that amount had risen to 60 percent. In 1790 the debt-to-GNP ratio in the United States was close to 40 percent, and by 1810 it had fallen to close to 10 percent (MacDonald,

2003, p. 306). The number of banks in the country also expanded steadily providing finance for the development of trade and manufacturing as predicted by Hamilton.

Cairú, in contrast, seems to have had a far more conventional view of the role of public debt and financial markets. It should be noted that a first Banco do Brasil was founded on 12 October, 1808 upon the arrival of the Royal family to Brazil. The bank was also the fiscal agent of the State and it did print paper money in emergencies. The bank was idealized by the Count of Linhares, who consulted Cairú on economic matters (Peláez and Suzigan, 1976, p. 39).[22] Cairú (Lisboa, 1810, p. 71) recognized the positive role of the banking sector in the case of the United States, and of a national public bank. However, he believed that in the case of Brazil the banking sector and manufacturing would flourish, since "public debt is almost insignificant," (idem). That is, for Cairú, it seems, the national bank was essential and public debt a hindrance to the development of domestic financial markets.[23]

The Banco do Brasil, however, did not stimulate the development of a private banking sector. In April 1826 with the return of the Royal family to Portugal the bank lost most of its assets, and it was finally liquidated in 1829. The lack of public debt and a set of taxes to fund interest payments certainly played a role in its demise. Steven Haber (1991, pp. 569–72) shows that the underdevelopment of the Brazilian banking sector affected negatively the development of the textile industry in comparison with that of the United States.[24]

In that respect, it seems that the inability of Brazilian elites to emulate the Anglo-Dutch system of public finance is at the heart of the country's backwardness in the first half of the nineteenth century. It is not sound finance – as it is sometimes claimed – that was lacking, but a sustainable and cheap system of public finance.[25] The notion that Hamilton's defense of tariffs was connected to his belief in the positive effects of public debt, rather than merely infant industry protection and the impressive development of the American financial sector, seem to corroborate that conclusion.

Concluding remarks

Conventional wisdom in Brazilian historiography suggests that, in part, the relative backwardness of Brazil with respect to the United States was the result of the economic liberalism of its elites, represented by José da Silva Lisboa, the Viscount of Cairú. The chapter argues that Cairú's defense of an open economy, integrated with the world economy, in which agricultural production would prevail over industrial interests, should be seen as a discourse for landowners and the mercantile class connected to the slave trade. It is also argued that, in contrast to Alexander Hamilton, Cairú and the Brazilian elites had a naive view of public finance that is central to understanding the backwardness of Brazilian financial markets. Political conservatism and financial underdevelopment are seen as more relevant than free trade – even though free trade also played a role – in explaining the relative backwardness of Brazil.

Notes

1 Assistant Professor, University of Utah. I would like to thank, without implication, Stephany Griffith-Jones, Carlos Mallorquín, José Antonio Ocampo, Maria Angela Parra, Esteban Pérez-Caldentey, Diego Sanchez-Ancochea and other participants for a stimulating debate. I also would like to thank Ken Jameson for his comments on a preliminary version.

2 See Furtado (1959, p. 101). Furtado argues that the British authorities also were more pragmatic and less fond of Adam Smith's doctrines than their Luso-Brazilian counterparts (ibid., pp. 93–4). According to Novais and Arruda (1999, p. 25), the negative view of Cairú in Brazilian historiography owes a great deal to Sérgio Buarque de Holanda and to Celso Furtado (see Holanda, 1936, pp. 199–200). Furtado's views are clearly more relevant for economists. See also Landes (1998, p. 314) for a recent restatement of the argument in the United States.

3 See Gerschenkron (1962) and Cameron (1967) on the influence of financial markets in economic development. For an analysis of the role of financial markets in American development see Sylla (1975), and for the Brazilian context see Peláez e Suzigan (1976), and Goldsmith (1986).

4 Cairú suggests that he had a role in the decision process, see Lisboa (1810). Cairú had read Adam Smith in the late eighteenth century, and had published his own Principles in Portugal in which he claims to be a disciple of Smith (Lisboa, 1804, p. 65). On Smith's influence on Luso-Brazilian authors see Almodovar and Cardoso (1998) and Lima (1978).

5 This goes against the traditional notion of comparative advantage. Comparative advantage was introduced in the first decades of the nineteenth century by David Ricardo, using British and Portuguese trade on cloth and wine as an example. For a critical perspective on the notion of comparative advantage see Felipe and Vernengo (2002–3).

6 Brazilian economic historiography tends to agree with that assessment, e.g. Roberto Simonsen (1936), and Caio Prado (1942). Furtado (1959, p. 94), however, warns against extreme simplifications and argues that the trade privileges conceded to the British were not the unique or even the fundamental cause of Brazilian underdevelopment in the first half of the nineteenth century.

7 In addition, on 28 April 1809 an Alvará protecting the local producers of new machines and innovations was introduced for a 14-year period (Lisboa, 1810, p. 48).

8 Cairú's ideas formed during his studies in Portugal – there were no universities in Brazil, one should emphasize – were certainly influenced by the ideas of Sebastião Carvalho e Melo, the Marquis of Pombal. Pombal was influenced by the English mercantilism he observed first hand as the Portuguese ambassador to England, and his policies tried to imitate the success of British mercantilism by developing international trade and economic activity in Portugal, and improving and expanding Portugal's merchant class. See Maxwell (1995).

9 According to Cairú land abundance and labor scarcity suggested that agriculture was the most productive activity in Brazil (Lisboa, 1810, pp. 46–7). Cairú suggested that, in contrast to the United States, Brazil lacked the free workers, artisans and manufacturers expatriated from Europe, who would constitute the skilled workers necessary for a considerable development of local manufacturing (ibid, p. 43).

10 Cairú lists the conditions necessary for the introduction of domestic manufactures, including abundance of capital, labor, raw materials, a relatively developed market, cost advantages, diffusion of knowledge, free trade (sic) and stimulus to inventors (Lisboa, 1810, pp. 59–60).

11 The Portuguese Royal family lived in Brazil from 1808 until 1821, when in the aftermath of a liberal constitutional revolt in the city of Porto, D. João VI decided to return to Portugal. Further, from 1815 on, Brazil and Portugal had the same status as a unified kingdom.

12 Novais and Arruda (1999, p. 26) suggest that their view is in stark contrast with conventional wisdom based on Sérgio Buarque de Holanda, Celso Furtado and Emília Viotti da Costa. They are particularly critical of Buarque de Holanda for establishing a negative view of Cairú. It appears that Buarque de Holanda's criticism was directed to the notion that Cairú was a modern and progressive thinker raised by Alceu Amoroso Lima – basically because he was well versed in the current developments in political economy – rather than a conservative and elitist author (see Holanda, 1936, pp. 83–5 and 199–200).

13 The classic work on Brazilian patrimonialism is Faoro (1957). On the development of liberal ideas in Brazil see Paim (1998).

14 As noted by José Murilo de Carvalho the contrast between Brazil and Hispanic America "was the presence of a national political elite, that is, of an elite that could aggregate interests of the dominant groups and protect them through the mediation of the state power," (in Merquior, 1986, p. 271). Note, however, that the State had some degree of autonomy. José Guilherme Merquior (1986, p. 274) argues that "what the crown bestowed upon the *fazendeiros* [landowners] was titles – and hence status, rather than power."

15 It is important to emphasize that the argument is not that trade was not important, but more precisely that it was not the only cause of Brazilian underdevelopment. In fact, from the Alves Branco Tariff of 1844 – which raised tariffs for most goods to a higher range, from 20 to 60 percent *ad valorem* – to the Silva Ferraz Tariff of 1860, a certain amount of protectionism was promoted, even though the reasons were connected to the fiscal needs of the State rather than industrial promotion (Buescu, 1974). This period saw a surge in industrial activity in Brazil, and the industrialist and banker Irineu Evangelista de Souza, Baron (later Viscount) of Mauá, became the symbol of the period.

16 Hamilton (1790, pp. 6–7) saw three main advantages related to the existence of a moderate amount of public debt. First, it allowed for increasing amount of trade, since debt permitted the expansion of the financial sector and this, in turn, increased the amount of credit available. Second, agriculture and manufactures – production in general – was promoted, again as a result of the positive effects of credit. Third, he believed that interest rates would fall, "allowing the public and individuals to borrow on easier and cheaper terms" (ibid., p. 7). These points show that Hamilton had a conceptual view of money as debt, and of the economic system as a framework of debt–credit relations backed by states and banks' promises to pay. These notions would later be developed by the Banking School in England and by several authors in the Keynesian tradition. For a review of those views, which are referred to as endogenous money, see Wray (1990).

17 The Bank of England acted as the creditor of the Treasury. The government was able to pay its liabilities in bank notes, and the Bank was able to issue bank notes up to the extent of its nominal capital. The ability to control credit laid the foundations of modern banking practices. Fundamentally, the system allowed public finance on cheap long-term debt. In the heyday of public borrowing during the Napoleonic Wars the debt-to-GNP ratio in Britain reached the incredible level of 300 percent, and between 1780 and 1845 it was never below 150 percent. As noted by MacDonald (2003, p. 355) "simplistic notions that national power and national debt are mutually incompatible are disproved by this single historical fact."

18 Swanson and Trout (1990, pp. 424–5) argue that Necker had a significant influence on Hamilton's views on public credit. In their view, Hamilton's emphasis on funding the debt by committing tax revenues to the payment of the interest on debt came directly from Necker.

19 MacDonald (2003, p. 287) suggests that the activity of land banks was supported by social and political forces in the colonies that benefited from a relatively devalued currency and moderate inflation.

20 The notion that the acceptability of money follows from the ability to use it for discharging tax payments, which is the domain of the State, is usually referred to as State or Chartal money. The origins of this notion lay in the German Historical School, in particular Georg Knapp. One of the precursors of the German Historical School was Friedrich List, who developed Hamilton's views on the need of domestic protection for national infant industries. See Wray (1990, pp. 38–44).

21 Irwin (2003) argues that Hamilton's views, in particular on his *Report on Manufactures*, have been mischaracterized, and that his nationalist views did not constitute an outright defense of economic autarky. In the same vein Harlen (1999) argues that classical economic nationalism, as proposed by Hamilton and later List, implied a mix of mercantilism and liberal policies in eclectic fashion.

22 It should be noted that if Cairú was influenced by Adam Smith, on monetary matters Smith was quite unorthodox. Smith was a defender of the real bills doctrine, and believed that money was created according to the necessities of trade. Hence, Smith saw the role of banks in the process of development in a positive light.

23 Brazil relied, in fact, more on foreign debt than on national public debt, and hence depended on export revenues to service its debt. One should note that when the first Latin American debt crisis occurred in 1825 Brazil did not default. However, access to foreign capital markets was limited and unreliable and could not be used to promote domestic manufacturing.

24 It should be noted that a second Banco do Brasil was established in 1853, on the basis of Mauá's private Banco do Brasil. Mauá was a "papelista," that is, a defender of paper money and banks, and his ideas resemble the British Banking School. Further development of the Banking sector in Brazil would have to wait until the proclamation of the Republic in 1889. However, by international standards the banking sector remained relatively underdeveloped.

25 Bordo and Végh (1998) seem to indicate that sound finance in the United States and lack of it in Argentina explains the lack of development of financial markets in the latter. It appears that rather than lack of sound finance – balanced budgets – Argentina lacked a proper system of funding national public debt.

References

Almodovar, Antônio and José L. Cardoso (1998) *A History of Portuguese Economic Thought*, London, Routledge.

Bairoch, Paul (1993) *Economics and World History: Myths and Paradoxes*, Chicago, The University of Chicago Press.

Bordo, Michael and Carlos Végh (1998) "What if Alexander Hamilton had been Argentinean?" NBER Working Paper No 6862, December.

Bourne, Edward (1894) "Alexander Hamilton and Adam Smith," *Quarterly Journal of Economics* 8 (3), pp. 328–44.

Buescu, Mircea (1974) *Evolução Econômica do Brasil*, Rio de Janeiro, Apec.

Cameron, Rondo (1967) *Banking in the Early Stages of Industrialization: A Study in Comparative Economic History*, New York, Oxford University Press.

Costa, Emília Viotti da (2000) *The Brazilian Empire: Myths and Histories*, Chapel Hill, University of North Carolina Press.

Faoro, Raymundo (1957) *Os Donos do Poder: Formação do Patronato Político Brasileiro*, São Paulo, Globo, 2001.

Felipe, Jesús and Matías Vernengo (2002–2003) "Demystifying the Principle of Comparative Advantage: Implications for Developing Countries," *International Journal of Political Economy* 32 (4), Winter, pp. 49–75.

Ferguson, James (1961) *The Power of the Purse: A History of American Public Finance, 1776–1790*, Chapel Hill, University of North Carolina Press, 1973.

Ferguson, Niall (2001) *The Cash Nexus: Money and Power in the Modern World, 1700–2000*, New York, Basic Books.

Furtado, Celso (1959) *Formação Econômica do Brasil*, São Paulo, Companhia Editora Nacional, 1987.

Gerschenkron, Alexander (1962) *Economic Backwardness in Historical Perspective*, Cambridge, MA, Harvard University Press.

Goldsmith, Raymond W. (1986) *Brasil 1850–1984: Desenvolvimento Financeiro sob um Século de Inflação*, São Paulo, Banco Bamerindus do Brasil; Editora Harper & Row do Brasil.

Haber, Steve (1991) "Industrial Concentration and the Capital Markets: A Comparative Study of Brazil, Mexico, and the United States, 1830–1930," *Journal of Economic History* 51 (3), pp. 559–80.

Hamilton, Alexander (1790) "Report on Public Credit," *Official Reports on Publick Credit, a National Bank, Manufactures, and a Mint*, Philadelphia, William McKean.

Harlen, Margerum (1999) "A Reappraisal of Classical Economic Nationalism and Economic Liberalism," *International Studies Quarterly* 43(4), December, pp. 733–44, 1821.

Holanda, Sérgio Buarque de (1936), *Raízes do Brasil*, São Paulo, Companhia das Letras, 1995.

Hume, D. (1955) *Writings on Economics*, Madison, University of Wisconsin Press, 1970.

Irwin, Douglas (2003) "The Aftermath of Hamilton's 'Report on Manufactures'," NBER Working Paper No 9943, August.

Landes, David, (1998) *The Wealth and Poverty of Nations: Why Some Are Rich and Others so Poor*, New York, Norton.

Lima, Heitor F. (1978) *História do Pensamento Econômico no Brasil*, São Paulo, Companhia Editora Nacional.

Lisboa, José da Silva (Viscounde de Cairú) (1804) *Princípios de Economia Política*, Rio de Janeiro, Pongetti, 1956.

—— (1810) *Observações sobre a Franqueza da Indústria e Estabelecimento de Fábricas no Brasil*, Senado Federal, Brasilia, 1999.

MacDonald, James (2003) *A Free Nation Deep in Debt*, New York, Farrar, Straus and Giroux.

Maddison Angus (2001) *The World Economy: A Millennial Perspective*, Paris, OECD.

Maxwell, Kenneth (1995) *Pombal: Paradox of the Enlightenment*, Cambridge, Cambridge University Press.

Merquior, José G. (1986) "Patterns of State-Building in Brazil and Argentina," in John Hall, (ed.), *States in History*, Oxford, Basil Blackwell, 1989.

Novais, Fernando A. and José Jobson A. Arruda (1999) "Prometeus e Atlantes na Forja da Nação," in José da Silva Lisboa (Viscount of Cairú), *Observações sobre a Franqueza da Indústria e Estabelecimento de Fábricas no Brasil*, Senado Federal, Brasilia.

Paim, Antônio (1998) *História do Liberalismo Brasileiro*, São Paulo, Mandarim.

Peláez, Carlos M. and Wilson Suzigan (1976) *História Monetaria do Brasil: Análise da Política, Comportamento e Instituições Monetárias*, Brasilia, IPEA/INPES.

Prado, Caio Jr (1942) *Formação do Brasil Contemporâneo*, São Paulo, Brasiliense.

Ricardo, David (1817) *On the Principles of Political Economy and Taxation*, (edited by P. Sraffa with the collaboration of M. Dobb), London, Royal Economic Society and Cambridge University Press, 1995.

Rocha, Antônio P. (2001) "Introdução," in *José da Silva Lisboa, Visconde de Cairú*, São Paulo, Editora 34.

Rotwein, E. (1955) "Introduction," in David Hume, *Writings on Economics*, Madison, University of Wisconsin Press, 1970.

Simonsen, Roberto C. (1936) *História Econômica do Brasil, 1500–1820*, Rio de Janeiro, Companhia Editora Nacional.

Smith, Adam (1776) *An Inquiry into the Nature and Causes of the Wealth of Nations*, (edited by R. Campbell and A. Skinner), Indianapolis, Liberty Fund, 1981.

Sylla, Richard (1975) *The American Capital Market, 1846–1914: A Study of the Effects of Public Policy on Economic Development*, New York, Arno Press.

Swanson, Donald and Andrew Trout (1990) "Alexander Hamilton, 'the Celebrated Mr. Neckar,' and Public Credit," *William and Mary Quarterly* 47 (3), pp. 422–30.

Winch, Donald (1998) "The Political Economy of Public Finance in the 'Long' Eighteenth Century," J. Maloney, (ed.), in *Debt and Deficits: An Historical Perspective*, Cheltenham, Edward Elgar.

Wray, Randall (1990) *Money and Credit in Capitalist Economies*, Aldershot, Edward Elgar.

Index